COURTS CROSSING BORDERS

COURTS CROSSING BORDERS

Blurring the Lines of Sovereignty

Edited by

Mary L. Volcansek
TEXAS CHRISTIAN UNIVERSITY

John F. Stack, Jr.
FLORIDA INTERNATIONAL UNIVERSITY

CAROLINA ACADEMIC PRESS
Durham, North Carolina

Library of Congress Cataloging-in-Publication Data

Volcansek, Mary L., 1948-
  Courts crossing borders : blurring the lines of sovereignty / by Mary L.
Volcansek, John F. Stack, Jr.-- 1st ed.
    p. cm.
  Includes bibliographical references.
  ISBN 1-59460-055-4 (alk. paper)
  1. International courts. 2. Judge-made law. 3. Sovereignty. I. Stack,
John F. II. Title.

  KZ6250.V65 2005
  341.5'5--dc22

                                                          2005001656

Carolina Academic Press
700 Kent Street
Durham, North Carolina 27701
Telephone (919) 489-7486
Fax (919) 493-5668
E-mail: cap@cap-press.com
www.cap-press.com

For Our Dearest Friends:
Mimi, Eva, Peggy, Kasha, Bella, Kotiti, Amanda, Amy, and Fitzy

CONTENTS

ACKNOWLEDGMENTS

We are pleased to acknowledge the assistance of several colleagues who made this volume possible. Dr. Thomas A. Breslin, former vice president for research at Florida International University (FIU), conceived of a series of conferences on contemporary public policy and provided financial support for eight conferences that led to the publication of six books, with the final two volumes now nearing production.

Thanks are due for the support of Dr. Mark B. Rosenberg, FIU's Provost and Executive Vice President of Academic Affairs, Dr. Ralph S. Clem, Director of the Center for Transnational and Comparative Studies, and Dr. Nicol Rae, Chair of the Department of Political Science. We are grateful to Professor Thomas E. Baker, Professor Michael Fischl, and Dr. Louis Fisher, who urged us to consider Carolina Academic Press, and for the support of Dr. Robert Conrow, our acquisitions editor at CAP. Our appreciation is also sent to Mr. Nicholas Eliopulos, who copyedited the manuscript with care.

This work would not have been possible without the support of the Jack D. Gordon Institute for Public Policy and Citizenship Studies at Florida International University and the tireless assistance of Ms. Elaine Dillashaw. We also wish to thank Dr. Harry Antrim, who dutifully read and commented on much of the manuscript.

COURTS CROSSING BORDERS

CHAPTER 1

COURTS CROSSING BORDERS

John F. Stack, Jr., Mary L. Volcansek

Europeans have suspected for some time that subtle inroads into national prerogatives are consequences of transnational organizations and their courts.[1] The successive treaties and the economic, legal, and political frameworks that have given rise to the European Union (EU) over the past fifty years have conceived an approach to state building that has incorporated the eighteenth century nation-state into a supranational structure that has stimulated economic growth.[2] In so doing, the power of courts above the level of states has been dramatically intensified as the various iterations of the European Union have sought to expand economic opportunities and integrate aspects of political processes.[3] Courts have played a seminal role in blurring lines of sovereignty among states in order to implement the economic and policy objectives of Europe's collective interests.[4] The European Court of Justice of the EU has ele-

---

1. Karen J. Alter, "The European Union's Legal System and Domestic Policy: Spillover or Backlash?", 54 (3) *International Organization* (Summer 2000).

2. Cesare P.R. Romano, "The Proliferation of International Judicial Bodies: The Pieces of the Puzzle," 31 *New York University Journal of International Law and Politics* (Summer 1999), 746.

3. Andrew Moravcsik, "Explaining International Human Rights Regimes: Liberal Theory and Western Europe," 1 (2) *European Journal of International Relations* (1995). Moravcsik roots the success of Western Europe in the further "improvement of democratic" regimes spanning several generations. "West European human rights regimes harmonize and perfect human rights and democracy among nations that already effectively guarantee basic human rights, rather that introducing them to new situations. . . . The most effective elements of the European human rights system are thus also the subtlest. The delicate process of legal harmonization proceeds slowly" (159).

4. Mary L. Volcansek, *Judicial Politics in Europe* (New York: Peter Lang Publishers, 1986): 267–70. Writing in 1986 as the accession of Spain and Portugal increased EU membership to twelve, Volcansek noted the critical roles played by both legitimacy and efficacy in the acceptance of European law: "if the judicial mandate is clear and communicated, if the environment is favorable to the ultimate policy, and if the body creating norms can

vated the treaties to the stature of a constitution, facilitated free movement of workers and capital among member states, and annulled national barriers to the free movement of goods and services.[5]

Americans have, however, been smugly less concerned about potential incursions into their national sovereignty, by courts or any other transnational bodies.[6] Yet, as the *New York Times* noted, a phenomenon similar to what has happened in Europe is occurring on this side of the Atlantic. "NAFTA's Powerful Little Secret" detailed the ways in which obscure tribunals, impaneled to enforce the rules of the North American Free Trade Agreement, are overriding national laws.[7] More recently, and more powerfully, Chief Justice Margaret Marshall of the Massachusetts high court was "surprised," according to an article in the *New York Times*, to discover that a case her court had decided and that the U.S. Supreme Court had declined to hear was under review by a North American Free Trade Agreement (NAFTA) court.[8] Less than two weeks after reporting about the Massachusetts case, the *New York Times* noted that a dispute settlement panel of the World Trade Organization (WTO) had ruled against the U.S. practice of subsidizing cotton producers, a ruling that, if upheld by the higher WTO judicial body, would likely end or seriously change the current model of cotton production in the United States.

---

achieve and maintain legitimacy as a symbol among interpreting publics, acceptance of legal norms can be expected" (270). See also Mary L. Volcansek, "Supranational Courts in a Political Context," in Mary L. Volcansek (ed.), *Law Above Nations: Supranational Courts and the Legalization of Politics* (Gainesville, FL: University Press of Florida, 1997).

5. Miguel Poiares Maduro, *We the Court: The European Court of Justice and the European Economic Constitution* (Oxford: Hart Publishing: 1998).

6. The literature on transnational organizations and transnational relations is enormous. The first works appearing in the early 1970s have, by and large, withstood the test of time. See, for example, Karl Kaiser, "Transnational Politics: Toward a Theory of Multinational Politics," 25 (4) *International Organization* (Autumn 1971); Robert O. Keohane and Joseph S. Nye (eds.), *Transnational Relations and World Politics* (Cambridge: Harvard University Press, 1971); Samuel P. Huntington, "Transnational Organizations in World Politics," 25 (3) *World Politics* (April 1973); Robert O. Keohane and Joseph S. Nye, "Transgovernmental Relations and International Organizations," 27 (4) *World Politics* (October 1974); Lawrence Juda, "A Note on Bureaucratic Politics and Transnational Relations," 4 (2) *International Studies Notes* (September 1977); Herbert C. Kelman, "The Conditions, Criteria, and Dialectics of Human Dignity: A Transnational Perspective," 21 (3) *International Studies Quarterly* (September 1977); and Robert O. Keohane and Joseph S. Nye, *Power and Interdependence* (Boston: Little Brown, 1977).

7. Anthony DePalma, "NAFTA's Powerful Little Secret: Obscure Tribunals Settle Disputes, but Grow Too Fat, Critics Say," *New York Times* (March 11, 2001), A-1.

8. *New York Times* (March 18, 2004), A-1.

Most Americans, even those in the legal community, are reluctantly recognizing that legal issues once thought of as domestic are now governed by a growing body of transnational law and a web of relatively obscure tribunals. Europeans experienced a similar awakening in the 1970s when they realized that the European Court of Justice was overruling domestic law on commercial issues and that the European Court of Human Rights was acting on issues of criminal law and civil and political liberties.

One side effect of the move toward globalization has been the development of a network of judicial bodies with wide-ranging authority to alter domestic policy and domestic law. What began as a mere side effect is now, as the chapters in this book explain, a major force in shaping legal practice in many regions of the world and in driving resolution of human rights, economic, and even criminal issues.[9] This book offers insights into the authority and implications of courts crossing borders.

Indeed, most multinational corporations are already keenly conscious of the power of tribunals acting under the auspices of the World Trade Organization (WTO) to review, modify, and overrule national policies. This book explores in a systematic fashion how transnational courts are blurring national sovereignty in Europe, in the Americas, and on a global scale.

The relentless motion toward transnationalism, resulting from the merging, mingling, and overlapping forces of technology, commerce, transportation, and communication processes, has wrapped individuals, societies, states, intergovernmental organizations, and corporations in growing webs of interdependence.[10] This does not mean that national borders are unimportant nor that any nation's sovereignty is about to be submerged into world federalism, but it does illustrate how business relations, especially in areas of mutual interest, are increasingly shaped by external conditions. In the case of Europe, transnational developments have proceeded further based on political consent and the necessity of making policy decisions reflective of neutral rules. Thus,

---

9. Ellen Lutz and Kathryn Sikkink, "International Human Rights Law in Practice: The Judicial Cascade: The Evolution and Impact of Foreign Human Rights Trials in Latin America," 2 *Chicago Journal of International Law* (Spring 2001). Lutz and Sikkink explore the evolution of transnational justice networks systematically pursuing foreign trials for "human rights violations often in the face of governmental indifference and recalcitrance" (3). The development of these networks illustrates the power of transnational networks pioneered by a small number of human rights lawyers and advocates.

10. Robert O. Keohane and Joseph S. Nye, *Power and Interdependence*, Third Edition (New York: Longman, 2001). The connections between transnational relations and interdependence are addressed from the perspective of globalization in Parts V and VI, underscoring the importance of the continued vitality of the study of transnational relations.

transnational courts have played fundamental roles in knitting together the states and peoples of Europe since the end of World War II.

The transnational phenomenon has been the target of nationalists on both sides of the Atlantic. In North America, demonstrators have taken to the streets in Miami, Seattle, Washington, and Quebec to protest the power of NAFTA, the International Monetary Fund (IMF), and the seemingly ubiquitous power of the World Trade Organization (WTO). But economic impulses and cross-border trade have made transnational agreements essential for economic survival. International organizations, like domestic bureaucracies, are governed by rules and procedures, and courts, especially in complex international organizations, are an essential condition for the functioning of inter-state organizations under the conditions of increasing levels of transnational relations. Similarly, the horrors of blatant violations of human rights have motivated political leaders to form regional organizations in order to foster the protection of human rights and to react when signatory nations violate those rights. Treaties negotiated, whether to advance trade or to protect human rights, are without teeth if there is no mechanism for the enforcement of their provisions. For that reason, dispute resolution systems—courts, if you will—have evolved as a crucial but largely unrecognized aspect of transnational agreements.

This book explores how courts are crossing borders and blurring sovereignty in a number of ways. Mary L. Volcansek explores the inevitability of transnational dispute settlement systems for the long-term viability of the growing number of regional trade organizations. Using the model of institutionalization that has been proposed to describe the evolution of supranationalism in Europe, she demonstrates the movement in transnational organizations from diplomacy to hard legalism that has served the purpose of enforcing compliance with treaty commitments. To illustrate the tendency toward hard legalism, she considers the cases of the European Union, GATT (General Agreement on Tariffs and Trade) and the World Trade Organization, NAFTA, MERCOSUR (Common Market of the South), and the Association of Southeast Asian Nations (ASEAN).

Miguel Poiares Maduro looks at the most successful and longest-lived transnational economic arrangement, the European Union, and how the European Court of Justice has been instrumental in transforming the EU into a political community from its origin as strictly a trading bloc. He notes the changing character of sovereignty in the EU as a result of the twin policies of Europeanization and constitutionalization and proposes that, at least within the EU, the concepts of plural constitutionalism and competitive sovereignty are most appropriate.

Joseph Jupille also looks at the European Union and the ECJ, but unlike Maduro, focuses on a single aspect of the ECJ's blurring of national boundaries. He argues that the ECJ has been instrumental, through its decisions on environmental policy, in reconciling natural, economic, and political borders. The ECJ's enforcement role in environmental policies has been pronounced and has clearly supported European policies over national ones. This chapter is highly illustrative, in a single issue area, of how a court can dramatically limit and alter a nation's freedom of action.

Doris Marie Provine looks at a different European Court, one that is not predicated on economics. She traces the evolution of the European Court of Human Rights (ECHR), the enforcement arm of the European Convention on Human Rights, in the field of non-discrimination. She found that the success of the ECHR has created its own problems. Because so many individuals approach the court, it has accumulated a backlog that precludes the timely resolution of cases. Furthermore, when considering equality issues the Court has been hesitant to find nations in noncompliance unless discrimination is coupled with a claim that another right enumerated in the convention has been abridged. The Court has, nonetheless, Provine concludes, established a credible jurisprudence of human rights on the European continent.

John F. Stack, Jr. assesses the most successful offspring of the European Court of Human Rights, the Inter-American Court of Human Rights established in 1979. The record of this court is mixed because of the continuing hurdles posed by sovereignty in the new world. The protection of human rights in the Americas remains very much a work in progress, but has been immeasurably advanced by the movement to establish accountable democratic political systems in the 1990s and the willingness of many countries to accept the compulsory jurisdiction of the Inter-American Court. The struggle to implement this human rights regime has benefited from numerous transnational human rights groups willing to confront repressive governments. The Court and the Inter-American Commission on Human Rights have utilized innovative strategies to expose states that violate human rights. Yet, absent the commitment of countries, especially the United States, to further institutionalize the Court, as in the case of Europe, the protection of human rights will advance episodically. While the institutional protection of human rights is at best incomplete, it is nonetheless a process that continues to increase the salience of human rights in the Americas. Given the historic levels of repression and the impunity with which states have violated human rights, the Inter-American system represents a major advance based in no small part on the activism of a courageous and innovative court, the globalization of human rights as a norm of democratic governments, and the work of thousands of non-governmental organizations and individuals utilizing transnational networks crossing the hemisphere and the globe.

David M. O'Brien looks at the ways in which sovereignty is blurred when the United States, Canada, and Mexico invoke the dispute resolution mechanisms of the North Atlantic Free Trade Association. As noted above, NAFTA is controversial for many Americans for whom the exportation of jobs and the weakening of the US economy are seen as the fault of the free trade area. Less well understood is NAFTA's dispute resolution mechanism that increasingly acts like a federal court without the oversight of the US Supreme Court. The NAFTA arbitration panels draw upon international and transnational law in a strikingly uninhibited fashion. Indeed, trade and other commercial transactions among the United States, Canada, and Mexico are governed by domestic laws as well as the NAFTA treaty and myriad international economic, commercial, and transnational treaties and laws. In many cases the implementation of trade and commercial transactions has been delegated to specialized bureaucracies among the participating countries, adding yet another level of complexity when disputes arise among them. The potential for heightened levels of judicial activism is, however, clearly present in the methods by which NAFTA panels frame and adjudicate disputes. This raises the stakes, O'Brien concludes, in the blurring of the lines of sovereignty in both economic and political spheres.

Confrontations between states and international and transnational courts established to punish the perpetrators of war crimes, crimes against humanity, and genocide inform the final chapters of the volume. Donald W. Jackson analyzes the development of the doctrine of universal criminal jurisdiction in the case of the European Court of Human Rights and globally in the case of the establishment of the International Criminal Court. Central to his analysis is the changing notion of sovereignty as an absolute bar against external interference in a country's domestic sphere when human rights violations such as genocide, war crimes, and crimes against humanity are at issue.

The concept of universal criminal jurisdiction allows that the perpetrator of a particular crime may be prosecuted in any country regardless of where the alleged crime occurred. Originating in the nineteenth century, universal criminal jurisdiction took the form of international agreements outlawing piracy and the slave trade. In the twentieth century, the Nuremberg Trials, the Geneva Convention of 1949, and subsequent United Nations Conventions on Genocide and Torture and the creation of the International Criminal Tribunals for the Former Yugoslavia and Rwanda, have also reinforced the concept that there are limits to absolute national sovereignty. Despite the controversial nature of the International Criminal Court for the United States government, Jackson illustrates how nineteenth- and twentieth-century U.S. policies have provided substantial legal and philosophical justifications for the establishment of the ICC.

The final chapter, by Kimi King and James Meernick, offers an assessment of the decisions handed down by the International War Crimes Tribunal for the Former Yugoslavia (ICTY) with respect to the mass sexual violence perpetrated on women. For the first time, an international court has squarely confronted the issues of sexual violence and placed it on the international legal agenda. The decisions of the ICTY shed light on the permissibility, availability, and utility of rape as an instrument of war and as an method of torture, and the Court is establishing landmark legal precedents in this area. The Court has handed down significant sentences for perpetrators, regardless of rank, underscoring the strict liability that attaches to sexual crimes and the accountability of individuals involved in sexual assaults during wartime. The judgments of the International War Crimes Tribunal for the Former Yugoslavia illustrate how sexual violence was used not only as a weapon of war but as a continuing method of control, humiliation, and torture. The ICTY has therefore heightened awareness of the gravity of mass sexual violence and established its ubiquity during times of armed conflict as a fundamental violation of human rights.

Taken together, the transnational judicial and quasi-judicial bodies considered in this volume illustrate the changing nature of sovereignty in a progressively globalizing world. Rather than simply deploring the march toward transnational judicial authority, the alternatives should be considered. Previously, treaties could be broken or ignored by nation-states without fear of sanction. Force seems a bit excessive to foster trade, and diplomacy is often too little. Subjecting transnational arrangements to the rule of law with enforcement by judges is surely preferable. Forfeiture of a measure of sovereignty is a small price for the potential of a world where human rights are protected and trade can benefit both prosperous and poor countries. Courts cross borders to achieve such noble goals.

CHAPTER 2

JUDICIALIZATION AND SOVEREIGNTY

Mary L. Volcansek, John F. Stack, Jr.

"Courts crossing borders" was chosen as a title to convey the convergence of two realities in international politics. The first is that the traditional meanings of national sovereignty and, indeed, possibly the nation-state itself, are undergoing a radical metamorphosis. Simultaneously, the international political sphere is becoming progressively "judicialized." By judicialization, we refer to a process explained by Torbjorn Vallinder as the "infusion of judicial decision-making and of court-like procedures into political arenas where they did not previously reside."[1] In some instances this process extends beyond formal courtroom proceedings and judicial deliberation and has come to dominate "nonjudicial negotiating or decision-making arenas by quasi-judicial (legalistic) procedures."[2] This book addresses that phenomenon at the transnational level, where courts or court-like bodies have encroached not only on what has typically been seen as the political sphere, but also on traditional notions of the nation-state and national sovereignty.

The judicialization of international politics has resulted from the creation of a growing number of transnational organizations whose aims are to promote economic or political integration or to protect human rights. These organizations have challenged notions of exclusive sovereignty "as control over population within a well-defined territory" because of concerns over "the implications on state action or inaction" on a range of issues. The state, as a re-

---

1. Torbjorn Vallinder, "When the Courts Go Marching In," in C. Neal Tate and Torbjorn Vallinder (eds.), *The Global Expansion of Judicial Power* (New York: New York University Press, 1995), 13.

2. C. Neal Tate and Torbjorn Vallinder, "The Global Expansion of Judicial Power: The Judicialization of Politics," in C. Neal Tate and Torbjorn Vallinder (eds.), *The Global Expansion of Judicial Power* (New York: New York University Press, 1995), 5.

sult, no longer is the primary actor in international relations, and "transnational, as opposed to interstate, relations have increased in importance."[3] The list of transnational organizations is long, and many of them have a tribunal of some sort embedded within them. These include the European Union, with its Court of Justice (ECJ), and the European Council, with its European Court of Human Rights (ECHR). There is also the Inter-American Court of Human Rights for the Organization of American States (OAS), and even the North American Free Trade Agreement (NAFTA) provides for bi-national panels. There are courts for the World Trade Organization (WTO), the Asian Free Trade Area (AFTA), and the Common Market of the South (MERCOSUR), as well as courts created to address a specific international issue, such as the International War Crimes Tribunal for Rwanda (ICTR) and the International War Crimes Tribunal for the Former Yugoslavia (ICTY). Perhaps the most ambitious is the newly created International Criminal Court that named its 18 judges early in 2003.[4] Whereas each of these courts possesses the capability to judicialize international relations and to erode national sovereignty, assertions of "universal jurisdiction" for human rights violations represent the most extreme threat. Universal jurisdiction possesses the potential to transcend or even obliterate protections traditionally afforded by national sovereignty for those accused of crimes against humanity.

Sovereignty

The modern state was born in Europe in the sixteenth century, and via Europe that political development extended across the entire world.[5] The theoretical bedrock of the nation-state was sovereignty, which received its first full explication by Jean Bodin. Sovereignty was understood as absolute, and necessarily so to resolve instability and disorder.[6] "Sovereignty" as a term, though, has always been, as Donald Jackson notes in his contribution, "a fickle word."

---

3. Robert O. Keohane, "International Relations, Old and New," in Robert E. Goodin and Hans-Dieter Klingemann (eds.), *A New Handbook of Political Science* (Oxford: Oxford University Press, 1996), 466.

4. Christopher Marquis, "U.N. Begins Choosing the Judges for New Court," *New York Times* (February 6, 2003), A5.

5. Samuel E. Finer, *The History of Government* (Oxford: Oxford University Press, 1997), 1261.

6. Gabriel A. Almond, "Political Science: The History of the Discipline," in Robert E. Goodin and Hans-Dieter Klingemann (eds.), *A New Handbook of Political Science* (Oxford: Oxford University Press, 1996), 58.

Sovereignty was initially conceived as absolute and indivisible and connoted a single source of power.

When most people today speak of sovereignty, they are referring to Westphalian sovereignty, associated with the 1648 Peace of Westphalia that ended the Thirty Years War. That view of sovereignty grants nations the authority, both *de jure* and *de facto*, to exercise a monopoly of power within their borders and implies that one nation cannot intervene in the domestic affairs of another nation.[7] Samuel Finer identified, however, variations within the understanding of sovereignty from the medieval era to the present, based on public and private rights and functional and territorial consolidation.[8] Not surprisingly, since variations on the concept of sovereignty have been present since the sixteenth century, degrees and deviations from a single understanding persist today.

The view of national sovereignty as monolithic eroded as cross-national transactions increased. The state lost its control over communication as transnational forms of broadcasting evolved, and direct private investment by multinationals and an increasing number of international non-governmental organizations have penetrated singular state prerogatives in the economic and social spheres. Interdependence has, of course, been a recognized phenomenon for more than thirty years.[9] The theme of the changing contours of national sovereignty recurs in discussions in this book, where various adjectives have been appended to the term—shared, pooled, limited, relative, and competitive, to note but a few.

Consensus exists among international relations scholars that globalization, in particular, has taken its toll on the traditional nation-state and its singular claim to sovereign power. Stephen Krasner notes, though, that at least three different definitions of sovereignty have been employed in addition to the Westphalian conception. Interdependence sovereignty focuses less on authority and more on control, in particular the ability of a nation to control its borders. People, ideas, goods, capital, and even diseases regularly transverse national borders on-line, on the ground, and in the air. Domestic sovereignty captures the more historical role of nation-states to control behavior within their territorial confines. International legal sovereignty is the diplomatic term for sovereignty that is based on mutual recognition and carries with it expectations that, among other things, diplomatic immunity will be respected and

---

7. Stephen D. Krasner, "Abiding Sovereignty," 22 *International Political Science Review* (2001), 234.

8. Finer, *The History of Government*, 1266.

9. Keohane, "International Relations, Old and New," 466.

that state actions are not challenged in courts of another country. A nation-state may have more or less of one form, but still retain a full measure of sovereignty in others. A world in which the nation-state remains sovereign and largely central to international relations will persist, Krasner argues, albeit in a still-evolving stage, just as it has over a period of several hundred years.[10]

Not all international relations scholars agree with Krasner's position that a nation-state-centered world is not obsolete, and they debate over the appropriate paradigm to replace earlier nation-state-centered understandings. Rosenau argues for a multi-centered international arena, in which nation-states are marginalized by a variety of non-state actors, such as international organizations and non-governmental organizations, individuals and firms, multi-national businesses and other transnational non-state entities.[11] Bertrand Badie concurs with Rosenau in his assertion that globalization has ended the state-centered version of the world, but argues that Rosenau's multi-centered view fails for its inability to account for an increasing number of transnational events, as for example ethnic and religious strife. He proposes a triangular conception of international politics, in which the nation-state is one of three major actors, flanked by and in competition with transnational networks and identity entrepreneurs. Transnational networks promote, in his model, inclusiveness, pragmatism, and utilitarianism, whereas identity entrepreneurs exploit primordial commitments, such as religion or ethnicity, and are exclusive to those who identify with the group.[12]

National sovereignty is, indeed, in a process of reinvention, but how it will look in a decade remains speculative. Remarkably, however, a volume of the *International Political Science Review* that was devoted to changing configurations of authority and sovereignty in the twenty-first century only noted the role of transnational organizations as catalysts in the process. Specific components of those organizations that are effectuating changes, notably courts, were not even mentioned. Generally, international or transnational organizations operate through traditional diplomatic channels of state-to-state or multi-state diplomacy, *except*, as the contributions to this volume demonstrate, where courts are part of the institutional framework.

Arjun Appadurai proposes that five "global flows" are eroding the nation-state: "ethnoscapes" as people move about the world in various capacities, "technoscapes" that result from flows of money and labor, "finance-scapes"

---

10. Krasner, "Abiding Sovereignty," 231–33.

11. James Rosenau, *Turbulence in World Politics* (Princeton: Princeton University Press, 1990).

12. Bertrand Badie, "Realism under Praise, or a Requiem? The Paradigmatic Debate in International Relations," 22 *International Political Science Review* (2001), 255–56.

that result from movements of global capital, and "mediascapes" and "ideoscapes" that are part of electronic communications systems.[13] We ask, why not "juriscapes," those landscapes and flows that are created by transnational judicial decisions?

Judicialization of Transnational Politics

Understandings of sovereignty have for centuries been linked to the nation-state, and similarly conceptions of judicial power have also been confined to the national level. In the United States, the extension of judicial power and challenges to its reach, at least at the level of the Supreme Court, have been acknowledged and often bemoaned for more than half a century. That recognition has come more slowly in other regions of the world, since many, like Europeans, were wed to a declaratory approach to the law: the judge is *la bouche de la loi* (the mouth of the law) and not a competitor with the legislative authority. That gap has narrowed, and the exercise of judicial power in Europe is now acknowledged as a limitation on other governmental actors.[14]

The direct and significant influence that a court can exert on the political process was first labeled as "juridification" by Alec Stone Sweet in his study of the French Constitutional Council. Stone Sweet noted that the Constitutional Council was able to set parameters for legislation in France through the weight and authority of its past jurisprudence and the threat of future censure.[15] He was describing what had been observed in the United States in instances in which judicial review serves as an *a priori* check on actions of the executive and legislative branches when the latter, cognizant through its precedents of likely Supreme Court responses to proposed actions, show a reluctance to pass legislation or take executive actions that might run afoul of the Court's authority to nullify acts that are offensive to the Constitution. What Stone Sweet accomplished was not only documenting that the judicial- legislative minuet was not restricted to the United States, but also giving it a label. What he called "juridification" became "judicialization."

---

13. Arjun Appadurai, "Disjuncture and Difference in the Global Cultural Economy," in B. Robbins (ed.), *The Phantom Public Sphere* (Minneapolis: University of Minnesota Press, 1993), 276–78.

14. Carlo Guarnieri and Patrizia Pederzoli, *The Power of Judges: A Comparative Study of Courts and Democracy* (Oxford: Oxford University Press, 2002), 4–5.

15. Alec Stone Sweet, *The Birth of Judicial Politics in France: The Constitutional Council in Comparative Perspective* (Oxford: Oxford University Press, 1992), 119.

Neal Tate then refined the meaning further, noting that there were two core elements of judicialization: first, "the process by which courts and judges come to make or increasingly to dominate the making of public policies that had previously been made...by legislatures and executives" and, second, "the process by which nonjudicial negotiating and decision-making forums come to be dominated by quasi-judicial (legalistic) rules and procedures."[16] This encapsulated the essence of judicial power, not only in the United States, but around the globe.

Stone Sweet later took the concept even further and posited that social life, not only the political sphere, was being judicialized. This occurs in any community, he writes, when a dispute settlement system accumulates power over the rule-making structure, and the rules that it makes determine how individuals interact with one another.[17]

That leaves unanswered the question of why this occurs. One answer is that in the post-World War II era, particularly in Western Europe, the long-term decline of laissez-faire economic policies led to the growth of welfare policies that opened a space for increased judicial activity in the public policy sphere.[18] The inclusion of judicial review in a number of post-World War II and now Third Wave of democratization constitutions provides an immediate opening for judicialization, since laws are subject to judicial scrutiny if challenged. Also, as Tate suggests, democracy, separation of powers, the politics of rights, use of courts by interest groups and by opposition groups, ineffective majoritarian institutions, and delegation by majoritarian institutions all foster the rise of judicial power.[19] The trend toward judicialization has been documented in democracies and emerging democracies around the world.

The new arena for tracing judicialization can be found in the growing number of transnational courts sprouting in all regions of the world. These courts present situations where the elements that have fostered an expansion of judicial power at the national level are not present. Transnational organizations are usually not democratic in their structures and sometimes involve nations that could hardly be considered democratic. Separation of powers is rarely found in any guise that Montesquieu might recognize, except possibly in the European Union. Many were created to foster trade and are not, therefore, di-

---

16. C. Neal Tate, "Why the Expansion of Judicial Power?", in C. Neal Tate and Torbjorn Vallinder (eds.), *The Global Expansion of Judicial Power* (New York: New York University Press, 1995), 28.

17. Alec Stone Sweet, *Governing with Judges: Constitutional Politics in Europe* (Oxford: University of Oxford Press, 2000), 13

18. Guarnieri and Pederzoli, *The Power of Judges*, 4.

19. Tate, "Why the Expansion of Judicial Power?", 28–33.

rectly linked to expanding welfare policies. Almost none have majoritarian institutions, effective or ineffective. The prerequisites cited in national contexts that may transfer to the transnational level include the politics of rights and the use of transnational judiciaries by interest groups and opposition groups.

Transnational Courts

The courts or court-like bodies discussed in this volume fall into two categories. Those designed to promote trade include the European Court of Justice, the bi-national panels of the North American Free Trade Association, MERCOSUR, WTO's Dispute Settlement Board, and the Asian Free Trade Area's Dispute Settlement Panels. Human rights are addressed by the European Court of Human Rights, the Inter-American Court of Human Rights, the International Criminal Courts for Rwanda and the Former Yugoslavia, and the broad assertion of universal jurisdiction. These courts emerged in different post-1945 eras, have distinctive missions and compositions, and reach different constituencies.

The authors do not hew to visions of sovereignty as singular, reposing in one institution or deriving from popular will. To most, new versions and divisions of sovereignty have been part of the international landscape since the Cold War era began. Sovereignty refers to a relativity, not to an absolute. Indeed, students of the EU have ceased discussing questions of national sovereignty since Charles de Gaulle left the center of French politics,[20] and discussions focus on federalism, intergovernmental relations, or simply levels of governance.[21]

In this volume, Donald Jackson bluntly asserts that "sovereignty has always had various and inconstant meanings," whereas David O'Brien sees "overlapping public and private spheres of governance…that transcend…old doctrines of national sovereignty." Miguel Maduro argues in his analysis of the ECJ (the oldest transnational tribunal considered) that sovereignty within the EU should be conceived as a competitive variety, in which "equal claims to independent political and legal authority…compete for final authority." The ECJ and the courts of the member nations of the EU are not, he proposes, hier-

---

20. John D. Donahue and Mark A. Pollack, "Centralization and its Discontents," in Kalypso Nicolaidis and Robert Howse (eds.), *The Federal Vision: Legitimacy and Levels of Governance in the United States and the European Union* (Oxford: Oxford University Press, 2001), 100.

21. Kalypso Nicolaidis, "Conclusion," in Kalypso Nicolaidis and Robert Howse (eds.), *The Federal Vision: Legitmacy and Levels of Governance in the United States and the European Union* (Oxford: Oxford University Press, 2001), 467.

archal, and the ECJ must therefore maintain a dialogue with national courts as they compete for rightful authority to apply EU law. Joseph Jupille looks at a single policy area of the European Union, environmental protection, and assesses the role of the ECJ in that process. He notes that sovereignty does not pose more than an artificial issue in environmental policies, since ecological borders have never been coterminous with political and economic ones and environmental problems cross national borders with impunity. Even so, he finds that decisions of the ECJ on environmental regulation have substantially eroded national sovereignty. Mary Volcansek, in her survey of selected courts and regional trade organizations, argues that courts or court-like structures are inevitable if regional trade organizations are to be effective and durable. Though she sees the creation of rules and bodies to enforce them as "necessarily compromising national sovereignty," she also envisions the resulting loss of sovereignty for nations in each trading regime to be variable—points on a continuum that runs from intergovernmental politics and soft legalism to supranational politics and hard legalism. Sovereignty is, in short, a matter of degree, rather than absolute.

Doris Marie Provine disregards the issue of sovereignty entirely in her embrace of the potential for the European Court of Human Rights to dismantle national mechanisms of discrimination. Indeed, since the ECHR allows citizens to bring suits directly, bypassing national institutions and often challenging them, sovereignty is reduced to an artificial construct. John Stack sees the Inter-American Court of Human Rights as an intentional challenge to the state, as an international, not national, society sets the norms and transmits them downward to nation-states.

The most direct and in many ways absolute affront to national autonomy comes from courts investigating war crimes and crimes against humanity. Kimi King and James Meernick's consideration of gender justice before the International War Crimes Tribunal for the Former Yugoslavia envisions a court that will end in all national settings "the culture of impunity" that has surrounded sexual assault as a weapon of war. Donald Jackson's analysis of universal jurisdiction reveals that its proponents intend to eradicate all lines of sovereignty when certain crimes are committed. Universal jurisdiction asserts "the authority of state courts or international tribunals with criminal jurisdiction to prosecute certain crimes recognized under international law, no matter where the offense occurred or regardless of the nationality of either the victim or the perpetrator."

Courts created explicitly to protect human rights have had differential successes, which translates into variable penetration of national sovereignty and national rules. The European Court of Human Rights is viewed by Provine primarily as creating a moral framework for governments, rather than adjudicating every wrong. Indeed, in her analysis of discrimination cases, she found that the ECHR ruled on a mere seven percent of the claims of discrimination that reached it. She attributes this anomaly to the fact that under the European Convention, the right not to be discriminated against is not a basic right. In other words, discrimination claims must always accompany an allegation that a basic right has been violated; if that argument fails or can resolve the case, the discrimination issue evaporates. Stack found that the most significant work of the human rights tribunal for the Americas lies in its strong denunciation of the practice of "disappearances of people" under authoritarian regimes. More importantly, the Inter-American Court has not only found national regimes guilty of disappearances, it also has levied and secured payment of fines and reparations by the offending nations. The problem of the European human rights body is that it now attracts too many complaints, whereas the Inter-American Court has had too few to fashion an overarching moral framework. Notably, the caseload of the European Court has increased since in 1998 the commission that had previously certified cases to the court was dismantled. In the inter-American system, the commission remains a gatekeeper to the Court and prefers diplomatic options to legal ones.

King and Meernick conclude that, despite criticisms from feminists, the International War Crimes Tribunal for the Former Yugoslavia has been successful in convicting and sentencing perpetrators of rape as an instrument of war and, thus, in breaking the culture of impunity. Universal jurisdiction to punish those who commit internationally defined crimes is still an evolving process, with the Belgian judiciary standing as the ones who are most willing to apply universal jurisdiction and to try other nationals in Belgian courts. The newly created International Criminal Court will serve as the largest test for the application of universal jurisdiction, but Jackson cautions that universal jurisdiction remains in an evolutionary state as a means to ensure that "no state has the right to violate human rights as part of its sovereign domestic jurisdiction."

The alphabet soup of courts at the transnational level has judicialized two types of transnational systems: human rights and economic policies. How and why each type has become more subject to judicial power than others is largely speculative. In the realm of trade or other economic issues, part of the answer may lie in the requirements of treaties. The NAFTA treaty represents an extremely detailed and carefully negotiated text, which should leave little room for judicial maneuvering. David O'Brien confirmed that out of the first thirty-six decisions of the bi-national panels, national regulatory agencies were reversed only once, though cases were remanded in some fashion fourteen times.

The treaties that undergird the European Union display more elasticity, most likely because so many different nations were involved in the negotiations and needed to be satisfied. Even so, the ECJ had few cases reach it during the early years of its existence. When even the first cases began to trickle in, the ECJ took the opportunity, as Maduro notes, to "constitutionalize the treaties." In the 1962 case of *Van Gend en Loos*, the ECJ declared that the treaty is not an agreement among states, but rather a pact made by the peoples of Europe. That decision had the effect, according to Maduro, of creating a European political community based on people, not nation-states.

Of the other economic organizations considered here, only the Common Market of the South has any aspirations beyond a free trade association or a customs union. The experience of the ECJ may, therefore, not be useful. Even so, the very success of the different economic blocs will, using Volcansek's logic, lead to the need for more regulations and, subsequently, to a body that is able to apply and enforce those rules. Even with the highly specific NAFTA treaty, O'Brien tells us that seventy-four cases were filed during the association's first seven years—an average of more than ten per year.

Courts, conventions, and treaties designed to try and punish human rights violators are just now proliferating. Stack explains this phenomenon, using the stages of development articulated by Risse and Sikkink, which emphasize the roles played by international non-governmental organizations and international networks as catalysts for the creation of human rights regimes. To achieve success, however, those efforts must be coupled with support for and internalization of norms at the societal level. Permitting direct access by aggrieved citizens is one means of forging the essential connection between the transnational norms and their efficacy. Notably, the ECJ, along with the ECHR and the Inter-American Court, all permit individual access, which facilitates a direct connection between citizens and judges, without the interposition of a national government between them. The number of citizen complaints reaching the European tribunals has soared, but that has not been the case for the Inter-American Court, where the Inter-American Commission filters the cases that will be adjudicated.

The International War Crimes Tribunal for the Former Yugoslavia is a criminal court, as is its parallel body for the atrocities committed in Rwanda. The victims of the crimes do not prosecute their own cases. In the cases of mass rape on which King and Meernick focus, the victims would be incapable of prosecuting their cases as all are civilians, and most were "severely traumatized." This tribunal and likely the International Criminal Court will evolve differently from what has been observed in the European and inter-American systems.

All of the courts or court-like bodies treated in this volume are transnational and, by definition, cross borders. The extent to which their pronouncements result in judicialization is variable at this time. Undoubtedly, the older bodies, such as the ECJ and ECHR and even the WTO, have already reached that place. When national policies are being formed, prior rulings by the courts are weighed and the language of legal proceedings permeates discussions and deliberations so as to escape judicial censure later. The Inter-American Court of Human Rights, the International War Crimes Tribunal for the Former Yugoslavia, and other relatively new courts for regional trade organizations have not yet accumulated a weighty jurisprudence that lends authority to their work. Obviously, assertions of universal jurisdiction to punish human rights crimes have, at this point in time, virtually no broadly accepted jurisprudence to direct political processes. The extent to which courts will effectively cross borders and blur lines of sovereignty will depend on the trajectories that the courts and those who bring cases before them set. If they follow the strategies of the older transnational courts, they, too, will judicialize politics and extend judicial power within their jurisdictions.

Stephen Krasner noted, when writing about the resilience of the nation-state and its attendant sovereignty, that the international system is anarchy, *unless* rules and institutions are in place to establish a hierarchy. These rules, he wrote, must be "recognized and consequential."[22] The key to making rules knowable and enforceable is the existence of a body charged with authoritatively interpreting and applying them and possessing the teeth to enforce decisions—a court, in other words. Hopefully, students of international relations will recognize the tenuousness of rules in the absence of dispute resolution systems and acknowledge the role, both current and potential, for transnational courts to enforce a hierarchy of norms and regulations and lend order to the chaotic international system.

---

22. Krasner, "Abiding Sovereignty," 229.

CHAPTER 3

COURTS AND REGIONAL TRADE AGREEMENTS

Mary L. Volcansek

Many new regional organizations have been born since 1980 in response to changing economic and political conditions worldwide and with an eye toward protecting intraregional trade under changed global rules. Trade was the driving force for most, but one regional arrangement for the protection of human rights also emerged. By 1999, more than one hundred trade associations had been registered with the World Trade Organization (WTO).[1] The proliferation of regional agreements carries potentially wide-ranging implications for both politics and economics, and the implication on which I focus in this essay is the apparent momentum, as cross-border transactions increase in number and intensity, to establish comprehensive rules and a mechanism to enforce them. The resulting rules and dispute resolution authority necessarily compromise national sovereignty.

The theory of "institutionalization" devised by Alec Stone Sweet and Wayne Sandholtz[2] to explain integration in the European Union offers a theoretical map for an examination of the drive to create dispute resolution systems in regional economic integration schemes. The institutional arrangements of the many newly formed economic alliances vary considerably,[3] and like those that began some three decades ago, there will be some successes and a lot of fail-

---

1. Sung-Hoon Park, "Regionalism, Open Regionalism and GATT, Article XXIV," unpublished paper presented at conference on Regional and Global Regulations of International Trade (Macao: Instituto de Estudos Europeus de Macau), 1.

2. Alec Stone Sweet and Wayne Sandholtz, "Integration, Supranational Governance and the Institutionalization of the European Polity," in Wayne Sandholtz and Alec Stone Sweet (eds.), *European Integration and Supranational Governance* (Oxford: Oxford University Press, 1998), 1-26.

3. E.D. Mansfield and H.V. Melner, *The Political Economy of Regionalism* (New York: Columbia University Press, 1997), 14.

ures.[4] Using the Stone Sweet and Sandholtz model as a guide, I argue for the inevitability of some mechanism for formal dispute resolution—a court, if you will—if regional economic cooperation is to be stable and durable.

Regional arrangements for protecting human rights seem, however, to be creatures quite distinct from those with economic motivations in both their origins and their approaches to dispute resolution. Global notions of human rights are recognized, but the international community "has not developed enforcement mechanisms for ensuring compliance," and that failure has opened doors for what Wheeler calls "humanitarian vigilantes" or "legal entrepreneurs."[5] The catalysts for both democratization and the protection of human rights can be located in transnational social movements[6] or in transnational advocacy networks that form critical international-domestic links.[7] The success of transnational human rights regimes seemingly depends on internal pressure from below, since there is rarely domestic leadership from the top.[8] Configurations of regional arrangements for the protection of human rights will likely be driven by forces distinct from those behind trade arrangements and are, thereby, beyond the reach of this piece.

Crossing Borders

The precise origins of the new forms of regional integration are murky, but there are a number of potential explanations for the explosion of regional customs unions, free trade areas, and other cooperative ventures in the waning years of the twentieth century.[9] The end of the Cold War and the breakdown of a bipolar world obviously coincided with the emergence of a new round of regionalism and may have opened a space for new economic configurations.

---

4. Walter Mattli, *The Logic of Regional Integration: Europe and Beyond* (Cambridge: Cambridge University Press, 1999), 187.

5. Nicolas J. Wheeler, "Humanitarian Vigilantes or Legal Entrepreneurs?" in Simon Casey and Peter Jones (eds.), *Human Rights and Global Diversity* (London: Frank Cass, 2001).

6. Alison Brysk, *From Tribal Village to Global Village* (Stanford: Stanford University Press, 2000), 286.

7. Thomas Risse and Kathryn Sikkink, "The Socialization of International Human Rights Norms into Domestic Practices: Introduction," in Thomas Risse, Stephen C. Ropp, and Kathryn Sikkink (eds.), *The Power of Human Rights: International Norms and Domestic Changes* (Cambridge: Cambridge University Press, 1999), 5.

8. Charles R. Epp, *The Rights Revolution: Lawyers, Activists, and Supreme Courts in Comparative Perspective* (Chicago: University of Chicago Press, 1998), 197.

9. Mattli, *The Logic of Regional Integration*.

Those events alone, however, cannot explain the increased propensity to embrace market-oriented economies in both industrialized and developing nations, North and South, East and West.[10] Acceptance of free trade and its inherently liberal market underpinnings are the result of a convergence of factors and, because of the presumed link between democracy and economic development, have been hailed as steps toward the end of dictatorial rule.[11] One important motivation for regional trade agreements can be found in a less lofty place: a provision of the General Agreement of Tariffs and Trade (GATT) that has been carried forward into the WTO. Article XXIV permits regional customs unions and free trade areas to maintain internal preferential treatment that need not be extended to non-member nations.[12]

The kaleidoscope of regional trade arrangements varies from customs unions and free trade areas to the European model of economic integration; their forms and their limits follow no single pattern, and they can be found on many continents. Some of the most prominent include MERCOSUR or the Common Market of the South (Argentina, Brazil, Chile, Paraguay, and Uruguay), ASEAN and AFTA (Association of Southeast Asian Nations and Asian Free Trade Area), APEC (Asia-Pacific Economic Cooperation), NAFTA (North American Free Trade Association), and the EU or European Union. Despite their obvious diversity, there may nonetheless be common threads in their development that are worth tracing.

Regions are by definition reflective of geographic proximity, but a "prior sense of belonging" together is not necessarily a causal factor in the new regionalism. The regional phenomenon of the last two decades has largely been a state-led attempt to devise strategies for meeting the new exigencies of economic globalization. The new regionalism is geographic, within an economic space, but it is also dynamic, inevitably changing in response to the winds of global trade.[13] Recognizing the dynamic quality of geo-economic arrangements is essential to understanding and projecting their development. Agreements that are reached among states can lead to "soft" or "hard" regionalism,

---

10. Miles Kahler, *Regional Futures and Transatlantic Economic Relations* (New York: Council on Foreign Relations Press, 1995), 3.

11. Samuel P. Huntington, *The Third Wave: Democratization in the Late Twentieth Century* (Norman, OK: University of Oklahoma Press, 1993), 311.

12. Frederick M. Abbott, "The North American Integration Regime and its Implications for the World Trading System," in J.H.H. Weiler (ed.), *The EU, the WTO, and the NAFTA* (Oxford: Oxford University Press, 2000), 173–77.

13. Jean Grugel and Wil Hout, "Regions, Regionalism and the South," in Jean Grugel and Will Hout (eds.), *Regionalism across the North-South Divide* (London: Routledge, 1999), 10.

with the former referring exclusively to economic ties and the latter indicating political ones.[14] Some are predicated on long-standing and natural affinities that pre-date any formal connections, as is the case of relations between Canada and the United States. Others are reactions to economic opportunism. Whereas most regional experiments of the last twenty or so years are intended only to nurture free trade, they often tend to "'harden' into formal agreements and international obligations...that extend well beyond the traditional goals of lowering or eliminating tariffs."[15]

Charting the progression from soft regionalism to a harder form is where experiences and conceptual models from the European experience can be helpful. The distinction between soft and hard regionalism is analogous to that often drawn in analysis of the European Union between intergovernmental and supranational governance. Regional relations and, indeed, most inter-state relationships do not fit neatly into one or the other category, for the distinctions rest on points between the two poles. As various regional arrangements mature or change, different aspects of inter-state or transnational relationships may move more closely to one or to the other.

Institutionalization

The framework of institutionalization presented by Stone Sweet and Sandholtz to explain differential integration within the EU is useful for understanding not only the etiology of regional agreements, but also their progression toward or into supranational arrangements or harder forms of regionalism. Institutionalization offers an explanation about how an interstate bargain in Europe was transformed into a "multidimensional, quasi-federal polity." The basic assertion of the theory is that European society first became transnational when economic, social, and political transactions and communications regularly transversed national borders. Non-state actors soon found that national legal rules created transaction costs and inhibited the generation of wealth and other collective goods. They then exerted pressure on national —that is state—decision makers, who quite naturally had their own vested interests in preserving state autonomy and control unhindered by external ties. Nation-states typically resist transnational agreements that potentially threaten their sovereignty, but in doing so, they risk blocking increased prosperity within their borders. State actors may enter into limited intergovernmental

---

14. Kahler, *Regional Futures*, 8.
15. Ibid., 9.

negotiations, but are thereafter in a position of reacting to pressure for increased integration.[16]

Non-state actors engaging in cross-border transactions in Europe sought broader rules to govern transaction costs and to lower the price of cross-border relationships. Transnational exchanges flow more efficiently when there is a single standard for customs requirements, health and technical standards, environmental regulations, commercial law, and currency rates. Once the rules are in place, however, there is a need for mechanisms to enforce them. When those mechanisms are created or institutionalized, the transition to hard or supranational governance begins. Stone Sweet and Sandholtz envision a continuum of integration that ranges from intergovernmentalism to supranational governance, with various points along it denoting different degrees of linkages among nations and transnational actors on different policies and in different realms. Intergovernmentalism or soft regionalism focuses on national actors, who bargain over different policies; it involves passive structures that enable more efficient state-to-state negotiations. At the opposite end is supranationalism, where centralized structures have some jurisdiction over the geographic area of all the states. These supranational bodies are then "institutionalized" and able to affect and constrain both national states and individuals; the institutions are, of course, equally susceptible to influences from states and other actors. Even in the European Union, a highly uneven pattern of integration has evolved, where supranational politics are paramount in some policy arenas, but where intergovernmental politics dominate in others.[17]

The key elements of the institutionalization thesis are (1) transnational society leads to interdependency, which in turn requires (2) supranational rules and (3) supranational organizations. The logic that has led to the European Union as it stands early in the twenty-first century also explains and may predict the direction of more recent regional trade agreements. The interests of economic elites of different nations in reducing the costs of cross-border transactions pressure national decision makers for formation of regional trading areas, since navigating multiple national trade regimes is inefficient and expensive. At some point, state interests and those of other social and economic actors converge, and intergovernmental bargaining occurs to create a customs union or a free trade zone within a confined geographic area. Soft regionalism is thereby begun. State interests are not, how-

---

16. Stone Sweet and Sandholtz, "Integration, Supranational Governance, and the Institutionalization."

17. Ibid., 1–16.

ever, monolithic, but are rather an amalgam of competing demands by interest groups. In the area of trade, economic elites, exporters, and investors are likely the ones who prevail, possibly over other interests, such as labor and environmental ones, to secure a reduction of cross-border transaction costs.[18]

The overarching trade regime in the post-World War II era was that of the General Agreement on Tariffs and Trade that was transformed in 1995 into the World Trade Organization. Non-discrimination among nations in trade forms the core of both the GATT and the WTO. The next level of trade integration is that of a free trade area, where tariffs and other restrictive measures are eliminated. Usually free trade areas reach services, capital, and goods, but apply only in a limited fashion to people. Customs unions are more integrated and entail prohibitions on tariffs and other restrictive measures, but also impose a common tariff on externally imported goods. Federal or complete economic integration can extend to political, social, and even security goals.[19] Once initial intergovernmental negotiations forming a free trade area or a customs union are completed, a number of factors many derail the process. Uncertainty and incomplete information interfere with transnational interactions unless there are other means to secure adherence to the rules, and more complex institutional arrangements often become necessary to guarantee the rules and police violations.[20] Rules emerge as essential to govern points of origin, restrictive measures, anti-dumping, subsidies, countervailing duties, non-tariff discrimination, and health and environmental standards. Such rules are necessary to insure that competition, even of a limited scope, is fair to all players and, once instituted, replace the earlier national trade norms.

Many regional experiments either break down or begin a course toward supranational governance when trying to administer the rules. Enforcement may be achieved through diplomacy and, when that fails, resort may be made to other measures. The ultimate alternative is dissolution of the trade agreement, and, indeed, though 184 regional trade agreements were at some point communicated to the GATT/WTO, at least 75 were not in force as of 1999.[21] The reasons for disintegration have not been systematically examined, but the inability to resolve competing claims or interests likely lies at the base of some failures. The absence of some form of enforcement mechanism can lead national commitments to regional trade arrangements to wax and wane with

18. Grugel and Hout, "Regions, Regionalism and the South," 176.
19. Abbott, "The North American Integration Regime," 173.
20. Mattli, *The Logic of Regional Integration*, 53–54.
21. Park, "Regionalism, Open Regionalism and GATT," 1.

each electoral cycle and subsequent shift in national administration. Transnational trade is obviously inhibited when the validity and enforceability of contracts, obligations, and rules cannot be assured beyond the term of office of an administration.

Some means separate from nation-state control must, in other words, exist to produce, monitor, and enforce the rules. Cross-border transactions create the need for transnational rules, but the efficacy of the rules depends on the mechanism to administer them. This is where a trajectory toward supranational governance begins. The Stone Sweet and Sandholtz framework does not suggest an inevitable motion toward diminution of sovereignty and a rise in federalism; rather, it recognizes a substantial variation by policy domain. The continuum from intergovernmental politics to supranational ones acknowledges unevenness across policies and makes placement of any specific policy arena dependent on both the presence and the intensity of transactions, rules, and organizations.[22] State-centered intergovernmentalism and diplomacy may remain the essential means of carrying out some policies, whereas supranational governance may predominate in others. The European Union anticipated, from its earliest days as the European Coal and Steel Community, a mix of national primacy and supranationalism. Most of the newly emerging regional trade associations envision no larger goal than establishment of a tariff-free trade area, administered at the intergovernmental level.

Rise of Dispute Settlement Systems

A process parallel to that sketched by Stone Sweet and Sandholtz has also been noticed in the tendency toward legalism in regional arrangements. Following in the wake of increased regionalism is the "less widespread move toward legalism in the enforcement of trade agreements."[23] The same adjectives that are used to describe regionalism, "soft" and "hard," are, according to James McCall Smith, also applicable to the realm of legalism. Hard legalism involves precise, binding legal obligations and a delegation of authority for interpreting and applying the law, whereas soft legalism refers to the absence of

---

22. Stone Sweet and Sandholtz, "Integration, Supranational Governance and the Institutionalization," 9.

23. James McCall Smith, "The Politics of Dispute Settlement Design: Explaining Legalism in Regional Trade Pacts," 54 *International Organization* (2000), 137–80.

those features.[24] Soft law is typical in international relations, but the goal of retaining policy discretion must give way in some circumstances to the desire to ensure treaty compliance. Discretion is retained when diplomacy is the vehicle, but compliance is more likely achieved through a harder from of legalism.[25]

As Figure 3.1 illustrates, the Stone Sweet and Sandholtz continuum from intergovernmentalism to supranational politics can be overlaid with that of Smith's soft-to-hard legalism. Intergovernmental politics rest on state-to-state diplomacy

Figure 3.1   Potential for Institutionalization and Legalization

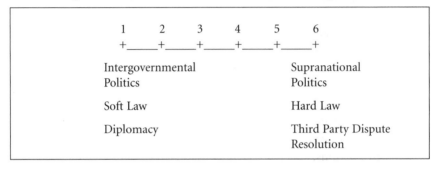

*Combination of concepts from Alec Stone Sweet and Wayne Sandholtz, "Integration, Supranational Governance, and the Institutionalization of the European Polity," in Wayne Sandholtz and Alec Stone Sweet, *European Integration and Supranational Governance* (Oxford: Oxford University Press, 1998); and James McCall Smith, "The Politics of Dispute Settlement Design: Explaining Legalism in Regional Trade Pacts," 54 *International Organization* (Winter 2000).

and with few elements of obligation, precision, or delegation of enforcement. Supranational politics involve high degrees of the elements of legalism, but there are points between those two anchors where some precision, some binding obligation, or some form of delegation to third party dispute resolution may lie.

At this stage in the evolution of regional trade agreements, few conclusions are certain. However, one of the motivating factors behind the growth of regional arrangements may be "a lack of confidence in the capacity of the GATT multilateral trading system to enforce a rule of law in trade relations."[26]

---

24. Kenneth W. Abbott and Duncan Snidal, "Hard and Soft Law in International Governance," 54 *International Organization* (2000), 421–56.

25. Smith, "The Politics of Dispute Settlement Design," 173.

26. Enzo Grille, "Multilateralism and Regionalism: A Still Difficult Coexistence," in Riccardo Faini and Enzo Grille (eds.), *Multilateralism and Regionalism after the Uruguay Round* (Basingstoke: Macmillan Press, 1997), 224.

That is undoubtedly only one of many explanations, but it nevertheless points to a problem that is central to the potential success of the new trade arrangements.

An obvious resolution to the problem of enforcing the rules of transnational trade is a formal dispute resolution system. The need to seek a neutral third party to resolve disputes is so natural as to require almost no elaboration. Richard Abel asserts that conflicts are part of the fabric of social and, implicitly, commercial relationships and are transformed into disputes when conflicting claims are asserted publicly. Most disputes never reach a judicial body, broadly defined. Some may simmer indefinitely without resolution, whereas others demand closure of some sort. Some disputes remain solely between the competing parties, whereas others gain momentum and are driven to a third party who is asked to intervene and apply the rules authoritatively.[27] The logic is so compelling that "courts have become a universal political phenomenon."[28]

The need is equally obvious at the inter-state level, but the potential parties are more reticent. At the inter-state level, the preference is usually to avoid soft law, hard law, or any of the points between. If the dispute remains solely between two nations, diplomacy is usually the preferred mechanism for resolution of the dispute. Of course, that option holds out the potential for no conclusion, and for that reason legalization is progressively being observed at the inter-state level. Most international actors prefer soft law—where obligation, precision, or delegation are absent—to avoid costs, threats to independence, and, of course, diminution of sovereignty.[29] Yet the intervention of a third party to resolve the dispute, whether authoritative or an application of soft or hard law, is becoming more common at the transnational level. Collective action problems can be solved by providing a means of punishing defection and enforcing cooperation.[30] At times, the simple act of providing a forum for dispute settlement can motivate the parties to resolve their conflict without involving an outside third party.

This logic has led to some form of outside, third party intervention mechanism in a number of international and transnational arrangements: the In-

27. Richard L. Abel, "A Comparative Theory of Dispute Institutions in Society," 8 *Law and Society Review* (1973), 217–347.

28. Martin Shapiro, *Courts: A Comparative and Political Analysis* (Chicago: University of Chicago Press, 1981), 1.

29. Abbott and Snidal, "Hard and Soft Law," 423.

30. Simon Hix, *The Political System of the European Union* (Basingstoke: Macmillan Press, 1999), 100.

ternational Court of Justice, the European Court of Human Rights, the Inter-American Court of Human Rights, the World Trade Organization's Dispute Settlement Board, and the European Union's Court of Justice. Other treaty arrangements provide for softer forms of norm enforcement, such as NAFTA's inclusion of dispute settlement panels for some types of conflicts or mandatory use of the WTO mechanism for others. For example, a panel of scientific experts is included in NAFTA to decide environmental and health issues, whereas some other categories of disputes are assigned directly to national courts for resolution.[31] One study of the newly emerging regional trade associations recognized the obvious need for a formal mechanism to resolve competing claims and strongly recommended that all such agreements should provide a mechanism for open forum dispute resolution and access to the Dispute Settlement Board of the WTO.[32] Notably, despite the logic of third party dispute resolution, most of the newly formed regional trade associations rely on the presumption of self-regulation.[33] Self-regulation of interstate agreements may be successful, but when it fails to achieve compliance, diplomacy is the only recourse. The General Agreement on Tariffs and Trade experience is instructive about the future of such a configuration: from its beginning, it used a diplomacy-based approach, but by 1979 legal mechanisms had evolved as central to its structure.[34] When it was transformed into the WTO in 1995, it adopted a system for adjudicating disputes that is both effective and sophisticated.[35]

Myriad potential problems inhere in state-to-state negotiations to resolve disputes. The most obvious is, of course, that no resolution may be possible. A second is the hierarchy among nations that prevents some from bargaining or asserting their claims on an equal footing. More fundamental, though, is the absence of a single, unified state interest when issues of trade are involved. Indeed, multiple competing interests are more likely. Labor and management seek different outcomes, consumers do not necessarily share

---

31. Mario F. Bognanno and Kathryn J. Ready (eds.), *The North American Free Trade Agreement* (Westport, CT: Quorum Books, 1993), 38.

32. Jaime Serra, *Reflections on Regionalism* (Washington, D.C.: Carnegie Endowment for International Peace, 1997), 54–55.

33. William D. Coleman and Geoffrey R.D. Underhill (eds.), *Regionalism and Global Economic Integration* (London: Routledge, 1998), 9–10.

34. Robert E. Hudec, *Enforcing International Trade Law: The Evolution of the Modern GATT Legal System* (Salem, NH: Butterworths, 1993), 11–15.

35. Robert Howse, "Adjudicative Legitimacy and Treaty Interpretation in International Trade Law," in J.H.H. Weiler (ed.), *The EU, the WTO and the NAFTA* (Oxford: Oxford University Press, 2000), 35.

the interests of producers, and importers and exporters may see trade advantages from opposite perspectives. Even though national solutions to many policy problems have lost their credibility,[36] the nation-state and its concern for sovereignty and authority can, nonetheless, overshadow those of free trade economies. Even so, states are being drawn into a "larger and more complex political structure that is the counterpart of the production and financial systems."[37]

Cases of Economic Dispute Regulation

The logic, if not the necessity, of adopting a third party approach to dispute resolution in regional trade agreements is best explained by looking at the experience of the most prominent of the regional arrangements. The European Union is the oldest, most stable, and most durable of them all, and its experience underscores the advisability of forging "an immutable link between law and legal processes, and integration [sometimes]...simplistically understood as a process leading towards greater centralization of governmental functions."[38] The oft-told story, familiar to European lawyers, is one whereby the judicial organ of the European Communities/Union, the European Court of Justice (ECJ), transformed the treaties into a constitution and established a system of supranational governance.[39] A brief version of that evolution begins with the Treaty of Paris, signed in 1951, to create the limited European Coal and Steel Community of six member nations. A decade later, the constitutionalization of the treaties began with an ECJ decision that established the doctrine of direct effect and enabled citizens of the various signatory states to assert their treaty rights in national courts and, thereby, transferred enforcement of treaty provisions from state-to-state negotiations to national courts.[40]

---

36. Daniel Wincott, "Political Theory, Law and European Union," in J. Shaw and G. Moore (eds.), *New Legal Dynamics of European Union* (Oxford: Clarendon Press, 1995), 308.

37. Coleman and Underhill, *Regionalism and Global Economic Integration*, 6.

38. Jo Shaw, "Introduction," in J. Shaw and G. Moore (eds.), *New Legal Dynamics of European Union* (Oxford: Clarendon Press, 1995), 3.

39. Miguel Poiares Maduro, *We the Court: The European Court of Justice and the European Economic Constitution* (Oxford: Hart Publishing, 1998), 7–30; J.H.H. Weiler, *The Constitution of Europe: Do the New Clothes Have an Emperor?* (Cambridge: Cambridge University Press, 1999), 221–24.

40. *NV Algememe Transport-en Expedities Onderneming Van Gend en Loos v. Netherlands Inland Revenue Administration*, Case 26/62 [ECR 1, 1963].

The doctrine of the supremacy of Community law over any conflicting national law was asserted by the ECJ the following year,[41] and those two complimentary doctrines elevated the stature of the treaties as fixing the rules of the game and placing courts, ultimately the ECJ, as the arbiter of those rules. Subsequently, even private law has been recognized as "Europeanized,"[42] and member states can be held financially liable for damages resulting from a failure to meet their obligations under the treaties.[43] The sum of the ECJ's jurisprudence led to the establishment of supranational governance in a wide range of legal questions, and the ECJ itself became a "catalyst in the integration process."[44]

In the international arena, however, the European Union also illustrates how nation-states always have the option of renegotiating the bargain. When national leaders became troubled by some of the decisions that the ECJ was making, they chose to limit the court's reach. Specifically, in the 1991 Maastrich Treaty, the ECJ was denied any role in new policy areas of the EU, particularly those in which national sovereignty was more directly implicated: justice and home affairs.[45] That turn of events underscores one particular quality of all international agreements: they can always be altered, through negotiation or dissolution.

The other long-lived trade arrangement is the General Agreement on Tariffs and Trade, which dates from 1947, and its successor, the World Trade Organization. The essence of the GATT commercial treaty is the principle of non-discrimination or the "most favorable nation" designation, whereby all members must accord to all other members the same trading privileges that it grants to any nation, whether or not that nation is a GATT member. As noted earlier, the various regional trade organizations benefit from the loophole that permits exceptions for the special treatment of regional trading partners. With each successive round of negotiations of the GATT, more and more trade regulations have been subsumed by it. Originally, states lodged complaints against one another only if diplomacy failed, and those complaints

---

41. *Costa v. ENEL*, Case 6/64 [ECR 585, 1964].

42. Christian Joerges, "The Impact of European Integration on Private Law: Reductionist Perceptions, True Conflicts and a New Constitutionalist Perspective," 3 *European Law Journal* (1997).

43. Takis Tridimas, "Member State Liability in Damages for Breach of Community Law: An Assessment of the Case Law," in Jack Beatson and Takis Tridimas (eds.), *New Directions in European Public Law* (Oxford: Hart Publishing, 1998).

44. Renaud Dehousse, *The European Court of Justice: The Politics of Judicial Integration* (New York: St. Martin's Press, 1998), 71.

45. David M. Wood and Birol A. Yesilada, *The Emerging European Union* (White Plains: Longman Press, 1996), 111–12.

were considered, first, by plenary sessions and, later, by ad hoc committees. As early as 1955, panels were recognized as the mechanism for dispute resolution. There was no fixed membership for panels, and nations could block the process at each stage, from forming a panel to reporting a decision. Panels were not intended to be juristic, but rather to "facilitate a satisfactory diplomatic settlement."[46] Rulings were intentionally vague and bore little resemblance to legal documents, but that was clearly by design.[47] By the end of the 1960s, the gentlemen's diplomatic approach was breaking down as nations preferred to avoid interference in various protectionist policies. The panels were reinvigorated by the 1980s, and lawyers replaced diplomats. The system assumed a more formal and legal texture, both in process and in decisions.[48]

As GATT membership grew, not only were more nations included, but also more incompatible values were represented. Old approaches that made the GATT system successful later emerged as its weaknesses: "secrecy, the centralized management of conflict and interpretation by bureaucrats, the exclusion of controversial material…all now served to rob the outcome of social legitimacy."[49] As a result, at the conclusion of the Uruguay Round and the advent of the WTO, a new panel system was put into place. The Geneva-based Dispute Settlement Board now oversees a bureaucracy for receiving complaints and establishing panels. Panels are convened only after negotiated settlements have proven impossible; decisions of panels may be appealed to the seven-person Standing Appellate Body; and the Dispute Settlement Board reviews all panel decisions. Enforcement is also supposed to be stronger under the WTO system than under the looser GATT panel system.[50] The system underwent a transition, in other words, from diplomacy to legalism, but nonetheless retains some of the more suspect elements of its earlier incarnation, such as secret pleadings and deliberations. Even so, the presence of an appellate body and the public nature of decisions, once rendered, make the system more transparent. That is, according, to Robert Howse, particularly important as panels must arbitrate and decide among competing values more and more.[51] In his analysis of the rulings of the Standing Appellate Body, he found that the recorded structure achieved greater social legitimacy through fair procedures, coherence and integrity in legal interpretation,

---

46. Alec Stone Sweet, "The New GATT," in Mary L. Volcansek (ed.), *Law Above Nations* (Gainesville, FL: University Press of Florida, 1997), 122.

47. Hudec, *Enforcing International Trade Law*, 12.

48. Stone Sweet, "The New GATT."

49. Howse, "Adjudicative Legitimacy and Treaty Interpretation," 39.

50. Stone Sweet, "The New GATT."

51. Howse, "Adjudicative Legitimacy and Treaty Interpretation," 39.

and institutional sensitivity.[52] In other words, the movement toward legalization of the trade regime has been accompanied by a parallel increase in legitimacy.

The North American Free Trade Area emerged, as David O'Brien explains in chapter 8, to facilitate trade between two adjacent nations, Canada and the U.S., which already had significant cross-border commercial transactions, and then expanded southward to include Mexico. The new regional trade agreement entered into force in 1997. Unlike the EU, the locus of authority remains at the national level and the union is more akin to a confederation.[53] NAFTA aimed at liberalizing markets, not, like the EU, at political integration, but even so, it too has developed a legalized approach to dispute resolution. Whereas the EU and the WTO adopted centralized mechanisms for resolving economic disputes under their umbrellas, NAFTA opted for a variety of mechanisms, depending on the particular issue. Despite its decentralization, NAFTA is among the "most highly detailed international trade agreements ever negotiated between governments" and includes twenty-two chapters detailing specific obligations of the member nations.[54] That extreme level of precision in enumeration of obligations ought to render dispute resolution less necessary. Ambiguity can be found, however, in any legal document.

Mechanisms to resolve disputes under the NAFTA document range broadly. For some conflicts, the WTO Dispute Settlement Board is mandated, and for others, national courts are the designated forum. A panel of scientific experts hears environmental and health issues, and a dispute settlement mechanism is available for other kinds of conflicts.[55] The last of these can be described as more akin to arbitration than to a legal forum, and ultimately the matter is referred to the national governments for a political resolution. There exists, however, another dispute resolution vehicle to address only anti-dumping and countervailing duties.[56] This high degree of specificity has been described as *ex ante* negotiation, intended to avoid later *ex post* renegotiation.[57] Unlike either the WTO or the EU, NAFTA involves no delegation of authority for (1) passage of secondary legislation, (2) selection of dispute settlement panels, or (3) incorporation of NAFTA norms into national legal systems. It does, however, allow for private parties to seek third party arbitration, with awards en-

52. Ibid., 68–69.
53. Abbott, "The North American Integration Regime," 171.
54. Frederick M. Abbott, "NAFTA and the Legalization of World Politics: A Case Study," 54 *International Organization* (2000), 324.
55. Bognanno and Ready, *The North American Free Trade Agreement*, 38.
56. Abbott, "The North American Integration Regime," 172.
57. Abbott, "NAFTA and the Legalization of World Politics," 525–28.

forced by national courts. Moreover, in anticipation that state-to-state nego-tiations may not succeed in resolving fundamental differences, NAFTA pro-vides for a state's exit from the agreement with six-month notice.[58]

MERCOSUR, or the Common Market of the South, was designed as a cus-toms union and could, as a result, be expected to be closer to the EU in form and trajectory than to the more limited free trade areas of NAFTA. Two previ-ous attempts at establishing free trade areas in that geographic area had failed, but MERCOSUR's objectives were more ambitious and seemed, in the wake of re-democratization in the Southern cone, more propitious. The Treaty of Asun-cion in 1991 committed Argentina, Brazil, Paraguay, and Uruguay to create a common market by 1995. If the NAFTA treaty stands as a model of *ex ante* bar-gaining and specificity, then the Treaty of Asuncion must merit the opposite des-ignation, leaving much of the detail and process of implementation available for *ex post* bargaining. Indeed, a dispute settlement system was included in the 1991 treaty, with the understanding that a more comprehensive means of managing conflict would be determined at the conclusion of the transitory period in 1994. The successor arrangement included the Commission on Trade that was charged, along with other tasks, with conducting preliminary reviews of allegations against member nations for violations of trading rules. The Protocols of 1994 established a consultative approach to dispute resolution as a first step. If the issue involved investment of foreign capital and if consultation were not suc-cessful, the case was directed to a national court in the country in which the in-vestment was made. Arbitration panels were designated as the last resort for for-eign investment issues or other conflicts. While much of this sounds extremely vague, particularly in comparison to WTO and NAFTA agreements, that was intentional. These designs were negotiated as conceptual frameworks to define what constituted prohibitions rather than affirmative duties.[59] Economic diffi-culties, most recently the Argentinean economic collapse of 2001, slowed, but did not halt progress toward the goals and realization of MERCOSUR.

The Association of Southeast Asian Nations or ASEAN offers a final case of how third party dispute resolution has evolved in regional trade agreements, and may constitute the most compelling one for the inevitability of devising a means of authoritatively settling conflicts if a regional trade agreement is to be effective and durable. ASEAN began in 1967 with an explicit commitment to the Asian penchant for diplomacy over law, but has subsequently chosen

58. Abbott, "The North American Integration Regime."
59. Lia Valls Periera, "Toward the Common Market of the South: Mercosur's Origins, Evolution and Challenges," in Riordan Roett (ed.), *Mercosur: Regional Integration and World Markets* (New York: New York University Press, 1995), 12.

legalization and employed other global institutions to resolve its disputes.[60] ASEAN began with the countries of Brunei, Indonesia, Malaysia, the Philippines, Singapore, and Thailand, each embracing the goal not only of greater economic cooperation, but also of more secure political relations. It now has thirteen members. ASEAN's origins are found in the desire of these nations to avoid fallout from the Vietnamese invasion of Cambodia. There was little economic interdependence among them and, indeed, both Japan and the U.S. had a greater volume of trade with each country than the nations had with one another. However, the end of the Cold War, the conclusion of the Cambodian conflict, and the rise of NAFTA all combined to encourage revitalization of the trade association. In 1991, the Southeast Asian countries launched their growth triangle strategy and endorsed the concept of achieving a free trade area, the Asian Free Trade Area or AFTA, within fifteen years.[61]

What began as a form of diplomatic cooperation evolved into an organization for trade and economic development. Similarly, where consultation and consensus building were the norm for dispute resolution initially, ASEAN has achieved a degree of legalization. Even with the advent of AFTA, which required a means for monitoring compliance with agreements, there was no movement toward legalization in the form of precision, obligation, and delegation. Indeed, the entire treaty document is only fifteen pages, and, for that brevity, AFTA gained the nickname of "Agree First, Talk After."[62] There was no obvious reason to adopt any formal method for dispute resolution, since the rules to be applied, interpreted, or enforced were virtually non-existent. That position changed, however, in 1996, in response to a dispute between Singapore and Malaysia over tariffs in which Singapore invoked the WTO dispute system against Malaysia. That situation highlighted the need for an internal means of settling disputes among the Asian nations and emphasized that disputes were likely to increase as the volume of inter-regional trade did. The result was a WTO-like mechanism, but with a shorter timeline and with a binding result. Final appeal is to the ASEAN Economic Ministers who decide, not by consensus, but by majority vote. Competition may be granted if compliance is not achieved, and as a last resort trade concessions may be suspended. The mechanism for authoritative resolution exists,

---

60. Miles Kahler, "Legalization as Strategy: The Asia-Pacific Case," 54 *International Organization* (2002), 550.

61. Lee Tsao Yuan, "Growth Triangles in Singapore, Malaysia and ASEAN: Lessons for Subregional Cooperation," in Edward K.Y. Chen and C.H. Kwan (eds.), *Asia's Borderless Economy: The Emergence of Subregional Economic Zones* (Sydney: Allen and Unwin, 1997), 97–100.

62. Kahler, "Legalization as Strategy," 554.

but the norm of consensual diplomatic resolution may still govern, since, as of 2000, the new dispute settlement system had not been invoked a single time.[63]

Courts, Institutionalization, and Trade

Only the most prominent of the regional trade organizations and the global WTO have been examined here, but a trend certainly emerges. In each case, there is an observable motion toward greater legalization, toward a formal mechanism for the resolution of disputes. GATT began in 1947 and relied on diplomacy, but by the time it evolved into the WTO in 1995 it possessed a highly structured dispute settlement system. The EU developed from the limited European Coal and Steel Community in 1951 into a highly integrated supranational organization, and the European Court of Justice has always been part of its structure. That court has, however, altered dramatically from its humble beginnings and has played an active role in propelling itself and an integrated Europe forward. ASEAN was next in chronological order, but it was relatively latent until 1991. It too has crossed the chasm from diplomacy to a formal dispute resolution system. MERCOSUR was born in 1991 and by the conclusion of its specified transition period had adopted a legalistic approach to resolving conflicts. NAFTA is the most recent of the regional trade agreements considered here, but it began with a highly articulated system of precision, obligation, and delegation.

If we return to Figure 1, illustrating the Stone Sweet and Sandholtz continuum from intergovernmental politics to supranational politics, with the Smith template of soft-to-hard legalism overlaying it, where would each of these trade organizations be placed? The closest to the soft-intergovernmental pole would be ASEAN and AFTA, where legalism is now in place but unused. MERCOSUR would join at that end of the spectrum. The EU would be the nearest to the other end, that of supranational politics-hard legalism, with the WTO next and NAFTA also on that side of the continuum. All three are closer to supranational governance, but none has fully reached that point. The first notable oddity about that grouping is that theoretically only customs unions that envision a more complete integration would be expected to approach supranational governance and hard legalization, but the WTO, which aims only at non-tariff discrimination, and NAFTA, which is clearly designed to be a free trade area, are both closer to that pole than to intergovernmental bargaining and soft legalism. MERCOSUR aspires to be a customs union, but

---

63. Ibid., 566.

is closer to soft legalization and intergovernmentalism along with ASEAN and AFTA, both with limited goals for further integration. Form and objective do not, therefore, predict placement on the continuum.

The age of the trade arrangement might be expected to be predictive. Indeed, the two oldest, the EU and the WTO, are both near the pole of hard legalism and supranational politics. Yet NAFTA, the newest of the regional trade organizations discussed here, is also on that side. ASEAN has a longer history than MERCOSUR, but the two associations are close in their positions to intergovernmentalism and soft legalism.

The hard-soft legalism points serve only to describe and not to explain. Along with age and stated nature of the organization, the terms merely convey what exists. My hypothesis was that regional trade agreements that are to be durable and effective will develop a dispute resolution mechanism, which implies a harder legalism. Durability is difficult to gauge for NAFTA, but the EU is obviously the most durable and effective of the regional trade agreements; MERCOSUR is, at this time, the least effective and its durability questionable.

The Stone Sweet and Sandholtz framework of institutionalization offers greater predictive power. Where transnational society is more highly developed and cross-border commercial transactions are frequent and intense, there is a drive by non-state actors to lower the costs of those transactions. Those costs, you will recall, stem from varying national rules on points of origin, dumping, non-tariff duties, health and environmental standards, currency exchange rates, and others. To reduce those costs, state-to-state bargaining is initiated. The more detailed those negotiations become, the more likely precision and legalization will occur. To ensure that the rules are obeyed and contracts fulfilled, legal obligation becomes necessary. That, in turn, often requires that a means of deciding disputes be institutionalized to enforce the bargains, rules, and obligations that have been agreed upon.

Moreover, if a trade agreement is successful and enhances the frequency and intensity of cross-border transactions, the potential for disputes also grows. NAFTA attempted to anticipate the sources of conflict and resolve them *ex ante*, whereas ASEAN/AFTA postponed those negotiations until concrete conflicts might arise. If the neo-liberal trade rhetoric is correct, improved economic development will continue to intensify and breed more competition that will in turn further present possibilities for conflicts that need to be resolved. All of this points to something close to an inevitability that dispute resolution bodies or courts will be part of successful trade associations.

Courts or other dispute resolution mechanisms have much to commend them for transnational arrangements, but nation-states have some good reasons to seek ways of mediating conflicts at the soft law or intergovernmental levels. Once an outside dispute resolution mechanism exists, states forfeit their ability to control the outcome in any specific case and, over time, the process of regionalism can become judicialized. In that situation, the power of the transnational adjudicative body is increased at the expense of national politicians, and judicial decisions begin to reach into more traditionally political spheres.[64] Transferring the power to settle disputes among trading partners from the negotiating table to a legal forum diminishes diplomatic options as well as political authority. Further, creation of a formal dispute settlement body does not ensure compliance. Enforcement of judicial decisions is hardly automatic even within the confines of a single nation-state,[65] and agreement on the substance of what a court has actually decided is often elusive. In other words, guarantees of compliance with transnational rules still depend largely on the trustworthiness of the contracting parties. The alternative is to accept that the rules are always subject to renegotiation, which protects sovereignty and vested national interests, but also guarantees the sovereignty and, therefore, impunity of neighboring trading partners. The experience of the European Union teaches, however, that one nation's suspicions about the intentions of its neighbors can be resolved better in an open legal forum and that there is greater compliance with decisions reached through hard legalism than through persistent renegotiation of the rules. Some external pressure to comply appears even more essential in regions where the trading partners are less homogenous.

The many regional trade arrangements in place are new and in many ways novel experiments. The character of each new organization is not yet set in stone; "changed priorities or altered alliances within states and/or change at the global level, will probably result in a renegotiation of policy."[66] With so many regional agreements emerging, undoubtedly there will be a great variety in the structures, longevity, and trajectories among them, but those that endure and that grow in intensity will likely find that having courts crossing borders serves to protect the interests of the signatory states.

---

64. Torbjorn Vallinder, "When the Courts Go Marching In," in C. Neal Tate and Torbjorn Vallinder (eds.), *The Global Expansion of Judicial Power* (New York: New York University Press, 1995), 13–14.

65. Bradley C. Canon and Charles A. Johnson, *Judicial Policies: Implementation and Impact* (Washington, D.C.: CQ Press, 1999).

66. Grugel and Hout, "Regions, Regionalism and the South," 12.

Chapter 4

Sovereignty in Europe: The European Court of Justice and the Creation of a European Political Community

Miguel Poiares Maduro

The processes of constitutionalization and Europeanization in the European Union can be related to the creation of a European political community that is a challenge both to state sovereignty and to the concept of sovereignty itself. I will first present those processes and demonstrate how they are linked to a claim of independent political and legal authority for a community of open and undetermined social goals. A European political community is emerging and with it a claim of European sovereignty that derives from claims of independent authority. In the second section, I will contrast the top-down character of the traditional rhetoric in the process of constitutionalization with the bottom-up legitimacy and process that supported it. I will highlight how the European Court of Justice (ECJ) found the support of a constituency of national actors for the processes of constitutionalization and Europeanization that it promoted. Some conclusions I will derive from the roles played by these actors. Next, I will highlight the pluralist nature of European constitutionalism and its relationship to national constitutionalism. The claim to independent political and legal authority on the part of EU law is not fully recognized by national constitutions that require us to assume a different understanding of how courts and the law operate in the context of competing political communities. This claim also highlights a form of competitive sovereignty. In conclusion I will explain why the European Court of Justice played such an important role in the development of the European Constitution and the consequences of the development of this European constitutional pluralism on both the European Constitution and the concept of sovereignty.

Sovereignty in Europe: Constitutionalization and Europeanization

Constitutionalization

The classic literature on the constitutionalization of European Community (EC) law[1] has described how the case law of the European Court of Justice developed a constitutional architecture with supremacy, direct effect, fundamental rights, an institutional rule of law (including separation of powers), enforcement mechanisms, and an autonomous and hierarchical legal order. According to J. H. H. Weiler:

> The constitutional thesis claims that in critical aspects the Community has evolved and behaves as if its founding instrument were not a Treaty governed by international law but, to use the language of the European Court of Justice, a constitutional charter governed by a form of constitutional law.[2]

The first step in this process of constitutionalization[3] was the construction of Community law with a legal order of its own, different from international law and operating directly on national legal orders. Furthermore, the principle of supremacy established that in case of conflict between national and Community law, the latter was to prevail.[4] As a consequence, Community law was to be understood as the higher law, the criterion of validity for national law. Many of the distinctive elements of Community law, such as direct effect and supremacy, can also be found in some instances of international law. In

---

1. In this text I will normally use the expression "EU law" to include both the law of the European Communities and the broader European Union. However, where referring to a particular historic period when the EU did not exist, I will use the expression "EC law."

2. J. H. H. Weiler, "The Reformation of European Constitutionalism," 97 *Journal of Common Market Studies* (1997), 98.

3. For a more detailed analysis, see, for example, K. Lenaerts, "Constitutionalism and the Many Faces of Federalism," 38 *American Journal of Comparative Law* (1990), 205; Eric Stein, "Lawyers, Judges and the Making of a Transnational Constitution," *American Journal of International Law* (1981), 1; G. F. Mancini, "The Making of a Constitution for Europe," *Common Market Law Review* (1989), 595; and J. H. H. Weiler, "The Transformation of Europe," 100 *Yale Law Review* (1990–91), 2403.

4. See *Costa v. ENEL*, Case 6/64 [ECR 585, 1964]. See also *NV Algememe Transport-en Expedities Onderneming Van Gend en Loos v. Netherlands Inland Revenue Administration*, Case 26/62 [ECR 1, 1963]; and *Walt Wilhelm*, Case 14/68 [ECR 1, 1969].

fact, some international lawyers as well as some domestic constitutional lawyers continue to argue that EU law remains, in its essence, a product of international law, the authority of which derives from the attribution to its norms of supremacy and direct effect in the national legal orders by national constitutions. However, such a vision ignores the true constitutional turning point of Community law: the claim of an independent political authority derived directly from the peoples of Europe rather than from the states.

It would indeed have been possible to explain the supremacy and uniform application of EU law without challenging the traditional conception of sovereignty and its locus in the state. In fact, as Bruno de Witte has powerfully explained, even the principles of supremacy and direct effect, usually identified as the cornerstones of the constitutionalization of EU law, could be developed and generally applied without changing, in a substantial manner, the character of the treaties and EU norms as international law.[5] There are other instances where international norms enjoy direct effect and supremacy without implying any challenge to the ultimate authority of national constitutions. On the contrary, it is often those constitutions that confer power to international rules. Even the claim of authority that is made by international rules under international monist theories of international law supremacy is not conceived as challenging the fundamentals of national constitutional sovereignty, since that supremacy is linked to a prior self-binding commitment of the states supported by *pacta sunt servanda*. In this case, these international instances of shared, pooled, or even limited state sovereignty do not really challenge state sovereignty, because those exercises of international sovereignty are delegated from the states and limited by the strict mandates of that delegation.

Why can't EU law supremacy and direct effect be traced back to such an understanding of international law and its relation to national constitutional law? Or why can't the supremacy and direct effect of EU law be seen as secured by the recognition of its authority by national constitutions in all member states? Such understanding safeguards a uniform application of EU law without challenging the ultimate authority of national constitutions and its connection with the source of the *pouvoir constituant* at national level. This vision is not the one embraced by the Court of Justice and, moreover, it does not fit with the nature and extent of the claim of authority made by EU law and the European political community. The Court of Justice based the direct

---

5. Bruno de Witt, "Direct Effect, Supremacy and the Nature of the Legal Order," in Paul Craig and Grainne deBurca (eds.), *The Evolution of EU Law* (Oxford: Oxford University Press, 1999), 181, 209.

effect and supremacy of Community law on a direct relationship between community norms and the peoples of Europe. The founding decision of the Court of Justice in *Van Gend en Loos* is, in effect, the declaration of independence of EU law from the authority of the member states. The treaty is presented as much more than an agreement among states; it is an agreement among the peoples of Europe that established a direct relationship between Community law and those peoples.[6] That source of direct legitimacy established a political link authorizing a claim of independent normative authority. Legal authority was therefore to be derived from an autonomous conception of the European legal order. This corresponded, in fact, to a claim of independent political and legal authority that meant that the European communities were, in the words of the Court, endowed with sovereign rights.[7]

The epistemological turning point in the locus of sovereignty and legitimacy in Europe lies in the direct relation found by the Court of Justice between the peoples of Europe and Community law. Once this direct political relationship was established, it was clear that the basic legal framework should be based on constitutional law and not international law. The latter regulates the relationship between states and their sovereign powers, whereas the former regulates the relationship among citizens and defines how their sovereignty is to be expressed in the political community. The constitutional reading of the treaties is, therefore, a consequence of an epistemological shift in the understanding of the political authority behind the project of European integration. This shift is what allowed the construction of a constitutional framework for Community law. The discourse that dominates its construction and relation with national legal orders became a constitutional dialogue: Implied competencies, separation of powers, fundamental rights, democratic legitimacy, and the rule of law are all constitutional concepts that form the cornerstone of the legal and political debates on the European Union and its legal order. These are also the concepts that have influenced the Court's approach to EU law.

The fundamental constitutional steps that determine the character of European integration are, in the last instance, dependent upon the will of the member states which, as masters of the treaties, can change or maintain the defining characteristics of EU law by revising the treaties in an intergovernmental forum subject (but only to some extent) to international law. Thus, there is always the hypothetical possibility that member states will reverse the

---

6. *Van Gend en Loos*, Case 26/62 [ECR 3, 1963].
7. Ibid.

process of constitutionalization by exercising their powers under the realm of domestic and international law. Under this conception, EU law would still be an expression of international law and state sovereignty would be safeguarded. This interpretation is based on a definition of sovereignty that, following Carl Schmitt, characterizes political and normative authority through the power of exception.[8] But should not the focus be instead on the normal operation of political and normative authority in a certain system? The power exercised collectively by states may still change the constitutional future of the Union, and the possible individual power of a state to exit the process of integration[9] may still constitute some ultimate claim to legal sovereignty. Both of these elements must be placed in the context of the day-to-day workings of EU law and its political and legal discourses. Moreover, it may be, de facto, impossible to exercise those powers of exception. Their shadows may never be seen. The legal effects that arise from the application of EU law by the European and national courts and the doctrines that shape and discuss that application are of a constitutional nature. And the forms of political action and discourse that underlie the process of European integration fit better with the dynamics of a traditional political community. In the same way, the degree of power already held at a supranational level in the European Union requires a form of limitation and organization that only constitutionalism can provide. Therefore, the Union is a constitutional legal order, although its constitutional authority may still be subject to the challenge of national constitutional authority.

All these elements are possible because of the claim to independent political and legal authority made by the European Court of Justice. This claim of sovereignty presents a difficult problem of compatibility, since the ECJ simultaneously respects state sovereignty and maintains the traditional conception of sovereignty itself. This conception is based on an indivisible notion of sovereignty, one that can be limited but not threatened by an ultimate authority or single origin of power (traditionally the state). In this light, some have naturally argued against the autonomy of European law. The EU could limit states' sovereignty in light of the states' delegation of authority, but it could not claim its own independent sovereignty in opposition to that of the state. The reality is, however, that such a claim of independent political and legal authority has been made by the European legal order and has been followed by an affirmation of EU powers well beyond those which can be traced

---

8. Carl Schmitt, *Political Theology: Four Chapters on the Concept of Sovereignty* (Cambridge: MIT Press, 1988).

9. A question that is legally controversial.

back to a delegation by the states. This claim, therefore, competes with that of the states and requires a notion of sovereignty that moves even beyond shared, pooled, or limited sovereignty. A notion of competing sovereignties is necessary.

Europeanization

The preceding section highlights the often underscored relationship between the process of constitutionalization and the development of a European political community. This European political community is both presumed in the Court's constitutional judgments and promoted by many of them. One can identify the promotion of a European political community with a broad process of Europeanization enhanced in the Court's case law, hand in hand with its constitutional steps.

The first element of the process of Europeanization is the promotion of individual allegiances in favor of European law, not only by promoting individual rights under the treaty but also by adopting a broad interpretation of such rights that allow individuals to use Community law as a form of second-guessing national policies that are incompatible with their particular interests. The second element in the process of Europeanization is the broader interpretation of community competencies adopted by the ECJ. The interpretation given by the European Court of Justice concerning either the functional competencies of the EC Treaty (those necessary to the achievement of the internal market)[10] or, together with the political process, the implied powers provision of Article 308 (granting the competencies which can be argued as necessary to achieve one of the broad goals of the European Community)[11] allowed a substantial growth in community competencies. In fact, the EU has become a political entity of almost universal goals. Most of all, its policies have become the result of an open political discourse among a mix of state, EU, and other social actors—not simply the product of a previous agreement among states. The emergence of a European political community was further favored by the exercise of EU competencies under the legal bases that provide for majority versus unanimous decision making.[12] This meant that not only were EU political goals extensive and undetermined but also the nature of its exercise changed from intergovernmental to majority decision making.

---

10. Articles 94 and 95.
11. Article 308.
12. Compare, for example, Articles 94 and 95.

A key role in the process of Europeanization has also been played by market integration rules in the treaty, notably by the free-movement rules. The Court extended the scope of application of these rules much further than that normally attributed to trade rules and used the free movement rules to review almost any area of national legislation that impacts the market. The extensive interpretation of free-movement rules led to a spillover of EU law and its rationale of market integration into political and social spheres at the national level. National legislation intervening in the market became subject to review under EU law independently of any protectionist intent or effects. This led to a process which Burley and Mattli refer to as substantial penetration of EC law[13] and what Sabino Casesse calls *"comunitarizazione' di funzione nazionali"* ("communitarizing" national functions).[14] Moreover, the European Court of Justice assessed the reasonableness of national regulatory policies in light of what could be called a majority perspective derived from the dominant regulatory choices in the different member states.[15]

It is possible to conclude that the process of constitutionalization was legitimized on the assumption of an emerging European political community founded on the peoples of Europe. At the same time, the process of constitutionalization, coupled with that of Europeanization, was part of a judicial strategy aimed at enhancing a European political community by conceiving the EU as an entity of open political goals and by shifting the focus of political action and allegiance of individuals to that entity.

Becoming Sovereign: How Was It Possible?

"Tucked away in the fairyland Duchy of Luxemburg and blessed with benign neglect by the powers that be and the mass media the Court of Justice created a new legal order with a federal architecture."[16] So goes one of the most famous sentences of European legal literature, describing how the European Court of Justice transformed Community law into a *legal order of its own.*[17] Eric Stein's wonderful description of the role undertaken by the Court of Jus-

---

13. Anne-Marie Burley and Walter Mattli, "Europe Before the Court: A Political Theory of Legal Integration," 47 *International Organization* (1993), 43.

14. S. Cassese, "La Costituzione Europea," *Quaderni Costituzionali* (1991), 487.

15. I deal extensively with this point in *We the Court: The European Court of Justice and the European Economic Constitution* (Cambridge: Hart Publishing, 1998), chap. 3.

16. Eric Stein, "Lawyers, Judges, and the Making of a Transnational Constitution," 1.

17. See *Costa v. ENEL*, Case 6/64 [ECR 585, 1964] ECR 585. See also *Van Gend en Loos*, Case 26/62 [ECR 1, 1963] and *Walt Wilhelm*, Case 14/68 [ECR 1, 1969].

tice has much truth in it but, at the same time, can be misleading in an attempt to understand how the emergence of a new sovereign legal order was possible and took place in Europe. Though the European Court of Justice certainly benefited from being "tucked away" in Luxemburg and neglected by the powers that be and the mass media, the sentence may also lead us to think that the Court of Justice developed this new legal order in isolation, *on its own.* That was not the case. In fact, the creation of the European legal order can be better understood as the product of a cooperative process involving a larger group of actors. A community of legal and social actors empowered the Court of Justice and legitimized the creation of a new supranational or federal legal order. This community of actors also influenced the content of the European Constitution.

The traditional rhetoric about the emergence of the European legal order describes the creation of the European Constitution as a product of the European Court of Justice. The stress is on an autonomous legal order with supremacy and direct effect as an expression of European legal sovereignty vis-à-vis national legal orders. The European Court of Justice itself emphasized this top-down vision of EU law and its relation to national legal orders. In great part, this emphasis followed the need for the Court to establish its authority and that of EU law in accordance with traditional views of law. Law has always been conceived as hierarchically organized. There was always some sort of basis—a *"Grundnorm,"* "a set of rules of recognition," or positivized natural law, conceived as the "higher law" of the legal system, serving as the criterion of validity for all other legal norms. The internal conception of the EU legal order was also made to fit this model. EU primary law is understood as the "higher law" of the Union,[18] the criterion for validity of secondary rules and decisions as well as of all national legal rules and decisions within its scope. Moreover, the Court of Justice is the higher court of this legal system and therefore is the ultimate authority on the interpretation of its rules. In a nutshell, while challenging the sovereignty of the states, this conception did not challenge the traditional conception of sovereignty.

The success of creating a European legal order was only possible because the Court looked for and found the cooperation of different national actors. For this, it also had to negotiate with those actors, in particular with national courts, but also with others. This need to negotiate was fundamental both in promoting the developments of the European legal order and in securing its legitimacy. The Court developed doctrines promoting the participation of a

---

18. One can even rank some rules higher than others, raised to the status of material limits on the revision of the Treaty of European Union; that is a discussion I will not engage here, however.

variety of national actors. Notably, it promoted the "subjectivation" of the treaties. By "subjectivation" I mean the movement from a state-based interpretation of the treaties into an individual-based interpretation: the treaties are not simply to be interpreted as an agreement among states, but as having been created for the "peoples of Europe." EU rules are directed to individuals and can be invoked by them. EU law becomes a new source of rights to which litigants can appeal. According to Ole Due, former President of the Court, "[I]t is remarkable...that those judgments which are often described as landmarks have generally contributed to promoting integration and at the same time to protecting the legal position of individual citizens and undertakings vis-à-vis both the authorities of the Member States and the Community institutions."[19] One could say, as did Burley and Mattli, that "the Court created a pro-community constituency of private individuals by giving them a direct stake in promulgation and implementation of Community Law."[20]

The Court was also quite open to questions posed by national courts and often relied on them to come up with original interpretations of EU rules. On the other hand, the role played by national courts in requesting rulings from the ECJ and in applying these rulings provided ECJ decisions in national legal orders with the same authority as national judicial decisions.[21] This created a dynamic that Mary Volcansek has characterized as "a pattern of positive reinforcement for national courts seeking preliminary rulings."[22] This dynamic promoted cooperation and discourse with national courts and helped to establish the autonomy and authority of Community law. National courts are responsible for the effective incorporation of EU law into national legal orders by accepting the principles of direct effect and supremacy and in promoting the use of EU law in national proceedings. Often lower courts promoted the incorporation of EU law since this new set of rules could be used to bring about decisions that national judges would prefer in terms of substantive jus-

---

19. Ole Due, "The Law-making Role of the European Court of Justice Considered in Particular from the Perspective of Individuals and Undertakings," 63 *Nordic Journal of International Law* (1994), 126.

20. Burley and Mattli, "Europe Before the Court," 60. See also J. H. H. Weiler, "A Quiet Revolution," 26 *Comparative Political Studes* (1994), 521.

21. Why national courts were willing and available to do so is another question. See J. H. H. Weiler, "Journey to an Unknown Destination: A Retrospective and Perspective of the European Court of Justice in the Arena of Political Integration," 31 *Journal of Common Market Studies* (1993), 60; and Burley and Mattli, "Europe Before the Court," 62.

22. In her words: "The Court of Justice accepted all conceivable requests from national courts and invited wide participation." *Judicial Politics in Europe* (New York: Peter Lang, 1986), 265.

tice. Essentially, the supremacy and direct effect of EU rules allowed national courts to set aside national laws whose application they did not favor. In these circumstances, EU law transformed all courts into constitutional courts. The empowerment of national courts through EU law explains much of their willingness to support the application of EU law[23] and also explains why they often brought forward some of the most expansive and creative interpretations of EU law.

The European Court of Justice found a constituency supporting the constitutionalization and Europeanization of EU law. But for this constituency, constitutionalization and Europeanization were frequently mere by-products of the use of EU law to change domestic policies and legislation. In other words, for many of the actors who supported the process of constitutionalization and Europeanization, support for the processes was a function of domestic politics and not of adhesion to a broad project of European integration. The foundation of EU law legitimacy for these constituents also depended, however, on cooperative national courts and the litigants involved in EU law. The establishment of a dialogue between national courts and individuals on the one hand and the European Court of Justice on the other was not limited to a single direction. Law is not the property of courts but is a product of the discourse among various actors in the legal community. In the case of EU law, the strong dependence of its legitimacy on this community of social and legal actors reinforced that discursive nature and impacted deeply the content of the European Constitution. Moreover, constitutionalization and Europeanization are often a functional result of the strategic use of EU law by national actors. EU law became a tool of domestic policies more than an instrument of European goals. This shift represents a different challenge to sovereignty: It is not so much a question of the erosion of state powers as it is a question of change in the patterns of representation and participation in domestic policies. The Europe Union challenges the sovereignty of states to define the balance of representation and participation in their domestic policies.

A good example of this phenomenon was the *Sunday Trading Cases* involving references made to the European Court of Justice by a variety of British courts on the validity of the British rules prohibiting trade on Sunday in light of Articles 28 and 30 (at the time 30 and 36) of the EC Treaty. In these cases, national economic actors used the free-movement-of-goods provision of the EC Treaty to challenge national rules that inhibited their economic free-

---

23. J. H. H. Weiler, *The Constitution of Europe: Do the New Clothes Have an Emperor?* (Cambridge: Cambridge University Press, 1999), 197.

dom by prohibiting trade on Sundays. The possibility for this challenge arose from the very broad interpretation traditionally given by the Court of Justice to the concept of a measure having an equivalent effect to a quantitative restriction (Article 28, EC Treaty). It was sufficient that a national regulation could affect trade for it to be considered such a measure, without any requirement of a de jure or de facto discriminatory impact on imported products. Once that was the case, the national measure would only be acceptable if necessary and proportional to the satisfaction of certain public interests.[24] Under this criterion, measures restricting the free movement of goods needed to be both necessary to the pursuit of a EU-recognized public interest and proportional to the goal to be achieved. In other words, the costs arising from the restriction imposed on the free movement of goods could not exceed the benefits derived from the public interest at which the measure was directed. What happened was that economic operators used the broad scope granted by the Court to restrict the free movement of goods in order to subject any national regulation of the market to a judgment of necessity and proportionality. This allowed the operators to promote redeliberation on different national policies at the European level, even where a concern with the freedom of trade between states did not exist. In the case of Sunday trading, the Court of Justice initially left that judgement of necessity and proportionality to national courts. That led to contradictory decisions on the validity of the prohibition of trade on Sunday because of the different assessments made by national courts on the necessity and proportionality of that prohibition. A broader analysis of the Court of Justice case law on the free movement of goods[25] (including its subsequent decision in *Keck & Mithouard*)[26] makes clear that the broad scope traditionally given to Article 28 by the Court of Justice was not intended to promote a review of all market regulation. The judicial aim was not to construct Article 28 as an economic due process clause controlling the degree of public intervention in the market,[27] but economic operators appropriated the

---

24. See Miguel Poiares Maduro, *We the Court.*

25. Ibid., chap. 3.

26. Joined Cases C-267/92 and C-268/91, *Keck and Mithourad* [ECR I-6097, 1993]. In this decision the Court restricted the scope of application of Article 30 in order to discourage "the increasing tendency of traders to invoke Article 30 of the Treaty as a means of challenging any rules whose effect is to limit their commercial freedom even when such rules are not aimed at products from other Member States." Even this decision did not prevent economic operators from continuing to develop new interpretations that allowed them to challenge national regulations limiting their economic freedom, even where those measures did not discriminate against out-of-state trade.

27. See Miguel Poiares Maduro, *We the Court.*

broad scope granted to the free movement of goods to, in effect, challenge virtually any regulation of the market.

The *Sunday Trading Cases* tell us that the scope and function of EU law is as much a function of national problems as it is of European issues. For national actors, EU law is simply a new source of arguments to be used in the context of conflicts that affect their interests. In these cases it was possible for domestic economic actors to challenge national regulatory policies through EU law and subject them to a second process of decision making outside the national political process. EU law becomes a terrain of national internal disputes over regulatory policies. As Rawlings says, EU law became "the European defence of domestic actors against national policies."[28]

Analysis of the processes of constitutionalization and Europeanization highlights a curious contrast between the discourse on EU legal authority put forward by the Court of Justice and the way in which its legal authority was actually supported. The first fits the traditional canons of legal sovereignty with a top-down presentation of the authority of EU law and its relationship with national law. The second demonstrates how the authority of EU law is to be found in its bottom-up construction and legitimacy. At the same time, the study of the role of national courts and other national legal actors is important in understanding how EU law is a product of a broad community of actors that cooperated with the ECJ in constitutionalizing and Europeanizing EU law. However, in that process, the community also promoted a particular vision of EU law and the European Constitution.

Competitive Sovereignty

We have seen how EU law is the product of a discourse among the actors of a broad European legal community in which the voice of some of those actors may even oppose the will of the Court of Justice. But can this discursive understanding be taken even further, to the point where it becomes the foundation for legitimacy of the European legal order and its distinctive element of identity? In other words, is that discourse related to a form of legal pluralism upon which the European legal order must be based? Or should that legal order also be subject to a hierarchical organization that grants to either the European Court of Justice or national constitutional courts the role of final

---

28. Richard Rawlings, "The Eurolaw Game: Deductions from a Saga," 20 *Journal of Law and Society* (1993), 313.

authority in deciding conflicts within the European legal community? These are the questions of legal sovereignty in Europe.

We have seen how the rhetoric of European law assumes that between EU law and national law, the final authority belongs to the former. We have also seen how that assumption is related to the need of fitting EU law into the classic conception of the law and sovereignty. But European integration attacks this hierarchical understanding of the law and the monistic conception of sovereignty. In reality, both national and European constitutional law assume, in the internal logic of their respective legal systems, the role of higher law and, when they coincide, challenge the idea of a monistic final authority. According to the internal conception of the EU legal order developed by the European Court of Justice, EU primary law will be the "higher law" of the Union, the criteria of the validity of secondary rules and decisions and of all national legal rules and decisions within its scope. Moreover, the Court of Justice is the higher court in this legal system. Yet a different perspective is taken by national legal orders and national constitutions. Here, EU law owes its supremacy to its recognition by a higher national law (normally constitutions). The higher law remains, in the national legal orders, the national constitution, and the ultimate power of legal adjudication belongs to national constitutional courts. As a result, the question of who decides has different answers in the European and the national legal orders[29] and when viewed from a perspective outside both national and EU legal orders, the question requires a conception of the law which is no longer dependent upon a hierarchical construction and a conception of sovereignty as single and indivisible. Such a conception of sovereignty has been under challenge by notions such as shared sovereignty, but what the relationship between the EU and national legal orders brings is an even more challenging notion—that of competitive sovereignty. The idea is one of equal claims to independent political and legal authority that compete for final authority in a model of constitutional pluralism.

An understanding of EU law and its relationship with national constitutions based on constitutional pluralism was first convincingly argued by Neil MacCormick[30] and more recently by Neil Walker.[31] Generally, national courts

---

29. Rossa Phelan has made a detailed analysis of the different viewpoints on the relationship between national and European legal orders, depending on whether one's observations come from the perspective of EC law, national constitutional law, or even public international law. See *Revolt or Revolution: The Constitutional Boundaries of the European Community* (Dublin: Sweet & Maxwell, 1997).

30. Neil MacCormick, "Beyond the Sovereign State," 56 *Modern Law Review* (1993), 1.

31. Neil Walker, "The Idea of Constitutional Pluralism," 65 *Modern Law Review* (2002), 317.

may tend to comply with the "European Constitution," but several national high courts still challenge the absolute supremacy of EU law. Such challenges are seen either in the description that national constitutionalism makes for itself or in the dependence of EU law effectiveness upon national law and national courts. To use the remarkable expression offered by Damian Chalmers, national law still holds a veto power over national law.[32] The shadow of such a veto is important even when it is not effectively exercised. The European legal order is characterized by both the "norm" (national courts' compliance with supremacy and direct effect) and, as Schmitt would argue, the power of exception still affirmed, but never exercised, by national constitutional courts. In fact, the possibility of the latter ends up also determining how the normal application and interpretation of EU law takes place.

There are therefore powerful pragmatic and normative reasons not to adopt a hierarchical alternative imposing a monist authority of European law and its judicial institutions over national law, or vice versa. That solution would be difficult to impose in practical terms and could undermine the base of legitimacy on which European law has developed.[33] Though the grammar used by EU lawyers in describing the process of constitutionalization may assume a top-down approach, the reality is that the legitimacy of European constitutionalism has developed in close cooperation with national courts and national legal communities. That, in turn, has had an increasingly bottom-up effect on the nature of the European legal order.[34] At the same time, in spite of their claims to ultimate authority and legal sovereignty, both the EU and national legal orders make more or less explicit concessions toward the claims of authority of the other legal order. They make the necessary adjustments to their respective claims in order to prevent an actual collision. EU law has introduced substantive constitutional changes, such as fundamental rights, in order to accommodate the claims made by national constitutions.[35] National constitutions have been interpreted in a manner that tends to prevent the review of specific EU acts.[36]

---

32. Damian Chalmers, "Judicial Preferences and Community Legal Order," 60 *Modern Law Review* (1997), 180.

33. In Chalmers's words, "the regime is able to develop provided it does not significantly disrupt the egalitarian relations enjoyed between national courts and the Court of Justice." Ibid.

34. Kamiel Mortelmans, "Community Law: More than a Functional Area of Law, Less than a Legal System," 1996 *Legal Issues of European Integration* (1996), 42–43.

35. See Miguel Poiares Maduro, "Contrapunctual Law: Europe's Constitutional Pluralism in Action," in Neil Walker (ed.), *Sovereignty in Transition* (Oxford: Hart Publishing, forthcoming).

36. Ibid.

Another reason to adopt a pluralist conception of the European legal order is related to a broader conception of the legitimacy of the process of European integration, one that finds legitimacy in its role of correcting the constitutional limits of national political communities and in the reform of the notion of constitutionalism that is associated with those political communities. This notion traditionally relates constitutionalism with a single political community and, at the same time, tends to concentrate power in a final authority through its hierarchical organization. However, in part, this notion contradicts constitutionalism itself, since it eliminates one of its forms of limited power. European constitutionalism promotes inclusiveness in national constitutionalism both from an external and internal perspective. From an external perspective, it requires national constitutionalism to take into account out-of-state interests that may be affected by the deliberations of national political communities and limits the possible abuses that could derive from the concentration of power on national communities inherent in the traditional conceptions of constitutionalism and sovereignty;[37] from an internal perspective, the challenges brought by European constitutionalism to the sovereignty of national deliberations under national constitutionalism also allow a new form of voice to disenfranchised national groups and often reintroduce true deliberation in areas where the national political process has been captured by a certain composition of interests or certain indisputable definitions of the public good. On the other hand, national constitutionalism serves as a guarantee that the traditional monistic conception of sovereignty is not going to be replicated at the European level. As long as the possible conflicts of authority do not lead to a disintegration of the European legal order, the pluralist character of European constitutionalism in its relationship with national constitutionalism should be viewed as a welcome discovery and not as a problem in need of a solution.

We have seen how the processes of constitutionalization and Europeanization have promoted the emergence of a European political community. Inherent in these processes is a claim to independent political and legal authority associated with a community of open and undetermined social goals. These processes were a product of the cooperation between the European Court of Justice and a particular set of actors. These actors were "used" by the Court to enhance the creation of a European political community, but the actors also "used" the Court to give a particular content to the European constitution and

---

37. Weiler refers to this function of European law as the principle of constitutional tolerance. J. H. H. Weiler, "The Principle of Constitutional Tolerance," in Francis Snyder (ed.), *The Europeanisation of Law: The Legal Effects of European Integration* (Oxford: Hart Publishing, 2000).

to change national policies and even constitutional settlements. At the same time, the sovereign claim involved in the emerging European political community and its constitution has never been fully recognized by national constitutions. The question of ultimate authority is an open one in Europe, giving rise to a form of constitutional pluralism in the relationship among these different political communities. The question has important consequences both for Europe and for the concepts of sovereignty and constitutionalism. I will conclude by highlighting some of those consequences.

The Limits of Judicial Constitutionalization

As a recent convention for discussing the future of Europe demonstrates, Europe's constitutionalism is in crisis. This crisis can be in part related to the inherent limits of the judicial process in performing such a constitutional role. The constitutional body created by the Court is revealed as deprived of a constitutional soul. In other words, Europe's constitutional developments appear as a purely functional consequence of economic integration without a real constitutional debate. Thus, the reliance of the European Constitution mainly on market integration rules creates a conflict between the functional legitimacy of market integration and the democratic legitimacy of national rules. The goal of market integration is no longer capable of explaining and legitimating the reach of the European Constitution into the member states' constitutional orders. The judicial origin of the European Constitution also means that it is mainly a product of representation and participation in that judicial process. To move the constitutional choices from the political process to the judicial process is not irrelevant. On the contrary, it alters the degree of voice of different actors in constitution making. Powerful corporations, for instance, tend to be "repeat players"[38] and thus are able to use and participate in the European legal discourse to a much higher degree than individuals. Moreover, multinational companies are much more able to promote Europe-wide litigation strategies and have higher stakes in organizing their participation in the judicial process when compared, for example, with consumer interests (which usually correspond to dispersed interests). Up to now, the litigation that has helped to mold the European Constitution has been based on market integration rules and dominated by some actors—notably companies that often appear as repeated litigants. Because of the character of those rules and the information and organization costs involved in participating in the EU judi-

---

38. See the example of *Sunday Trading* in Rawlings, "The Eurolaw Game," 315.

cial process, mainly companies have started the discovery process of EU law and the European Constitution. The European Constitution is a product of judicial construction fueled by litigation arising from certain actors. This has led many to see this Constitution as "market biased" and its underlying political community as excluding some citizens. For many, the current constitutional process should serve precisely to promote a true constitutional moment in Europe. In doing so, it would enlarge the scope of participants in the process of European integration and help create a European political identity among the peoples of Europe. Only such a political identity will be capable of supporting the claims of sovereignty that the Union already makes. Even if, as argued in this paper, the form of European constitutionalism should remain essentially plural and respect a plurality of equally legitimate claims of independent political authority, it appears obvious that such an ethos must now be subject to a broad public discourse that should no longer be controlled by the European Court of Justice and its limited constituency of social actors.

Judicial Preferences

Structural limits also prevent the Court of Justice from developing further European constitutionalism. The growing workload of the Court is affecting both the quality of its judgments and the capacity of the Court to deal with other constitutional issues. The Court is often perceived to be paying more attention to national political malfunctions than to the problems of constitutional organization internal to the Union. However, the growth in EU competencies and in the majoritarian character of the European political process requires the Court to devote more of its resources to review the activity of the EU legislator and, therefore, to limit its activity in other constitutional areas. This shift of resources must come hand in hand with a reform on the issue of participation and representation in the EU judicial process. This issue must not continue to be the domain of a particular set of social actors or of particular national courts. We must focus on the composition and construction of the European legal community when reforming the EU legal order. This issue requires the question of democracy in Europe to be extended to the question of how to democratize the EU legal and judicial discourses.

The Consequences of Pluralism

Studying the role of national courts and other national legal actors is important in understanding the legitimacy and effectiveness of EU law and the way in which the latter is developed by the Court of Justice. But such a study is also particularly important in epistemological terms for a true knowledge of the EU legal order. The latter is as much a product of its construction by the Court of Justice as it is a product of the national legal communities' appropriation of that body of law. Therein lies a third consequence: Not only is EU law the product of a broader legal community but, as a result, it can be really known only in that light. We need to pay more attention to the national European courts and the way in which they interpret and apply European law.[39] Otherwise we may be mistaking the tree for the forest. For example, we should pay attention to the cases where national courts have gone further than the ECJ in extending the protection granted by EU law in cases of horizontal direct effect and discrimination against a state's own nationals.[40] At the same time, Europe's constitutional pluralism makes the coherence and integrity of the European legal order dependent on a dialogue that must also occur among different national courts or, broadly, among the different national legal communities. A coherent EU legal order will require both vertical discourse (between the ECJ and national courts) and horizontal discourse (among national courts). Finally, Europe's constitutional pluralism challenges the autonomy of different deliberative processes once any decision can be challenged in a different political forum. At the same time, the use of the different levels of governance becomes a consequence of the balance of representation and participation in those different levels and not of a particular theory on the allocation of competences between different levels of governance. In this light, the scope of EU law and policies is as much a function of national problems as it is of European issues. For national actors, EU law often is simply a new source of arguments to be used in the context of whatever conflicts affect their interests, whether or not they have a European dimension.

---

39. See Anne-Marie Slaughter, Alec Stone Sweet, and J. H. H. Weiler (eds.), *The European Courts and National Courts* (Oxford: Hart Publishing, 1998). The editors speak of the "European Courts of Justice" to refer to this characteristic of EU law.

40. Examples of the first have been referred to by national judges in the context of a project on the application of EU labor law by national courts, subsequently collected by S. Sciarra (ed.), *Labour Law in the Courts—National Judges and the ECJ* (Oxford: Hart Publishing, 2000). For examples of the second, where national courts applied EU law in cases that the European Court of Justice had excluded from the scope of application because it considered them as purely internal to the state, see *Cour de cassation, chambre crunelle, Comite national de defense contre l'alcoolisme,* C. Sossie de Montalera and others, June 16, 1983 and *Tribunal d'instance de Bressuire (greffe de Thouars), commissaire de police de Thouars,* C. M. Cognet, *Centre Leclerc,* April 10, 1987.

The Nature of the Challenge to Sovereignty

The most commonly presented challenge to sovereignty is the erosion of the autonomy of a political community in determining its policies (self-government)—its power to independently exercise the traditional functions of governance. In some cases, it is the freedom and capacity to exercise such functions of governance that is challenged. In other cases, we even assist a transfer of some functions of governance to new forums of decision making. But the process of European integration, particularly in its legal dimension, highlights other challenges to sovereignty. The relevance of national dynamics to the application of EU law demonstrates that the challenge to national sovereignty often does not lie in a transfer of competences from the states to the Union. The Europeanization of national political and legal disputes often corresponds to an attempt by certain national actors to shift the balance of participation and representation in the resolution of those disputes at the national level. Frequently, what changes is the balance of representation and participation between different national actors in the definition of a certain policy and not so much in the European or national character of the policies. Such change is a strategic form of Europeanization, not an ontological one. This strategic Europeanization changes the balance of participation and representation of different national actors in domestic policies and in this way represents a different challenge to sovereignty. It challenges the political sovereignty of the state that is identified with its autonomy by defining the scope and patterns of representation and participation in the framing of domestic policies. In other words, it challenges the autonomy of a political community by defining participation and representation in that political community.

European integration also challenges another form of sovereignty—the ultimate source of power in the political and legal organization of society. In strict legal terms, this source corresponds to the validating norm of all other rules and exercises of normative power in a given legal system. The attribution of this ultimate authority to the states is questioned by the claim of EU law to such ultimate authority. These competing claims imply a challenge to the traditional notion of sovereignty linked to the recognition of ultimate legal and political authority. Sovereignty as a monopoly on power has long been under challenge, but now the idea of sovereignty as ultimate authority is also challenged by the emergence of competing political communities in the same political and legal arenas. In this light, European integration does much more than challenge state sovereignty. It challenges sovereignty itself.

CHAPTER 5

NATURAL, ECONOMIC, AND POLITICAL BORDERS: TRADE AND ENVIRONMENTAL PROTECTION BEFORE THE EUROPEAN COURT OF JUSTICE

Joseph Jupille

International, transnational, or supranational courts definitionally cross or transcend state borders. Yet, in most cases, the legal territories over which such courts operate conceal a multiplicity of spaces, neither identified in nor coterminous with the lines and shadings of our political maps. Among them, ecosystems and markets have often been credited with blurring the lines of sovereignty, in that neither necessarily respects national borders. What is more, natural and economic borders stand in complex relationships to each other. Reconciling the tensions among natural, economic, and political borders represents a key function of transnational courts, whose border crossings offer insights into the present and future of sovereignty.

This chapter addresses these issues by considering attempts by the European Court of Justice (ECJ) to reconcile free trade and environmental protection in an emergent and rapidly changing supranational/federal polity (the European Union or EU). The court's efforts at reconciling these various borders—natural, economic, and political—provide a lens through which to examine more general dynamics of courts crossing borders and the perhaps attendant blurring of the lines of sovereignty. I argue that the ECJ's activity in this area represents an imperfect and impermanent reconciliation of the complex pressures of ecology, economy, and politics. Indeed, a blurring of the lines of sovereignty appears as an enduring characteristic in a world in which complex ecosystems, complex economies, and complex polities coexist.

Figure 5.1   Natural, Economic, and Political Spaces (Borders)

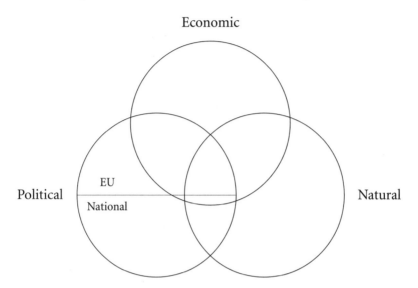

My argument can be broken into four parts. The first is a very brief elaboration of the complexities that arise when natural, economic, and political borders are considered simultaneously. The next part provides an abstract theoretical sketch of what we should expect of courts, and specifically the ECJ, when natural, economic, and political borders conflict. The third part considers these expectations in light of evidence from the ECJ's "trade-environment" jurisprudence, including both doctrinal development and patterns of litigation and outcomes. The last part summarizes the argument and findings and assesses what the interaction of natural, economic, and political borders tells us about the nature of contemporary sovereignty in the European Union and beyond.

Nature, Economy, and Polity: The Complexity of Borders

At the risk of oversimplification, it seems clear that ecosystems, the market, and politics occupy partly overlapping and partly distinct spaces, as in Figure 5.1.

Some issues fall exclusively within one category or at least privilege one category so much that the others can be ignored for analytic purposes. For example, we might imagine a private transaction, one that creates no externalities and poses no enforcement problems, as residing wholly within the domain of the market, posing no or only trivial political or ecological issues. Similarly, we might imagine "purely" political issues—say, freedom of speech - that do not impinge meaningfully upon the economy or the ecology. Finally, the proverbial tree falling in the woods may exemplify an issue with natural, but no (or trivial) economic or political consequences.

More interestingly, we can imagine a whole host of issues (arguably the vast majority) that fall into two or more domains. Markets affect and are affected by politics. Natural borders and environmental protection can have profoundly important political consequences, and environmental protection is quite explicitly politically determined. The relationships between economy and ecology are, quite simply, myriad and profound. Finally, all of these relationships can operate across numerous borders and thus complicate allocation of control and authority within the "political" category alone, as well as its relationship to the other issues. We can, in short, easily understand that both economic and environmental spheres have political elements and consequences and that nature and the market each affect the other in multiple ways; and politics, in addition to its own complexity, influences and is influenced by markets and ecosystems. Sometimes, the unenviable task of sorting out these contradictions, reconciling these ambiguities and tensions, and attempting to make ecological, economic, and political sense of the whole mess falls to courts.

Courts Crossing Borders in the European Union

These issues are all present in the European Union that, even prior to the enlargement, comprised a vast and ecologically differentiated territory of over one million square miles, an $8 trillion annual GDP that accounts for approximately 20% of world trade, and complex but highly evolved supranational political and legal structures that increasingly commingle with those of its 15 constituent member states, with all of their various political traditions, languages, cultures, and tastes among 380 million citizens. These issues are difficult to resolve politically and may also be subjected to a vertically integrated legal order, established by the EU's treaty/constitution, at the pinnacle of which stands the European Court of Justice. The treaties, interpreted by this supranational Court, ultimately guide any would-be resolution of the multiple tensions inherent in the misfit between natural, economic, and political borders.

In this context, what should we expect of a court that finds itself in such an unenviable position? The two standard approaches to understanding the ECJ, known as neofunctionalism and intergovernmentalism, differ sharply in their answers to this question and offer strikingly clear predictions about what will animate the court. Neofunctionalists tend to suggest that the court will favor economics over politics and ecology, and supranational over national authority. Intergovernmentalists suggest, on the other hand, that political logic dominates economic and ecological considerations (though good politics might involve making better markets or better environmental policies), and that national authority trumps the supranational. Let me briefly develop each in turn.

Neofunctionalism

I will refer to a body of literature, developed by Alec Stone Sweet and his collaborators and concerning the judicial role in the EU, as neofunctionalism,[1] which represents an analytical upgrading of Ernst Haas's early neofunctionalist concepts[2] and a fusion of them with a transactionalist logic more consistent with the work of Karl Deutsch.[3] At the heart of this approach lies the proposition that a virtuous circle exists among transnational market exchange, triadic dispute resolution (TDR), and rule making. Exchange begets TDR, TDR begets rules, rules facilitate exchange, and so forth. In terms of process, this model expresses exchange as key, privileges the roles of traders (transnational business) and supranational elites (the European Commission and Court, especially), and downplays the roles played by EU member states. Things are a bit more vague in terms of outcomes, but Stone Sweet's model

---

1. Alec Stone Sweet and Wayne Sandholtz, "Integration, Supranational Governance, and the Institutionalization of the European Polity," in Wayne Sandholtz and Alec Stone Sweet (eds.), *European Integration and Supranational Governance* (New York: Oxford University Press, 1998); Alec Stone Sweet and James A. Caporaso, "From Free Trade to Supranational Polity: The European Court and Integration," in Wayne Sandholtz and Alec Stone Sweet (eds.), *European Integration and Supranational Governance*, (Oxford: Oxford University Press, 1998); Alec Stone Sweet and Thomas Brunell, "Constructing a Supranational Constitution: Dispute Resolution and Governance in the European Community," 92 *American Political Science Review* (1998); Alec Stone Sweet, "Judicialization and the Construction of Governance," 31 *Comparative Political Studies* (1999); Alec Stone Sweet, *The Judicial Construction of Europe* (Oxford: Oxford University Press, forthcoming).

2. Ernst Haas, *The Uniting of Europe: Political, Social and Economic Forces, 1950–1957* (London: Stevens and Sons, 1958).

3. Karl W. Deutsch et al., *Political Community in the North Atlantic Area: International Organization in the Light of Historical Experience* (New York: Greenwood Press, 1957).

basically expects the Court to be pro-EU and, I would add, implies that the Court should be pro-trade (as against environmental protection), though the latter is not explicit.

Intergovernmentalism

A second approach reverses some of these priorities and remains agnostic about others. Intergovernmentalism, as the term implies, suggests that EU member states largely dominate the EU's politico-legal landscape and that consequently the European Court of Justice must attend to member state preferences and possible responses when contemplating its own best course of action.[4] The Court, then, must strike a balance in any given case between the demands of legal consistency (which underpins its perceived legitimacy and the continuing aggregate support of member states for the ECJ) and the demands of political expediency. In terms of process, this model privileges the role of member-state governments and the EU's Council and strongly downplays the independent roles of the Commission and the Court. As with neofunctionalism, intergovernmentalism has little specific to say about environmental protection versus the promotion of free trade. The balance it strikes, on this account, reflects its strategic circumstances and specifically the preferences of the member states.

The Evidence

In assessing evidence from the ECJ's behavior and jurisprudence in the trade-environment area, I seek less to test rival theories than to get the empirical lay of the land. I thus use the theoretical perspectives as touchstones to guide my inquiry into the Court's negotiation of the difficult boundaries between nature, economy, and polity.

Aggregate Evidence

In assessing the evidence, it makes sense to begin with the twin neofunctionalist claims that transnational and supranational actors dominate states

---

4. Geoffrey Garrett, "The Politics of Legal Integration in the European Union," 49 *International Organization* (1995), 171–82; Geoffrey Garrett, R. Daniel Kelemen, and Heiner Schulz, "The European Court of Justice, National Governments, and Legal Integration in the European Union," 52 *International Organization* (1998), 149–76.

Figure 5.2   Trade, TDR, and Rules: Environment, 1975–2001

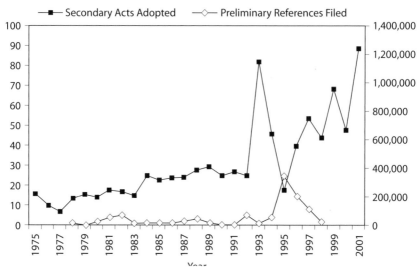

Sources: (1) For preliminary references, Alec Stone Sweet and Thomas Brunell, *Data Set on Preliminary References in EC Law* (San Domenico di Fiesole: Robert Schuman Center, European University Institute, 1999). (2) Author's calculations from Celex (secondary legislation). Search conducted February 5, 2002 for all secondary legislation adopted in Celex sector 15.10. (3) Eurostat (trade).

in the political process and that the market trumps environmental protection. Consider first the hypothesized virtuous circle among exchange, the density of legal norms (the production of EU secondary legislation), and the development of a transnational legal system linking private litigants, national judiciaries, and the ECJ. Neofunctionalists expect that these three variables will be highly positively intercorrelated. Figure 5.2 graphs the relevant time series.

Several observations seem warranted. First, least surprisingly, exchange has risen steadily. Neofunctionalists hypothesize that this will give rise to (and, partially, reflect successful) demands by transnational business elites both for dispute resolution in the form of preliminary references to the Court and to the creation of Euro-rules or secondary legislation. Second, as expected, the density of legal norms (production of Euro-rules in the form of secondary legislation in the environmental sector) is also clearly increasing over time, which empowers the ECJ insofar as it stands at the pinnacle of the judicial system charged with interpreting those norms. Third, both

Table 5.1   Environmental Preliminary References by Judicial Outcome, 1976–1998

	Reference pattern			
Judicial outcome	National v. EU	Transposition of directive	EU env'l. v. EU trade	Total cases
Inconsistent with EU	13	2	3	18
Consistent with EU	5	13	2	20
Total cases	18	15	5	38

Source: Rachel A. Cichowski, *Litigation and environmental protection in the European Union, Max-Planck-Projektgruppe Recht der Gemeinschaftsgüter*, Table 3 (Bonn: Max-Planck, 2000), 13.
Note: For column three, read as "inconsistent (consistent) with EU trade law."

secondary legislation and preliminary references correlate positively to transnational exchange (respectively, R=.56 and R=.65, p<.01 [one-tailed] for both).

In sum, these data suggest that, as expected by neofunctionalists, the expanding scope and level of exchange or demands to expand exchange incite policymaking at the political level more commensurate with the (European) scope of the market, both of which create demands for transnational adjudication. Transnational rule making and adjudication, in turn, presumably reinforce trends toward more exchange. Insofar as neofunctionalism privileges these dynamics (and the transnational and supranational elites presumably behind them), the data largely support it.

Cichowski provides additional indications—though these too carry certain ambiguities—that these trends are operating to reinforce the primacy of supranational and transnational elites (the Commission, Court, and business) over the state. She reports the outcomes of all preliminary rulings made by the ECJ in the environmental area between 1976 and 1998, and I reproduce her results in Table 5.1.

The first column reports the outcomes of cases involving a clash of domestic with European laws. Here, the ECJ most often rules in favor of supranationalism. When asked to determine the compatibility of domestic laws intended to implement European law obligations (second column), the

Figure 5.3   Preliminary Rulings as Percentage of New ECJ Cases, 1953–2000

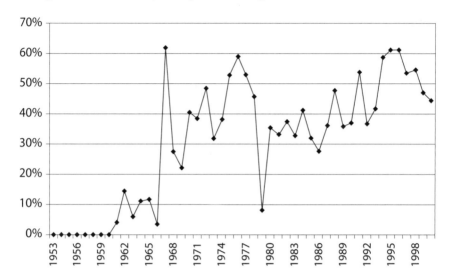

Source: European Court of Justice, *Statistics of General Activity of the Court of Justice* (Luxembourg: ECJ, 2000), Table 16. <http://curia.eu.int/en/stat/st00cr.pdf>, consulted on February 11, 2002.

Court is much more likely to find member states in conformity. This result can only be characterized as theoretically ambiguous, since it could be interpreted as indicating either ECJ deference to member states (the intergovernmentalist position) or effective fusion of domestic and European legal orders (the neofunctionalist position). The last column gets to the Court's resolution of clashes between EU environmental and EU free trade norms. Here, according to Cichowski, the Court strikes a balance between the two competing policy priorities, though the small numbers involved render any conclusions preliminary.

While suggestive, the data presented are incomplete insofar as they consider only preliminary rulings, which, while singularly important in the "constitutionalization" of the treaty, tend to represent less than half of the Court's workload (Figure 5.3), and may give us a skewed picture of its jurisprudence.

Of the remaining types of legal procedures, infringement proceedings, in which the Commission challenges member states' fulfillment of their EU legal obligations before the Court, comprise the lion's share. Indeed, with specific reference to the environmental sector, the Court's own summary of leading cases cites 63 cases, of which 36 (57%) take the form of infringement proceedings.[5] Accordingly, and given the ambiguity inherent in the support given by the Court to member-state implementing measures, I calculated judicial outcomes in the leading environmental infringement cases as identified by the ECJ's website.[6] Of the 36 cases, member states were unambiguously victorious in only 3 (8.3%), in another 3 cases (8.3%) won mixed results, and in the remainder (over 83%) witnessed a victory by the European Commission over the offending member state. This analysis, then, vindicates the neofunctionalist expectation that supranational actors (here, the Commission and Court) will largely control the litigation process, at member states' expense.

One final point concludes this aggregate discussion of Court proceedings. It concerns data presented in Table 5.2.

The bottom line here is that the Court's enforcement role is pronounced in the environmental sector, as the first column of the table confirms. Perhaps more importantly, the far-right column reports all-time use by the European Commission of the Article 228 procedure, which allows it to ask the Court to fine member states found repeatedly to be in noncompliance with their EU law obligations. The implications of this procedure for state sovereignty cannot be understated. Here, supranational actors are given an effective "stick" to force member states to comply with supranational law. As with enforcement in general, environmental cases comprise almost 45% of the Article 228 procedures undertaken. The Court itself has had occasion to rule on such a case only once and took the opportunity to fine Greece 20,000 euros per day for its noncompliance with Community waste law.[7] And, lest there be any doubt as to the effectiveness of this provision, at the end of 2000 Greece duly paid the 1.8 million euros it owed from the date of the judgment though the third quarter of that year.[8] The ECJ appears to behave clearly in favor of supranationalism in environmental affairs.

The aggregate figures on court activity in the area of environmental protection and free movement of goods tend, in short, to vindicate neofunctionalist expectations. Where EU and national laws clash, the ECJ supports

---

5. European Court of Justice, *Jurisprudence Relative à La Communauté Économique Européenne (CEE / CE)*, 1954–1999, Category B-21 (environnement). < http://curia.eu.int/common/recdoc/reperjurcomm/cee/b-21.htm>, consulted on February 4, 2002.

6. Ibid.

7. *Commission of the European Communities v. Hellenic Republic*, Case C 387/97 [ECR I-5047, 2000].

8. Commission of The European Communities, *Eighteenth Annual Report on Monitoring the Application of Community Law (2000)*, COM (2001) 309 final, volume I, July 16, 2001, 17. <http://www.europa.eu.int/eur-lex/en/com/rpt/2001/act309en01/com2001_0309 en01-01.pdf>, consulted on February 4, 2002.

Table 5.2   Infringements Pursued by Sector, 30 July 2001

Sector	Cases before ECJ		Article 228 Cases	
Environment	105	31.44%	21	44.68%
Internal Market	59	17.66%	4	8.51%
Agriculture	2	.6%	0	0%
Enterprise	12	3.59%	1	2.13%
Social Affairs	21	6.29%	5	10.64%
Customs and Taxation	29	8.68%	1	2.13%
Energy and Transport	44	13.17%	9	19.15%
Competition	7	2.1%	0	0%
Information Society	4	1.2%	1	2.13%
Consumers	29	8.68%	4	8.51%
Fisheries	8	2.4%	1	2.13%
Financial Affairs	6	1.8%	0	0%
Budgets	3	.9%	0	0%
Education, Culture, Audiovisual	4	1.2%	0	0%
Personnel	0	0%	0	0%
Enlargement	0	0%	0	0%
Regional Policy	0	0%	0	0%
Justice and Home Affairs	1	.3%	0	0%
Secretariat General	0	0%	0	0%
Legal Service	0	0%	0	0%
Total	334		47	

Source: European Commission Secretariat General. <http://www.europa.eu.int/comm/
secretariat_general/sgb/droit_com/pdf/infr_statserie2_table24_en24092001.pdf>,
consulted on February 2, 2002.

EU laws. Where questions arise as to whether member states have properly implemented their EU law obligations, the Court preponderantly supports (implemented) EU law against private litigants, but overwhelmingly supports the Commission when it alleges that member states have been less than faithful. The evidence is less clear in terms of the trade-environment balance, in part because the aggregate statistics include so few cases. In an effort to confirm these findings and perhaps resolve remaining ambiguities, I will attempt to triangulate my analysis with a brief doctrinal analysis of the Court's trade-environment jurisprudence.

Doctrinal Analysis

Court doctrine reveals a rather more nuanced picture both in terms of the relative importance of trade and environment and in terms of the relative powers of member states and the supranational Union, as can be seen in my following quick summary of the key cases in the Court's trade-environment jurisprudence. This analysis suggests that national environmental measures may retain significant future prospects, even in the face of demands for transnational exchange and supranational empowerment. I begin with a rapid overview of the constitutional underpinnings of EU free trade and environmental law and then move to the Court's own judgments.

The constitutional bases of Community action provide insights into provisions for the free movement of goods as well as for the protection of the environment, and on the tensions between the two. Substantive provisions for the free movement of goods are provided for in the EU's founding Rome Treaty in Articles 28 and 29 (ex-Articles 30-34). In particular, Article 28 declares that "quantitative restrictions on imports and all measures having equivalent effect shall be prohibited between Member States," where the notion of "equivalent effect" provides a blanket justification for striking down member state provisions deemed restrictive of trade. Article 29 establishes the identical principle for exports.

In opposition to Articles 28 and 29, which prohibit trade-restrictive measures, Article 30 (ex-Article 36) explicitly allows for such measures as long as they are grounded in concerns for, inter alia, "public morality, public policy, public security, or the protection of health and life of humans, animals, or plants." However, "the Court has consistently held that, since article [30] derogates from a fundamental principle of the Treaty, it must be construed narrowly. Thus the grounds listed in article [30] justifying restrictions on free movements are exhaustive."[9] Article 30 does not enumerate the environment as a factor justifying derogation from the free trade provisions of Articles 28 and 29, and according to the above logic the Court will not likely include the

---

9. David T. Keeling, "The Free Movement of Goods in EEC Law: Basic Principles and Recent Developments in the Case Law of the Court of Justice of the European Communities," 26 *International Lawyer* (1992), 470.

environment by way of a wide reading of the article. Use of Article 30 is also limited by the principles of proportionality, according to which national measures that restrict trade may do so only as little as is necessary for the goal to be achieved, and of non-discrimination, which requires that trade-restrictive measures be indistinctly applicable to all of the goods in question, whether foreign or domestic.[10] Although EU leaders have long considered amending the treaty to include the environment as one of the enumerated categories for derogation capable of being invoked under Article 30,[11] in the absence of such a modification trade-restrictive environmental measures must continue to rely on already-enacted treaty amendments and case law for justification.[12]

The 1986 Single European Act or SEA entered into force in 1987 and fundamentally amended the Treaty of Rome by adding explicit provisions for the environment in its newly created Title VII, encompassing then-Articles 130r-t (post-Amsterdam Articles 174-176). Symbolically, this addition codified Community environmental "action" and gave it an explicit legal basis that it had previously lacked. More substantively, Article 130t held that EC-level environmental action would "not prevent any Member State from maintaining or introducing more stringent [environmental] protective measures" which were otherwise compatible with the treaty, i.e., the free movement of goods.

The implications of another SEA "amendment" to the treaty—Article 100a(4) (now Article 95(4))—are also of potential importance for the environmental and the free movement of goods regime. This article, included in the SEA at Danish insistence,[13] allows member states to maintain "national

---

10. For the development of the proportionality doctrine see *Criminal proceedings against Léon Motte*, Case 247/84 [ECR 3887–3907, 1985] and *Ministère Public v. Claude Muller and Others*, Case 304/84 [ECR 1511–1530, 1986].

11. See, for example, the work of the Reflection Group prior to the intergovernmental conference that produced the Amsterdam Treaty, signed in 1997 and entered into force in 1999. Reflection Group's Report, 5 December 1995, point 63.

12. Note that GATT Article XX, paragraph (b) (relating to species preservation) and paragraph (g) (relating to the conservation of natural resources) come closer to explicit environmental references than does EEC Article 36, although the latter is loosely based on the former. See Robin Griffith, "International Trade Treaties and Environmental Protection Measures,"1 *Review of European Community and International Environmental Law* (1992), 25–27; Ernst-Ulrich Petersmann, *International and European Trade and Environmental Law after the Uruguay Round* (Boston: Kluwer Law International, 1995). On GATT Article XX see Steve Charnovitz, "Exploring the Environmental Exceptions in GATT Article XX," 25 *Journal of World Trade* (1991).

13. Jean-Paul Jacqué, "The 'Single European Act' and Environmental Policy," 16 *Environmental Policy and Law* (1986); "Denmark Wins Assurances From EEC Partners That National Laws Will Not be Compromised," *International Environment Reporter* (February 12,

provisions" or unilateral environmental policies not only for the grounds enumerated in Article 30, but also for "major needs... relating to the protection of the environment or the working environment," on condition that they notify the Commission of these measures. Although termed "controversial" and "problematic," Article 95(4) allows member states opposed to a particular piece of free trade legislation to "opt out" of the Community measure in order to protect the environment.[14] The harmonization of production conditions foreseen by Article 95, intended to facilitate the completion of the internal market, could not, because of paragraph 4, be undertaken at the expense of extant environmental legislation contradicted or potentially undermined by Community measures.[15]

This provision remained untouched by the 1991 Maastricht Treaty (ratified in 1993), as did Article 130t, but at the same time Maastricht elevated "sustainable... growth respecting the environment" to the level of a fundamental task of the Community, thereafter on a level on par with completion of the internal market. Other than the renumbering of treaty articles undertaken at Amsterdam, neither Maastricht nor the Nice Treaty (agreed upon in December 2000, signed in February 2001, and as of this writing not yet in force) made significant changes to the trade-environment balance, with the sole exception that the "environmental guarantee" in the internal market section of the treaty applied, post-Amsterdam, to new or existing measures rather than simply to existing ones.[16]

EU treaty law on the free movement of goods has been supplemented by numerous important ECJ decisions that have served two broad purposes.

1986), 29; "Danish Government Puts EC on Notice that it Values Environment Above Unity," *International Environment Reporter* (August 12, 1987), 370.

14. C.D. Ehlermann, "The Internal Market Following the Single European Act," 24 *Common Market Law Review* (1987); Claus Gulmann, "The Single European Act—Some Remarks from a Danish Perspective," 24 *Common Market Law Review* (1987); James Flynn, "How Will Article 100a(4) Work? A Comparison with Article 93," 24 *Common Market Law Review* (1987); Bernd Langeheine, "Le rapprochement des législations nationales selon l'article 100a du traité CEE: l'harmonisation Communautaire face aux exigences de protection nationales," 328 *Revue du marché commun* (1989).

15. For an interpretation of Article 95(4) (ex-Article 100a(4)) in light of developments since the SEA, see Robert D. Sloan and Pascal Cardonnel, "Exemptions from Harmonization Measures under Article 100a(4): The Second Authorization of the German Ban on PCP," 4 *European Environmental Law Review* (1995).

16. Member states could thereafter enact new measures environmentally stricter than the EU norm, where previously the article only authorized them to maintain existing high-standard measures. See Ludwig Krämer, *E.C. Treaty and Environmental Law* (London: Sweet and Maxwell, 1998), 110.

First, the ECJ has defined the scope and limits of the free movement of goods regime; and second, it has begun to specify the relationship between trade and the environment, although it has not as yet struck a definitive balance between them.

Two cases are particularly important in defining the scope and limits of the free movement of goods in the European Union. The first is the July 11, 1974 decision *Procureur du Roi v. Dassonville*, which struck a decisive blow in favor of trade liberalization in the EC. In *Dassonville*, when confronted with the legality of a Belgian decree requiring that spirits bearing a designation of origin, e.g., Scotch whiskey, be accompanied by an official document certifying the validity of that designation, the Court struck down the Belgian law as constituting an excessive restriction on trade. More generally, the Court held that "all trading rules enacted by Member States which are capable of hindering, directly or indirectly, actually or potentially, intra-Community trade are to be considered as measures having an effect equivalent to quantitative restrictions," as those apply to Articles 30 and 34.[17] With one stroke, *Dassonville* greatly increased the number of measures that would be considered as illegal restrictions on trade.[18]

The second case in this mold is the famous *Cassis de Dijon* case of February 20, 1979. *Cassis* is perhaps best known for its establishment of the "mutual recognition doctrine," which holds that products manufactured legally in one member state may be marketed in others. This provision is seen as a landmark in the creation of the common market because it no longer requires the harmonization of product standards at the European level. After *Cassis*, all that is required for a good to qualify for free movement is that it be recognized and legally marketable in only one member state. However, in a provision that has generally received less attention, *Cassis* also established that restrictions on trade which satisfy so-called "mandatory requirements," relating to the protection of public health, consumers, the effectiveness of fiscal supervision, and so on, must be allowed.[19] The doctrine of mandatory requirements came to be known as the "rule of reason" and opened a gap in the European Community's free trade regime that amounts to a de facto extension of Article 30 (ex-Article 36). Henceforth, barriers to the free movement of goods could be justified on more than just the "exhaustive" derogations found in that article. The

---

17. Point 5 of the judgment in *Procureur du Roi v. Benoit and Gustave Dassonville*, Case 8/74 [ECR 852, 1974].

18. Eric L. White, "In Search of the Limits to Article 30 of the EEC Treaty," 26 *Common Market Law Review* (1989), 235.

19. *Rewe-Zentral AG v. Bundesmonopolverwaltung fur Branntwein* ["*Cassis de Dijon*"], Case 120/78 [ECR 662, 1979], point 8.

door was opened for a host of potentially valid "mandatory requirements" including, the Commission explicitly noted in 1980 and 1981, environmental protection.[20] Although it would take several years for the Court to embrace this possibility, it nonetheless remained an important potential limit to the free movement of goods, nuancing considerably the strong liberalizing line taken in *Dassonville*.

The second broad function fulfilled by the ECJ's jurisprudence has been to clarify, however tentatively and at times contradictorily, the relationship between environmental protection and the free movement of goods, and necessarily the broader political question of the relationship between national versus supranational competence.

From the mid-1970s, member states had, at least partly at the behest of the Commission and the European Parliament,[21] enacted a series of environmental measures, despite the fact that such measures had no explicit legal basis in the treaty. In fact, the Council cast these not as environmental measures but, for the most part, as measures aimed at facilitating the free movement of goods. It based legislation in this area on Articles 100 (harmonization of national provisions for the purpose of promoting the common market) and 235 (akin to an "implied powers" clause). Despite greatly varied opinion as to the legality of this practice,[22] the Court in this period first confirmed the status

---

20. Communication from the Commission concerning the consequences of the judgment given by the Court of Justice on February 20, 1979 in Case 120/78 (*Cassis de Dijon*), OJ C 256, October 3, 1980, 3; answer given by Mr. Thorn on behalf of the Commission (October 28, 1981) to Written Question no. 749/81 by Mr. Bonde, OJ C 309, November 30, 1981, 7.

21. European Commission, SEC(72) 666 final, Communication de la Commission au Conseil sur un programme des Communautés Européennes en matière d'environnement, March 22, 1972; European Parliament, PE Doc. 161/70, Rapport fait au nom de la commission des affaires sociales et de la santé publique sur la lutte contre la pollution des eaux fluviales et notamment des eaux du Rhin [Rapporteur: M. Boersma], November 11, 1970.

22. Michel Carpentier, "L'action de la Communauté en matière d'environnement," 153 *Revue du Marché Commun* (1972); Jean Touscoz, "L'action des communautés européennes en matière d'environnement," 9 *Revue trimestrielle de droit Européen* (1973); Wolfgang E. Burhenne and Thomas J. Schoenbaum, "The European Community and Management of the Environment: A Dilemma," 13 *Natural Resources Journal* (1973); Alain Gerard, "Les limites et les moyens juridiques de l'intervention des Communautés Européennes en matière de l'environnement," 11 *Cahiers de Droit Européen* (1975); Eberhard Grabitz and Christoph Sasse, *Competence of the European Communities for Environmental Policy: Proposal for an Amendment to the Treaty of Rome* (Berlin: Erich Schmidt Verlag, 1977); Heinhard Steiger, *Competence of the European Parliament for Environmental Policy* (Berlin: Erich Schmidt Verlag, 1977); Konrad Von Moltke, "The Legal Basis for Environmental Policy," 3

quo ante in two series of judgments. In the 1980 *Detergents* judgment, the Court confirmed that the fundamental justification for an EU environmental policy was the preclusion of distortions to trade and competition. The ECJ held that EU environmental measures were justified since "provisions which are made necessary by considerations relating to the environment…may be a burden upon the undertakings to which they apply and if there is no harmonization of national provisions on the matter, competition may be appreciably distorted."[23] Accordingly, Articles 100 and 235 provided sufficient legal basis for the adoption of Community "environmental" measures, even if the measures were actually aimed at preventing barriers to free trade in the form of national environmental policy.

The Court held, in turn, in the 1983 *Inter-Huiles* case that France had contravened EU free trade rules by banning the export of regulated waste oils in order to ensure their proper disposal in state-licensed facilities. The Court was particularly concerned that the French measures were discriminatory and treated foreign and French disposal facilities differently, and in 1983 it was unwilling to countenance such trade-restrictive measures for the purpose of protecting the environment.[24]

The Court undertook initial movements away from this free trade baseline and toward a definition of the relationship between trade and environment in the February 7, 1985 *Waste Oils* judgment. In this case, the Court was asked to determine the compatibility of portions of the EC's waste oils directive and

---

Environmental Policy & Law (1977); George Close, "Harmonisation of Laws: Use or Abuse of the Powers under the EEC Treaty?", 3 *European Law Review* (1978); House of Lords Select Committee on the European Communities, *Approximation of Laws Under Article 100 of the EEC Treaty*, Session 1977–78, 22nd Report (London: Her Majesty's Stationery Office, 1978); House of Commons Select Committee on European Legislation, *First Special Report*, Session 1983–84, HC 126-iv (London: Her Majesty's Stationery Office, 1984); Eckard Rehbinder and Richard Stewart, *Integration Through Law: Europe and the American Federal Experience, vol. 2: Environmental Protection Policy* (New York: Walter de Gruyter, 1985); John A. Usher, "The Scope of Community Competence—Its Recognition and Enforcement," 24 *Journal of Common Market Studies* (1985); John A. Usher, "The Gradual Widening of European Community Policy on the Basis of Articles 100 and 235 of the EEC Treaty," in Jurgen Swarze and Henry G. Schermers (eds.), *Structure and Dimensions of European Community Policy* (Baden-Baden: Nomos Verlagsgesellschaft, 1988).

    23. *Commission of the European Communities v. Italian Republic*, Case 91/79 [ECR 1099–1113, 1980].

    24. *Syndicat National des Fabricants Raffineurs d'Huile de Graissage and Others v. Groupement d'Intérêt Économique 'Inter-Huiles' and Others*, Case 172/82 [ECR 555–582, 1983]; Caroline London and Michael Llamas, *Protection of the Environment and the Free Movement of Goods* (London: Butterworths, 1995), 50.

in particular its Article 5, under which member states could divide their territories into zones and assign waste collection and disposal rights to certain undertakings within them with inter alia the Community's free movement of goods requirements. In an historic judgment, one that both heralded the evolving balance between trade and the environment and elevated the legal status of environmental protection, the Court held that "the principle of freedom of trade is not to be viewed in absolute terms but is subject to certain limits justified by the objectives of general interest pursed by the Community."[25] Environmental measures such as the one the Court was judging had to "be seen in the perspective of environmental protection, *which is one of the Community's essential objectives*."[26] The balance had begun to shift in the ECJ's jurisprudence. Environmental measures still could not be justified under Article 36 (now Article 30) or the *Cassis* rule of reason, nor could they be countenanced if they were discriminatory; even so, the idea that environmental protection might justifiably hinder the free movement of goods was beginning to take hold.

The Court followed its own reasoning to its logical conclusion in a famous 1988 judgment. The September 20, 1988 decision in *Commission v. Denmark* or the "Danish Bottles" case involved a classic trade versus environment issue. The European Commission, supported by the United Kingdom, challenged the validity of Danish legislation that required that beer and soft drinks be marketed only in containers for which an adequate system of collection and refilling, approved by the competent Danish authority, had been established. The Commission and the UK argued that the Danish rules breached free movement of goods requirements by in practice favoring Danish beverages over imported ones, and also that the rules were unnecessary to achieve the stated aim of environmental protection. Denmark replied that its policy was non-discriminatory and proportionate to the environmental aim it pursued, adding that the Commission was doggedly pursuing the free movement of goods at any price despite growing ecological awareness on the part of the public.

The Court explicitly established for the first time that "the protection of the environment is a mandatory requirement which may limit" the free movement of goods, consistent with the *Cassis de Dijon* rule of reason.[27] Because the Dan-

---

25. *Procureur de la République v. Association de défense des brûleurs d'huiles usagées*, Case 240/83 [ECR 531–552, 1985].

26. Ibid.

27. *Commission of the European Communities v. Kingdom of Denmark*, Case 302/86 [ECR 4630, 1988].

ish legislation served the mandatory requirement of environmental protection, and because it did so, the Court held, in a way that was both non-discriminatory and proportionate to the aim to be achieved, the two requirements that an Article 30 rule of reason restriction on trade must satisfy, the Court's ruling must be considered a legal restriction on free trade in the legitimate interest of environmental protection.

Although the Danish Bottles decision was "cautious about any interpretation relating to the future of Community policy" and did "not offer a general solution" to the reconciliation of liberalized trade and environmental protection,[28] it did arguably serve notice that trade and environmental protection would thereafter be on more comparable footing. The Court had altered the terms of the trade-environment discourse.

A 1990 judgment of the Court, the so-called "Scottish Grouse" case, provides additional indications of the complexity facing the ECJ in the area of environmental protection. The case involved questions surrounding the legality of provisions of the Dutch law on birds, prohibiting the import or sale of certain bird species, some of which, like the Scottish grouse, were not indigenous to the Netherlands. The case thus turned on the extent to which EU law and specifically the EU's directive on the conservation of wild birds allowed member states to enact strict environmental measures that might hinder EU trade. The directive had explicitly allowed stricter national measures only with respect to endangered species occurring within the territory of the legislating member state, and the Court relied on these limitations to prohibit application of the Dutch law to Scottish grouse.[29] Two conclusions suggest themselves in this connection. First, despite rejection of the Dutch provisions, the judgment can be seen as reinforcing national sovereignty to the extent that the judgment prohibited extraterritorial legislation. To the extent that a rejection of extraterritoriality lies at the heart of the doctrine of sovereignty, the latter can be seen as reinforced. Second, though, the judgment arguably gave some comfort to environmentalist concerns by leaving the door open to national regulation to protect birds that were both migratory and endangered.[30] Read this way, Scottish Grouse seems more consistent than inconsistent with the ECJ's evolving trade-environment jurisprudence.

The July 9, 1992 "Walloon Waste" case raised a number of legal issues surrounding the free movement of goods that are extremely complex and cannot

---

28. Pascale Kromarek, "Environmental Protection and Free Movement of Goods: The Danish Bottles Case," 2 *Journal of Environmental Law* (1990), 107.

29. *Gourmetterie van den Bourg*, Case C-169/89 [ECR I-2143, 1990].

30. R. Daniel Kelemen, "The Limits of Judicial Power: Trade-Environment Disputes in the GATT/WTO and the EU," 34 *Comparative Political Studies* (2001), 644.

be considered in detail here.[31] At issue was 1987 Belgian legislation, under which the importation of waste for disposal into the region of Wallonia, including that from other Belgian regions, was forbidden, subject to certain exceptions. The Commission challenged the legislation as being against existing Community Directives 75/442 (Waste Framework Directive) and 84/631 (Transfrontier Shipments of Hazardous Waste) and Community free trade rules. The Court rejected the applicability of the 1975 Directive and held that Belgium was in breach of the 1984 legislation to the extent that the latter allowed member states to prohibit hazardous waste shipments for disposal only on a case-by-case basis, rather than absolutely as in the Walloon ban.

However, the court upheld the legality of the Walloon ban as it applied to non-hazardous waste. By establishing that "waste, whether recyclable or not, should be regarded as a product the movement of which must not in principle, pursuant to Article 30 EEC [now Article 28], be impeded,"[32] the Court explicitly defined waste as goods subject to Community free trade rules. It ended long-standing speculation about whether waste is even in principle subject to the same trade rules as more traditional "goods." Furthermore, the Court did find *Cassis*-line justification for the Belgian measure because, it held, waste is intrinsically damaging to the environment. The real problem for the Court in this case was that it could not uphold the Belgian legislation with reference to *Cassis*-derived "mandatory requirements" justification, because the measure in question was explicitly discriminatory: the rule of reason had been construed, as had Article 36 (now Article 30), to preclude such discriminatory measures from being justifiable derogations from free trade. However, it appeared that the Court very badly wanted to uphold the legislation, and to do so it had to do something of a legal two-step: after first establishing that waste was a good, subject to free trade rules, the Court went on to establish, second, that waste is sui generis and is attached to its location of production because of the waste management principles of proximity and self-sufficiency, and the environmental policy principle of the rectification of damage at its source. Because it is attached by these principles to its place of generation, "foreign" waste and "local" waste are in fact, the Court implied, different goods, and legislation banning the first but allowing for disposal of the second could not therefore be considered as discriminatory.[33]

---

31. For comments on the judgment see L. Hancher and Hanna Sevenster, "Comment," 30 *Common Market Law Review* (1993); and Marina Wheeler, "The Legality of Restrictions on the Movement of Wastes under Community Law," 5 *Journal of Environmental Law* (1993).

32. *Commission of the European Communities v. Kingdom of Belgium*, Case C-2/90 [ECR I-4431, 1993], point 28.

The Court went through these legal contortions and in the process perhaps obscured rather than clarified the relationship between trade and environmental protection, in order to "have its cake and eat it too"; in other words, the Court sought to uphold the Walloon import ban while not unacceptably widening Article 36 (now Article 30) and/or the mandatory requirements doctrine to permit discriminatory measures. This unprecedented move has been widely criticized and interpreted as possibly opening a wide breach in the free movement of goods regime.[34] However, Walloon Waste certainly confirms the "trend by which environmental protection outweighs the principle of free trade."[35] The extent to which this case can serve as a precedent—and, if so, what kind -remains unclear. The Court's legal doctrine continues to permit considerable tension between the goals of trade liberalization and environmental protection, a tension that will likely require political, rather than legal, efforts to be resolved.

In sum, the ECJ's jurisprudence has come increasingly to favor environmental protection over free trade where the two goals conflict. In my reading, the ECJ has also come increasingly—and this is not separable from the first point—to support *national* environmental measures at the expense of *EU* free trade rules. The picture is far from clear, and the law is arguably far from settled. The extent to which this narrative supports intergovernmental claims depends in part upon the sequence of Court judgments, other supranational actions, and member-state actions such as treaty revisions. While this point is a bit removed from the core interest of this chapter, let me just suggest that both approaches can find support in ECJ jurisprudence. The ECJ's initial judgments seemed more responsive to member state precedents, such as the use of Articles 100 and 235 for EU environmental law, and arguably led the member states in identifying environmental protection as a fundamental objective of the EU; those early cases followed the Commission in extending the *Cassis* rule of reason to this class of measures. The ECJ arguably again followed member states' lead in allowing for significant national autonomy in the environmental area. Neither explanation finds decisive support, and each accounts for part of the picture. The ECJ's trade-environment jurisprudence, on this account, can be read as highly imperfect and arguably impermanent, reflective of the continuing fluidity of natural, economic, and political borders in the EU.

---

33. Ibid., point 36.

34. Hans Somsen, Comment on Case C-2/90, *European Environmental Law Review* (1992), 112.

35. Wheeler, "The Legality of Restrictions on the Movement of Wastes," 148.

Conclusion

I have suggested that the interaction of non-coterminous natural, economic, and political borders poses special problems for transnational courts and may offer meaningful insights into the nature of contemporary sovereignty. Applied to the EU context, this suggests that the ECJ faces a delicate balancing act in reconciling the demands of environmental protection, market exchange, and national and supranational political and legal authority. Using the prevailing theoretical formulations of neofunctionalism and intergovernmentalism as guideposts, I have examined the delicate interplay of nature, economics, and politics in the ECJ's trade-environment jurisprudence.

The evidence paints a rather ambiguous picture of Court behavior. On the one hand, aggregate indicators drawn from both preliminary references to the Court and infringements decided by it suggest that the ECJ privileges supranational over national authority. The Court consistently upholds EU laws over national laws in the case of conflict, and consistently follows the Commission in identifying and enforcing breaches of EU law obligations by member states. Notwithstanding intergovernmentalist claims to the effect that the whole enforcement system serves member states, this analysis suggests rather clearly that the Court is not only directing the process, but directing it in a supranational direction. On the other hand, the doctrinal analysis shows ever-increasing sensitivity by the Court to the legitimate need for environmental protection, which has the ancillary effect of reinforcing national competence at the expense of European competence. Indeed, Kelemen has traced through the same line of case law and concluded that it reveals a court highly aware of, sensitive to, and constrained by its strategic relationship with member states.[36] Overall, it seems clear that the court has striven to strike a balance among the often-conflicting demands placed on it by the environment, the market, and politics, but locating the precise nature, much less future, of this compromise proves impossible.

What does all of this tell us about the dynamics of courts crossing borders and about the nature of contemporary sovereignty? If one subscribes to the notion that ecological, economic, and political borders remain in a constant state of development, redefinition, and flux, then it seems safe to conclude that sovereignty is, and for the foreseeable future will remain, blurred. On this analysis, the ECJ's messy jurisprudence reflects rather than creates the blurred lines

---

36. Kelemen, "The Limits of Judicial Power."

of sovereignty. At the same time, these trends within and across the various borders will reinforce a court's own centrality in the process. Any action, whether predominantly focused on the market or environmental protection, on the state or the suprastate, must increasingly survive tests of legality, with the ECJ as the chief architect of the legal discourse. Continued fluidity, while perhaps not of the Court's design, will likely redound to its benefit as cases continue to come before it. Ultimately, in that sense, the ECJ specifically and the EU generally may indicate broader trends that transcend Europe's own various borders and might inform developments in other regions, as well as a global trend. As borders multiply and blur, it will fall to courts to cross, delimit, and otherwise define them.

CHAPTER 6

HOW RIGHTS EVOLVE: THE CASE OF NON-DISCRIMINATION IN THE EUROPEAN COURT OF HUMAN RIGHTS

Doris Marie Provine

Sensitivity to individual rights is growing in Europe, but in a distinctively European way. This is a movement within individual states, but also among them. The duality is significant. Litigation over individual rights at both the national and supranational level is helping Europe develop a sense of constitutional identity, a complex accomplishment with far-ranging implications. Judges are key players in this development. Empowered by the establishment of constitutional review in the past fifty years, and by treaties that recognize judicial review, judges have become more activist. At this point, as Alec Stone Sweet and others have pointed out, the judicialization of politics is well underway in Western Europe, and it is an irreversible process.[1] This process is opening new doors for advocates of social change, even as it imposes new constraints on legislatures and executives.

While judicial responsiveness to rights claims in national courts and constitutional-review bodies is part of the story, the really striking development

---

1. C. Neal Tate and Torbjorn Vallinder, "The Global Expansion of Judicial Power: The Judicialization of Politics," in C. Neal Tate and Torbjorn Vallinder (eds.), *The Globalization of Judicial Power* (New York: New York University Press, 1995); J.H.H. Weiler and Ulrich R. Haltern, "Constitutional or International? The Foundations of the Community Legal Order and the Question of Judicial Kompetenz-Kompetenz," in Anne-Marie Slaughter, Alec Stone Sweet, and J.H.H. Weiler (eds.), *The European Court and National Courts—Doctrine and Jurisprudence: Legal Change in its Social Context* (Oxford: Hart Publishing, 1998); and Alec Stone Sweet, *Governing with Judges: Constitutional Politics in Europe* (Oxford: Oxford University Press, 2000).

of recent years is the rise of litigation at the supranational level, with its multiple implications for national sovereignty. Having empowered individuals to make claims against their governments, Europe's supranational courts—the European Court of Justice, the war crimes tribunal in The Hague, and the European Court of Human Rights—are laying the groundwork for the emergence of European norms and a sense of European citizenship in their decisions.[2] The process has gone far enough in the commercial realm that a constituent assembly has recently been created to draft a written constitution for the European Union. Developments at this level complement and encourage the trend within individual nations toward adjudication of constitutional principles.[3] The European Court of Human Rights, the subject of this chapter, is an important part of this story of dynamic, multi-level litigation and expanding rights consciousness.

The European Court of Human Rights

The European Court of Human Rights is based in Strasbourg, France, territory that has enormous strategic and historic significance in Europe because it has been both German and French territory, depending on the outcome of war. The Court hears suits brought by individuals against their governments for violations of the European Convention on Human Rights. Litigants come to the Court after their appeals at the national level are exhausted. When a litigant wins a judgment from the European Court, the national courts recognize the decision, not just as a case resolution, but, typically, as binding law for future cases within their jurisdiction because the signatory states have promised that the rights and freedoms outlined in the Convention will be secured for their citizens. The Convention protects citizens against various forms of government over-reaching and intrusiveness. It is a document designed to protect political freedoms and privacy, not economic rights or social benefits. The rights are, for the most part, familiar. What is striking about this arrangement is not the rights protected, but the idea that a court with jurisdiction beyond the borders of the nation-state is directly available to citizens.

---

2. Weiler and Haltern, "Constitutional or International"; Neal Dorr, "An Introduction to Human Rights Developments since 1945," in Liz Heffernan (ed.), *Human Rights: A European Perspective* (Dublin: Round Hall Press, 1994); and Miguel Poiares Maduro, "The European Court of Justice: Constructing a European Political Community," in this volume.

3. Luke Clements, *European Human Rights* (London: Sweet and Maxwell, 1994); and Igor I. Kavass, *Supranational and Constitutional Courts in Europe: Functions and Sources* (Buffalo: William S. Hein, 1992), 6–7.

The establishment of the European Court of Human Rights and its growth as an institution, not surprisingly, parallel the development of scholarly thinking about human rights. As a basis for limiting the power of governments to act to the detriment of their citizens, human rights is not a new idea. As Forsythe observes, "Human rights is an old subject precisely because it addresses a persistent question of human existence—the relationship of person(s) to state and society—that reoccurs not only across time but across cultures."[4] The ancient Greeks, Enlightenment thinkers, and many others have made contributions. What *is* new is the idea that human rights can be a basis for international diplomacy, protest, and litigation.[5] The idea that nations can and should scrutinize each other's record on individual rights started to gain ground only in the aftermath of World War II, and the international infrastructure to make such criticism meaningful began to develop at about the same time. The issue of enforcement, highly controversial at first, was finally resolved in the 1950s in Europe. At that point, leaders in most of the countries of Western Europe signed on to the European Convention on Human Rights and set up the machinery to enforce it. They established, in the words of one analyst, "the most advanced and developed framework and structure for the international protection of human rights anywhere in the world."[6]

How does this institution articulate with rights-mindedness in local communities? The Court's large—indeed, overwhelming—caseload suggests widespread popular acceptance of this institution. Its geographical remoteness seems not to interfere with its broad base of support. Consider, for a moment, the relationship of the Court to Oñati, the small, historic city in the heart of Basque country where I began to write this chapter. On one level, the Court represents the intrusion of distant government. The Basque region is an area that strongly prefers local to national governance; separatist leanings are common. Some even consider Pais Vasco a stateless nation. If Spain is an intrusion in daily life, what of a court created by European states? But in terms of the Court's role in fostering European ideals, there is a deep resonance with the fabric of local life in Oñati. This is a court designed to reign in the excesses of state power, to force states to respect their citizens. The European Court of Human Rights is thus a place to assert the sense of grievance that permeates this region.

This historic city is also a reminder of the power of human rights consciousness to shape thinking about what governments do. Oñati gets its name

---

4. David P. Forsythe, *The Internationalization of Human Rights* (Lexington: Lexington Books, 1991), 14.

5. Clements, *European Human Rights*.

6. Dorr, "An Introduction to Human Rights," 17.

from an imperial Spanish family, made famous by one of its Mexican-born members, Don Juan de Oñate, a colonizer who founded the first European settlements in the southwestern United States. Don Juan de Oñate blazed the Pass of the North in 1598 with 500 settlers and 7,000 animals more than two decades before the English Pilgrims arrived at Plymouth Rock. In the process, he apparently subdued the rebellious Acoma tribe by cutting off the right feet of dozens of young warriors. This ancient story became newsworthy recently when El Paso, Texas commissioned a large statue of Oñate astride a rearing stallion as part of its sculpture walk through downtown El Paso. The statue would be the largest bronze equestrian statue in the world and something of an engineering marvel. The decision to move forward with this $1.2 million project has created outrage among the Pueblo people, who have always reviled Oñate.[7]

The power of the European Court of Human Rights arises, not from cases of spectacular violence like the Oñate mutilations, but from the accumulation of more mundane instances of institutionalized violence, deprivation of benefits, and state-sanctioned discrimination. This chapter will briefly review the organization of the Court and discuss its growing workload, but my central concern is with jurisprudence: How do the Court's judges create persuasive legal norms from the materials and ideas available to them? How have they successfully positioned themselves as the conscience of Europe?

Judges on Rights

The analysis that follows proceeds from the conviction that judges enjoy considerable discretion when deciding cases and that they are generally aware of their role in defining rights. Judges are political decision makers who operate within boundaries set by tradition and power. These boundaries pose some restraints, but there is play in this system too. In the words of Alec Stone Sweet: "Legal discourse is insular and self-referential, driven by its own concerns, but it is not completely divorced from socio-political contexts."[8] Thus judicial reasoning is politically significant, not only because it resolves particular cases, but, more importantly, because it contributes to the normative basis of state power. [9] This is particularly true in the ever-expanding realm of

---

7. Ginger Thompson, "As a Sculpture Takes Shape in Mexico, Opposition Takes Shape in the U.S.," *New York Times* (January 17, 2002).

8. Stone Sweet, *Governing with Judges*, 28.

9. Ibid., 29.

human rights, where judges create a moral framework for governments' operations that must be taken into account by other political actors.

For Americans habituated to giving the U.S. Supreme Court the last word on rights, the idea that judges define the limits of government authority is not new. Receptivity to judicial authority came much later in Europe, only after Nazism and the ravages of World War II made the need for change obvious. And even this concession has been somewhat grudging by American standards. Igor Kavass notes that, while the American example provoked much interest in nineteenth-century Europe, "most European politicians believed that the interests of the people were best served by their elected representatives."[10] They were also loath to give up power to judges. European suspicion of the judiciary dates back to pre-Napoleonic times. World War II changed this perception and encouraged a serious re-thinking about the role of the judiciary and the importance of recognizing human rights. Neal Dorr argues that the horror of the Holocaust, with its slave labor and methodical slaughter, dehumanization, and brutality, had the greatest impact:

> Can there have been, at any point in history, such an explicit and direct antithesis of the individual dignity and worth of each human person—the concept on which human rights must rest? The Nazi policy was the precise opposite of Kant's injunction to treat every person as an end and not a means. And it came not from barbarism but from the heart of our western civilization; from a culture which had produced Kant himself—and Hegel, Goethe, Beethoven and Mozart.[11]

One way to get a sense of how rights jurisprudence has developed in the European Court of Human Rights is to look closely at how the Court has interpreted a single article of the governing convention. The Convention, through a series of articles and protocols, binds the signatory European nations to observe enumerated civil and political rights. Here I examine cases based on the guarantee of non-discrimination, a provision that occasioned considerable controversy when it was first suggested for inclusion in the United Nations Charter of Rights that preceded the Convention. The racially exclusionary policies in effect in many member states in the 1940s explains their hesitation. At this point, however, the promise of non-discrimination incorporates widespread, popular aspirations for equal treatment under law. Every state has signed on to this provision without qualification.

---

10. Kavass, *Supranational and Constitutional Courts*, 4.
11. Dorr, "An Introduction to Human Rights Developments," 5.

Article 14 promises that the rights and freedoms that the Convention guarantees are equally available to all, without regard to race, sex, language, belief, or status. It bears a distinct resemblance to the equal-protection clause of the Fourteenth Amendment to the United States Constitution, which requires that: "No State shall…deny to any person within its jurisdiction the equal protection of the laws." Equal protection of the law has proven a surprisingly complicated ambition in the American context. The scope of the guarantee is also proving difficult to define in the European Court of Human Rights. The pattern in the two venues, superficially at least, is quite similar. In both Europe and the United States, suits claiming infringement are very common, while judicial rulings providing relief are very rare. This means that an important part of the jurisprudence of non-discrimination is negative, consisting of reasons why the government need not act differently. The reasons for non-action, however, differ in each case. For the American Supreme Court, the issue is when to move beyond a historically specific set of fundamental concerns about racial equality, based on the outcome of a bloody war, to a wider domain appropriate for modern conditions. In the European Court of Human Rights, the question is how to build from a broad statement of coverage that reaches all conceivable types of questionable legal distinctions, but that lacks historical roots that might indicate the scope and depth of the commitment undertaken.

The political dilemma facing judges of the European Court of Human Rights is obvious. They must be responsive to the goal of securing human rights in Europe and yet remain aware of the delicacy of their mission. Requiring nations to change their laws inevitably causes resentment, particularly when the court mandating the changes is made up almost entirely of non-nationals. Only one member of the affected state sits on a bench that is growing larger every year. The tension is well captured in this response from Marc Thiessen, a critic of the European Court of Human Rights and other efforts to develop human rights at a supranational level, to the assertions of Mark Leonard, a defender of the Court:

> Mr. Leonard insists that the new global order is fully democratic, but then declares that it is OK for a supranational court to overrule Britain's domestic laws banning gays in the military. Why? Because said law is "offensive." Who says the law is offensive? The British people? Was there a referendum I missed? Did their elected representatives vote in Parliament to repeal the law? No, they did not. Strasbourg made the decision for them.[12]

---

12. John T. Rourke, *Taking Sides: Clashing Views on Controversial Issues in World Politics* (Guilford, CT: Dushkin/McGraw Hill, 2002), 27.

The specific questions examined here are three: How has the Court developed a sense of what is and is not covered by the non-discrimination guarantee from the paltry language and ambiguous history of Article 14? Has it acknowledged tension between equal enjoyment of rights and the increasingly unequal distribution of goods among citizens? What is the likely terrain for expanding equality guarantees in the European system?

The Institutional Setting for European Human Rights

The impetus for the European Convention on Human Rights, as noted earlier, was the rise of Nazism and the subsequent experience of a devastating world war. Many of the statesmen of the era had experienced imprisonment,[13] and a widespread sense had developed that individual rights, particularly political rights, had to be more adequately protected from internal, as well as external, threats. Fear of dictatorship, as Robertson and Merrills note, had made Europeans value democracy. Human rights were thought to be a precondition of democracy and the rule of law.[14]

The European Convention on Human Rights is, in a sense, a byproduct of the effort to set up the United Nations immediately after the war. The 1945 U.N. Charter, with 50 nations participating in the drafting, was a compromise document. It set forth a commitment to human rights, a first in an international agreement, but not in enforceable terms. After much discussion, words like "promote" and "encourage" were adopted instead of "guarantee" or "safeguard."[15]

In 1948, the U.N. adopted a more elaborate statement of rights, the Universal Declaration of Human Rights, describing it as "a common standard of achievement for all peoples and all nations."[16] The document contained a listing of political and civil rights, as well as economic and social rights. The Universal Declaration has no legally binding force, but it inspired fifteen Western European nations to create an enforceable instrument based on the portion of the Universal Declaration containing civil and political rights.[17] The Conven-

---

13. A.H. Robertson and J.G. Merrills, *Human Rights in Europe: A Study of the European Convention on Human Rights* (Manchester: Manchester University Press, 1993), 2.

14. Ibid., 3.

15. Dorr, "An Introduction to Human Rights Developments," 7.

16. Ibid., 10.

17. See Rosalynn Higgins, "The European Convention on Human Rights," in Theodore Meron (ed.), *Human Rights in International Law* (Oxford: Clarendon Press, 1984).

tion, which they signed in Rome in 1950, is clear about the source of the rights it contains and the decision to make these rights enforceable: "Being resolved, as the governments of European countries which are like-minded and have a common heritage of political traditions, ideals, freedom and the rule of law, to take the first steps for the collective enforcement of certain of the rights stated in the Universal Declaration."

The Convention has fourteen articles offering specific protections ranging from the right to life (Article 2), fair trial (Article 7), and family life (Article 8), to freedom of thought (Article 9). Some articles are accompanied by protocols drafted in later years to set forth new freedoms and conditions; the signatory states subscribe in varying numbers to these additional provisions. The Convention initially split the function of rights protection into three parts. A Commission of Human Rights accepted and screened complaints, attempted settlements, and passed on those cases that it could not resolve to a Committee of Ministers of the Council of Europe or to the European Court of Human Rights. The Ministers, political actors with political skills, were to attempt settlement when they thought appropriate, while the Court, as an expert legal body, was to elucidate the meaning of the Convention as it decided cases referred to it. The expectation was that most cases would be brought by states on behalf of their citizens, not by individuals complaining about actions taken by their own governments. There was, however, a provision (Article 25) that allowed for suits by individuals against their own governments if permitted by the signatory state.

The founders were wrong in predicting a manageable caseload made up mainly of state-initiated petitions. The original signatory states were under pressure to allow individuals to sue them, and eventually, all of them agreed to it. Eventually permission to sue became automatic when it became a condition for membership in the Council of Europe. As the number of signatories grew, so did the influx of work for the Commission and Court. During the 1980s and 1990s, the number of petitions increased by significant amounts annually. Most of these were declared inadmissible, that is, not falling within the technical requirements for resolution. Figure 6.1 maps the growth in applications declared inadmissible over time.

The number of decisions by the Court increased dramatically as well, growing more than tenfold between 1980 and 1995 to more than one hundred cases a year, and continuing since then on the same steep upward trajectory. Figure 6.2 maps the growth in judgments over time.

In 1997 it was decided to merge the Commission and Court, and in November 1998, a new protocol came into effect, replacing the formerly part-time Court and the Commission with a single full-time Court. This newly consti-

Figure 6.1   Applications Deemed Inadmissible over Time

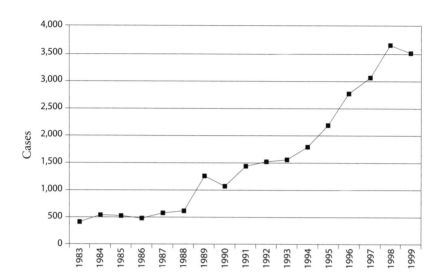

Figure 6.2   Growth in Judgments over Time

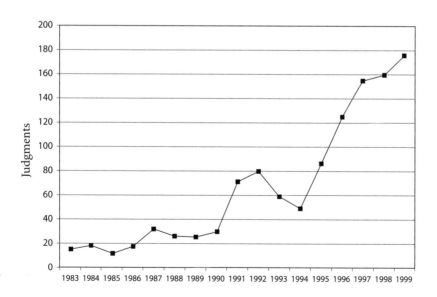

tuted Court gained power to set its own agenda and to divide itself into sections, committees, and chambers to increase its decisional capacity. A Grand Chamber of 17 judges meets only to hear cases a section deems most significant. Most cases now go to three-member committees or seven-member chambers. These changes significantly increased the decisional capacity of the Court, to about 700 cases per year. They have not, however, been sufficient to relieve the pressure of a growing caseload. The Court rejects nearly 65 percent of the cases coming to it as non-admissible, but the cases that remain must somehow be resolved. The problem grows worse every year. The number of signatory states, now 43, is likely to grow larger, and so is the inclination to petition. The result is an awesome backlog. In 2001 the number of pending applications was 15,858.

The pressure of unresolved cases is of enormous concern to the Court, but is intractable without further significant structural adjustments. Within a year of the consolidation of the Court, its Registrar noted that "the continuing steep increase in the number of applications to the Court is putting even the new system under pressure. Today we are faced with nearly 10,000 registered applications and more than 47,000 provisional files, as well as around 700 letters and more than 200 overseas telephone calls a day."[18] Not long afterwards, the President of the Court, Luzius Wildhaber, complained that the judges had experienced a 500 percent increase in the number of applications over the past seven years. He warned that the backlog would continue to grow and that "there will come a point at which the system becomes asphyxiated."[19]

This brief discussion merits at least three observations. One is that Europe, with the adoption of the Convention on Human Rights, clearly demonstrated a commitment to develop a regional human-rights regime with teeth and the potential for a robust jurisprudence. This commitment was made significantly before Europe undertook commercial integration. Second, the idea of European human rights has proven very popular, indeed too popular for the efficient functioning of the Court. The Court's growing caseload, however unmanageable, demonstrates a broad-based public attachment to human-rights adjudication. Finally, it should be noted that the nations of Europe have continued to support the idea of litigation for human rights, even as the Court's power and reach have grown with the passage of time.

---

18. Press Release, August 6, 2000.
19. Ibid.

Tailoring Demand to the Court's Resources

In 1997 I noted the relative paucity of decisions favorable to women under the European Convention. I blamed the framing of Article 14 and the litigation process itself. I speculated, however, that even narrowly focused decisions build a sense of social engagement with the rights of individuals:

> Dramatic action is unlikely in this forum, either for women or any other group that suffers deeply embedded social discrimination. Occasionally, exceptions occur, and even in routine cases, human rights litigation generates a jurisprudence of social concern for individual rights. Legitimacy in this metanational setting is thus not simply a question of constraint, but a process of creation. The commission and court help to create a milieu of rights whose ultimate direction is hard to discern.[20]

In this chapter I return to Article 14, but within a broader framework. My concern here is with the growth of a general jurisprudence of relief under this article, not with discrimination against women per se. I found that even with this broader ambit of concern, the pattern remains one of judicial caution. Still, there is an inexorable increase in judicial engagement with individual rights. As cases in which petitioners were successful accumulate, they become a foundation for future growth. And when non-judicial elites commit themselves to full citizenship for homosexuals, women, religious minorities, immigrants, and the disabled, courts have a tendency to fall in step. An analysis of the past decade of cases defining Article 14 non-discrimination norms demonstrates these trends.

The Parameters of Judicial Concern

Article 14 of the European Convention on Human Rights states:

> The enjoyment of the rights and freedoms set forth in this Convention shall be secured without discrimination on any ground such as sex, race, colour, language, religion, political or other opinion, national or social origin, association with a national minority, property, birth or other status.

---

20. Doris Marie Provine, "Women's Concerns in the European Commission and Court of Human Rights," in Mary L. Volcansek (ed.), *Law above Nations* (Gainesville, FL: University Press of Florida, 1997), 5.

As noted above, litigants often invoke Article 14, but the Court seldom accepts the invitation to respond in those terms. A violation of Article 14 was claimed in 212 of the cases the Court resolved with final judgment between 1991 and 2001. The Court found a violation of Article 14, however, only fifteen times in this period. This remarkable fact should be read both as an indication of the salience of discrimination as an issue in European politics and as a sign of its still-undefined contours as a legal doctrine.

Article 14 remains undefined in part because of the way it is framed in the Convention. The right not to be discriminated against is not a primary right, like the right to religious freedom, security of one's home and possessions, or procedural rights in litigation. Rather, the Convention promises non-discrimination in the enjoyment of these rights. Cases that lose on the primary right also fail in their Article 14 claim. Indeed, this is what befell the vast majority of Article 14 claims in the cases the Court decided with full opinion. They failed, in other words, because litigants were unable to convince the Court that basic guarantees were violated. Note that these "lose/lose" cases represent a small part of the overall picture of failed rights claims. The vast majority of claims get no hearing at all. Claimants generally fail to get a hearing on the merits either that they do not convincingly show that they have exhausted the remedies available to them, or because they are unable to show that their claim falls within the guarantees of the Convention.

Even when litigants get past the initial test of showing a violation under the Convention, most equality claims get only cursory attention. Sometimes this happens because the complaining parties state at the outset that, if they win on one claim, they will drop the others. The 1998 *Tinnelly v. U.K.* is a good example, where the applicants, a contracting firm based in Northern Ireland, complained of discrimination against them in bidding for a government demolition contract. The gist of the complaint was that their religious beliefs had been a factor in their failure to get the contract, and the applicants had set forth claims under Article 8 (respect for private life), Article 6 (right to a hearing), and Article 13 (right to an effective remedy); Article 14 was paired with the Articles 6 and 8 to create additional claims. At the hearing, however, the applicants stated that they were willing to rest their case entirely on Article 6 and, if successful, would not pursue the others. The Court granted relief on that ground, and the inquiry stopped there.[21]

---

21. *Tinnelly & Sons, Ltd. and Others and McElduff and Others v. United Kingdom* (October 7, 1998, Section IV) #20390/92 and #21322/93.

The Court also tends to give short shrift to a discrimination claim when other motives can explain state action. This appears to have happened in a case involving a man who had been convicted three times for advocating Kurdish separatism and for publishing a brochure calling for a separate state of Kurdistan. The Court found that the applicant's Article 10 right to free expression had been violated, but did not accept his assertion that he had been prosecuted because of his Kurdish ancestry. The Court found that, even though the state had acted illegally, its rationale *could* have been that the brochure was a threat to security. With this plausible reason in hand, the Court was unwilling to assume that the applicant might have been prosecuted on the basis of his ethnicity (Section 83).[22]

The most frequent reason that Article 14 claims fail to get full consideration in judgments, however, is that the Court finds them superfluous. In these cases, as in the two just described, success on other grounds is enough to resolve the issue. The difference is that the Article 14 claim is not dropped by the applicants or rejected by the Court. Rather it is simply treated as unnecessary to resolve. This is how the Court handled *Association Eakin v. France*.[23] The case concerned a book produced in Spain that supported violence in pursuit of Basque nationalism. The French courts justified confiscating the book and banning its circulation on national security grounds, using a statute designed to control foreign books. The applicant argued that his freedom of expression had been infringed upon (Article 10) and that he had suffered discriminatory treatment because a book produced in France would not have been treated the same way. The Court agreed on the freedom of expression point, summarily dropping the Article 14 claim as "unnecessary" to decide (point 65).

As a survey of recent cases demonstrates, the Court handles cases in other areas the same way. A good example is *Grande Oriente D'italia de Palazzo Giustinani v. Italy*,[24] where the claim was infringement of freedom of association. The applicant's success on that ground was used to justify dropping his discrimination claim. In *Caballero v. U.K.*[25] the issue was discrimination in the context of pretrial detention without bail for attempted rape. The government conceded that bail should have been available, so the Court dropped consideration of the Article 14 claim. See also *Platakou v. Greece*,[26] where the complaint was discrimination in the context of inequitable adjudication (Article 6). In all of

---

22. *Askoy v. Turkey* (October 10, 2000, Grand Chamber) #18635/95, #31071/96, and #34535/97.

23. (July 17, 2001) #39288/98.

24. (August 2, 2001) #35972/97.

25. (February 8, 2000, Section III) #32819/96.

26. (January 11, 2001) #38460/97.

these cases the Court found it unnecessary to determine whether the acts complained of were discriminatory because it supported the applicant on other grounds. This formula for avoiding Article 14 follows the familiar prescription in Anglo-American jurisprudence that a judge should not go further in legal analysis than is necessary to resolve a dispute. The consequence in this context, however, is that judicial reticence prevents development of Article 14 case law except when discrimination is a central part of the claim.

How Article 14 Jurisprudence Grows

The fifteen cases over the past ten years that did use Article 14 in reaching a judgment most often concerned clear legal distinctions in law, that is, *de jure* discrimination. These cases arose when a statute or administrative decision prevented the applicant's full enjoyment of rights protected by the Convention. Discrimination was the basis for the complaint. In deciding these cases, the Court drew no distinction among rights and freedoms protected by the Convention, though there are some patterns. For example, property rights claims were the most numerous and also the most varied.

To anyone accustomed to thinking about discrimination in terms of historically disadvantaged minority groups, Article 14 cases span an unusual gamut. For example, the Court discussed, but ultimately rejected, a discrimination claim brought by a Swiss group promoting vegetarianism. The complaint alleged discrimination in Switzerland's failure to air an anti-meat commercial.[27] In a 1997 case the Court found that Greece had discriminated against the Catholic Church in denying it the right to sue in its civil courts,[28] and in a 1999 case it found that Cyprus had discriminated against a private tenant because it gave public authorities more power to evict than private landlords.[29]

What is most important to observe, however, is that, despite differences in applicants and in specific rights claimed, the Court was able to maintain a consistent, indeed formulaic, approach in elucidating the meaning of Article 14. The Court always began by noting that a difference in treatment is discriminatory if it "has no objective and reasonable justification." The aims of the legislation must be legitimate, and the means used to reach them must

---

27. *Vgt Verein Gegen Tierfabriken v. Switzerland* (June 28, 2001) #24699/94.

28. *Canea Catholic Church v. Greece* (December 16, 1997, Reports 1997-VIII) #25528/94.

29. *Larkos v. Cyprus* (Feruary 18, 1999, Reports of Judgments and Decisions, 1999-1) #29515/95.

be reasonable and proportional. Distinctions are problematic if they cannot be explained in these terms. The Court then would go on to note that states enjoy a certain "margin of appreciation" that must be taken into account in making these assessments. This formula could allow considerable "wiggle room" for states, but the Court resisted that approach when the legal distinction itself seemed questionable, as in cases involving sex discrimination and national origin. In these cases the Court always notes that "very weighty reasons" would need to be put forward before a difference in treatment could be justified.[30]

The applicants who were successful in their Article 14 claims were often, but certainly not always, the social or economic underdogs envisioned by those who drafted this article. One Article 14 "upper-dog" was a company that relied on a promise that it could build a warehouse in an area reserved as a greenway, and it successfully claimed that it should have been compensated when permission was denied.[31] Even more striking is the pattern in sex-discrimination cases. Three of the four cases successfully claiming sex discrimination in this ten-year period involved claims by men to tax exemptions traditionally enjoyed by women. I noted this pattern in my earlier study of sex-discrimination claims, as did Alpha Connelly in her study of gender in the Court's judgments:

> It is interesting that many of the complaints under the Convention have been brought by men challenging assumptions about the traditional roles of men and women in relation to children. They have concerned the private sphere of human relations, the sphere to which women have often historically been confined. Complaints from women about their rights in the public sphere have been less common....[32]

One might be tempted to conclude at this point that the Court is hopelessly conventional in its approach to equality. The judges, after all, are establishment types proposed by their governments for service on this prestigious court. Until recently, the bench was almost entirely male and is still dominated by senior male figures who have been highly successful in earlier careers in public service, law, or legal education. The Court's disinclination to explore the outer limits of Article 14 unless absolutely necessary is, one must remember, due in part at least to the way Article 14 was drafted. That

---

30. See, for example, *Burghutz v. Switzerland* (February 22, 1994, A280-B) #162213/90 and *Schuler-Zgraggen v. Switzerland* (June 24, 1993, A263) #14518/89.

31. *Pine Valley Developments Ltd. v. Ireland* (November 29, 1991) #12742/87.

32. Alpha Connelly, "Ireland and the European Convention on Human Rights: An Overview," in Liz Heffernan (ed.), *Human Rights*, 283.

article provides relief only within the boundaries of the Convention, so a case cannot be successful unless the applicant shows a violation of another article. Similarly, as troubling as the male preponderance of applications under Article 14 is, the Court has no responsibility for the cases that are filed. Protections designed for women are vulnerable to litigation under the Convention, while many of the social and economic burdens facing women are not.

There *are* signs of healthy growth in the way the Court handles claims of discrimination under Article 14. One is the Court's growing hostility to assumptions about group differences in laws, administrative rulings, and judicial decisions. This chapter has already noted the Court's suspicion of racial and gender categorization in law, and significantly, the judges appear to be growing more sensitive to issues of sexuality. A good example is the Court's 1999 decision in *Salgueiro da Silva Mouta v. Portugal*.[33] The Court's unanimous decision overturned a Portuguese appeals court that had denied custody to a father who was living in an openly gay relationship. The Portuguese court had based its decision partly on its conclusion that homosexuality is "an abnormality" to which children should not be exposed. The European Court, perhaps in deference to the fact that it was over-ruling an appellate judge, noted that it was "forced to find" a violation (Section 36).

The Court also makes good use of its opinion format to teach lessons about discrimination. It refuses to accept technical excuses for denying basic rights, laboriously showing where a government's excuses fall short. It presents the facts involving denial of benefits in a way that reveals how pernicious stereotypes lead to bad decisions. In *Schuler-Zgraggen v. Switzerland*,[34] for example, the Court showed how an insurance court had based its judgment that a woman was not interested in going back to work on an assumption that mothers of small children prefer to stay home with their children. The problem, the Court pointed out, is that it would not have made this assumption had the case concerned a male. This is obviously a useful strategy when the case involves discrimination against women or unpopular targets, such as homosexuals, immigrants, and religious minorities. But even male-initiated sex-discrimination cases give the Court occasion to denounce gender stereotypes, as occurred in *Karlheinz Schmidt v. Germany*,[35] a 1994 case addressing a requirement that men, but not women, pay a fire service levy in lieu of service on the fire brigade.

---

33. (December 21, 1999, Section IV) #33290/96.
34. (June 24, 1993, A263) #14518/89.
35. (July 18, 1994) #13580/88.

Another educational technique the Court often employs is citation to a progressive source, such as the recommendations of the Council of Europe or the European Social Charter. *Mazurek v. France*[36] is an excellent example of this approach. The Court was faced with a French statute that made distinctions between the inheritance rights of legitimate and illegitimate children. The Court's opinion cited statistics on the increasing number of illegitimate births in France, quoted testimony of various experts working to reform the law, and noted relevant provisions of the United Nations Convention on the Rights of the Child. It concluded that "France stood out in the Council of Europe by its maintenance of an excessively restrictive and discriminatory position on this question" (Section 31) and found the French law in violation of the Convention. In overturning the statute, the judges noted that their interpretations of provisions are "necessarily dynamic." They could not ignore "a distinct tendency in favor of eradicating discrimination against adulterine children" (Section 52).

The Court has also taken tentative steps toward the idea that a state may be obliged to recognize differences in order to be non-discriminatory. *Thlimmenos v. Greece*,[37] a 2000 decision, was brought by a Jehovah's Witness who had been turned down for appointment as a chartered accountant on grounds of a previous felony conviction. His conviction arose from conscientious refusal to serve in the Greek military. Greece at that time made no exceptions for religious opposition to military service, so Mr. Thlimmenos was forced to go to prison for his beliefs. The validity of the initial conviction under the European Convention was not at issue in this case. The question was whether Greece could enforce its neutral rule against this applicant. The Court said no. It required Greece to distinguish between felonies: "The right not to be discriminated against in the enjoyment of the rights guaranteed under the Convention is also violated when States, without an objective and reasonable justification, fail to treat differently persons whose situations are significantly different" (Section 44).

Finally, the Court also appears to be increasingly drawn to the idea that there are sometimes positive duties involved in upholding the guarantees of the European Convention. The matter arises most often in cases involving Article 8, which guarantees respect for private and family life. An example is *A v. United Kingdom*,[38] a 1998 case that arose from the caning of a "difficult" boy by his stepfather. The stepfather was prosecuted, but the juvenile judge advised the jury that "it is a perfectly good defense that the alleged assault was merely the correcting of a child by its parent." The prosecution, in this

---

36. (February 1, 2000) #34406/97.
37. (June 4, 2000) #34369/97.
38. (September 23, 1998, Reports 1998-VI) #25599/94.

judge's view, was obliged to show that the caning was unreasonable. The jury found for the stepfather. The European Court found that this approach provided inadequate protection to children against torture or inhuman or degrading treatment (Article 3). As in other cases, it did not find it necessary to examine the Article 14 claim. The case is important here as a marker of judicial sensitivity to the state's affirmative duty to ensure the rights of all of its citizens.

Affirmative duties, however, are a sensitive matter for the Court, as illustrated by its handling of a 1998 case brought by a wheelchair-bound Italian man who wanted to visit the seaside and enjoy the beach.[39] Italian law requires local authorities and the private concessions that lease public property to provide access to the handicapped. Italy did not enforce these rules, however, and Mr. Bota's complaints and lawsuits to force compliance were unavailing. In resolving the dispute, the European Court noted that government is sometimes obliged to act affirmatively to prevent discrimination, but found that these cases are rare. It cited failure to deal with toxic pollution that destroys a people's enjoyment of their homes, failure to provide a criminal sanction for rape of a retarded person, and failure to provide for legal aid in a marital separation proceeding as examples of affirmative duties. In this case, however, the Court apparently believed that Mr. Bota lived too far from the beach to benefit from this affirmative obligation. It found Bota's claim so "broad and indeterminate" that there was "no conceivable direct link between the measures the State was urged to take in order to make good the omissions of the private bathing establishments and the applicant's private life." Without a violation of Article 8, there was no right to relief under Article 14. The implication of this case is that the handicapped have no generalized right of access to public facilities under the European Convention.

Conclusion

The Court has a serious access problem of its own. The influx of applications threatens to overwhelm the institution. The backlog is already huge, as noted earlier, and it continues to grow. The applicants and the governments they sue seem more inclined to wait for a ruling than to settle their disputes. Recent organizational changes have not been enough to deal with this problem. What should the Court do? If it imposes more severe admissibility crite-

---

39. *Bota v. Italy* (February 24, 1998, Reports 1998-I) #21439/93.

ria, the applicants who succeed in getting a hearing will tend to be the ones with more funds and better lawyers. If the admissibility criteria grow more technical, states new to the process will be significantly disadvantaged. If the Court does neither, the average time to decision could grow to a decade, from the current five years. The issue is embarrassing because timeliness in adjudication is one of the promises of the European Convention. This issue must be resolved if the Court is to live by its own rules.

The solution probably does not lie with the Court itself. The signatory states will have to commit to a two-tier system of adjudication, with discretionary review at the highest level. Were such a system to be established, it would create an extraordinary opportunity for the development of human-rights law. The European Court could choose cases for their significance, much as the United States Supreme Court does now.

The fundamental question is how the European Court of Human Rights came to garner so much interest. The process of bringing the broad guarantees of the Convention to life was slow at first. The number of applications refused hovered at around 500 per year through the 1980s, and there were fewer than twenty-five judgments per year (see Figures 6.1 and 6.2). The Court currently operates in a vastly different milieu, explained in part by growth in the number of member nations, the requirement that states allow themselves to be sued, and the ever-growing list of protocols. But the Court's own work is also part of the answer. The Court has successfully negotiated delicate political terrain to establish a credible jurisprudence of human rights. This is a significant accomplishment that deserves analysis.

What do the Article 14 cases during the past ten years teach us about the evolution of human rights in this forum? First, the Court has developed a reasonably clear sense of what is and what is not covered by Article 14. The judges have taken to heart the constrained approach to equality incorporated in the Convention, which limits consideration to rights set forth in the document. Failure to make out a claim under one of these provisions dooms a non-discrimination claim. Ironically, success often has the same effect. Still, the Court has found occasions to declare that Article 14 applies, and it has developed a clear approach to balancing the state's discretion in making and implementing policy and the individual's right to be free of discrimination. The Court has drawn this line without undue deference to governments, and it has used the techniques of explication and incorporation of expert judgment to educate officials about their responsibilities.

The Court has not moved very far in acknowledging the dampening effect of personal hardship and economic disadvantage on the enjoyment of rights, though it has not been oblivious to the impact of poverty on the ability to enjoy rights. It has long acknowledged that economic hardship must be taken into account when it defeats basic procedural guarantees. And it does seem drawn to the idea that states may sometimes be duty-bound to take affirmative action to protect vulnerable individuals. Still, its unwillingness to offer any relief to Mr. Bota is troubling. Bota, in attempting to gain access to the beach, had not asked for anything the government had not already offered to provide. His claim was not speculative, as the Court alleged. The Court appears to be afraid of a slippery slope in which government's affirmative duties grow out of control. This is unfortunate, especially when a government has already accepted certain responsibilities toward its citizens.

What is the likely direction of future Article 14 decisions? The current rules for limiting the reach of equal rights jurisprudence will likely stay in place: the limitation of jurisdiction to issues elsewhere named in the Convention, the margin of appreciation that gives states wiggle room in reaching fundamental goals, and the reasonableness standard that allows more than one avenue to reach legitimate goals. The more likely areas for growth and change lie in the gradual elimination of stereotypes embedded in law and in judicial recognition of more positive duties toward citizens. I make these predictions for two reasons. One is social pressure. As other institutions rethink the policy implications of illegitimacy, homosexuality, and other sensitive status issues, the Court will pay attention. It has already declared itself in opposition to stereotypical thinking and has announced that it sees the non-discrimination guarantee in dynamic terms. The Court is also likely to add to the range of affirmative obligations of states. Here also the pressure of elite opinion will have an effect. But one should also be optimistic about the expansiveness of rights because of the nature of adjudication, which tends to build on itself. Precedents encourage litigants to file claims. At the same time precedents give courts grounds to move forward toward a more expansive view of the state's duties toward its citizens.

CHAPTER 7

CONSTRUCTING HUMAN RIGHTS IN THE AMERICAS: INSTITUTIONAL DEVELOPMENT AND PRACTICE IN THE NEW WORLD

John F. Stack, Jr.

A number of recent, important contributions to the literature of supranational judicial institution building consider how courts have developed the capabilities to enforce decisions limiting the sovereignty of nation-states in the twenty-first century.[1] Mary Volcansek, for example, argues for the momentum, if not inevitability, of certain dispute resolution mechanisms in trading blocs when economic conditions are both "stable and durable."[2] The success of economic integration in Western Europe and the proliferation of regional trading pacts including both the North Atlantic Free Trade Association (NAFTA) and the World Trade Organization (WTO) auger well for even greater strides toward judicial institution building as cross-border transactions ratchet upward "in number and intensity, to establish comprehensive rules and...mechanism[s] to enforce them."[3]

---

1. See, for example, Alec Stone Sweet and Wayne Sandholtz, "Integration, Supranational Governance, and the Institutionalization of the European Polity," in Wayne Sandholtz and Alec Sweet Stone (eds.), *European Integration and Supranational Governance* (Oxford: Oxford University Press, 1998); and Mary L. Volcansek, "Courts and Regional Trade Agreements," in this volume.
2. Volcansek, "Courts and Regional Trade Agreements," 23.
3. Ibid.

This chapter provides an alternative perspective to that of the Europe case where transnational courts have attained some considerable measures of supranational authority, especially in the areas of rulemaking and compliance. In the New World, the developing human rights regime is removed from the conspicuous achievements of supranational law, policymaking, and economics that characterize the European context. Yet an examination of the inter-American system reveals how both the Inter-American Commission on Human Rights and the Inter-American Court of Human Rights have made important strides forward even in light of the strong emphasis on state sovereignity. The evolution of a human rights regime in the Americas illustrates the power that transnational forces have exerted in creating institutions and practices that challenge unfettered state abuses of human rights during the past thirty years.

Constructing a Human Rights Regime

The chapter draws on the work of Thomas Risse and Kathryn Sikkink that describes the establishment of transnational human rights regimes based on "principled ideas" and their incorporation in the "collective understandings about appropriate behavior which then lead to changes in identities, interests, and behavior" of citizens, states, and regions.[4] Invoking the work of Hedley Bull, Risse and Sikkink underscore that socialization, especially in the arena of human rights, can work only in the context of a defined "international society."[5] Such an international society is not based on the existence of mere sovereign states under international law, but rather on a process that induces individual states to accept new rules of the game as the price of admission into "international society."[6] Risse and Sikkink state:

> [T]he goal of socialization is for actors to internalize norms, so that external pressure is no longer needed to ensure compliance....Because a state's political identity emerges not in isolation but in relation to and in interaction with other groups of

---

4. Thomas Risse and Kathryn Sikkink, "The Socialization of International Human Rights Norms into Domestic Practices: Introduction," in Thomas Risse, Stephen C. Ropp, and Kathryn Sikkink (eds.), *The Power of Human Rights: International Norms and Domestic Changes* (Cambridge: Cambridge University Press, 1999), 11.

5. Ibid. See also Hedley Bull, *The Anarchical Society: A Study of Order in World Politics*, (New York: Columbia University Press), 1977.

6. Risse and Sikkink, "The Socialization of International Human Rights Norms," 11.

states and international non-state actors, the concept of socialization may be useful in understanding how the international society transmits norms to its members.[7]

The process of internalizing new sets of beliefs and values is a transnational process by its very nature as the "political identity" of the state is realigned in association with intergovernmental organizations (IGOs) and non-state actors and in relation to other states from which the evolving "international society transmits norms to its members."[8] In constructing such an international society, "the diffusion of international norms in the human rights area crucially depends on the establishment and the sustainability of networks among domestic and transnational actors who manage to link up with international regimes, to alert Western public opinion and Western governments."[9] The viability of "such advocacy networks" are essential to a much longer-term socialization process that results in (1) placing "norm violating" countries on an international agenda, (2) energizing domestic opposition groups and providing some protection for such groups against continuing state repression, and (3) creating human rights regimes both above the state (transnationally) and below the state (trans-societally), simultaneously assisting in the application of pressure on the offending government.[10] Risse and Sikkink further identify three sets of "causal mechanisms" that result in the internalization of norms at four separate stages in the development of human rights regimes:

- processes of instrumental adaptation and strategic bargaining;

- processes of moral consciousness raising, argumentation, dialogue, and persuasion;

- processes of institutionalization and habitualization; and

- internalization of norms, identities, interests, and behavior.[11]

The movement from one stage to another results in the further entrenchment or "spiraling" of human rights-related norms to such an extent that each stage challenges/transforms the behavior of governments as the human rights regime is strengthened.[12] The initial reaction to the developing human

---

7. Ibid.
8. Ibid.
9. Ibid, 5.
10. Ibid.
11. Ibid., 5, 13.
12. Ibid., 3, 5, 17–22.

rights regimes impinging on the states from above (the transnational) and from below (the trans-societal) may well result in a merely transparent process of instrumental and strategic bargaining by governments. State action may reflect no commitment to underlying human rights norms and values, but be calculated to remove an irritant, whether it is an IGO, bilateral/multilateral sanctions by states, or unwanted negative publicity. The power of principled ideas in human rights regimes over time, however, is reflected in the deepening transformation of norms into legitimate values of the society, followed by their institutionalization and habituation by governments. The model presupposes a power that is constructed in human rights regimes within states that deepens overtime. The final process results in the internalization of norms in identities, interests, and behavior by the state itself.

Such a constructivist perspective works well under conditions of "hard" regionalism as described by Stone Sweet, Volcansek, and others, when socioeconomic benefits provide additional material incentives for state compliance. But the social constructivist perspective also underscores the independent power of ideals and norms embedded in even developing human rights regimes. Such a perspective emphasizes "that communicative processes define in the first place which material factors are perceived as relevant and how they influence understandings of interests, preferences, and political decisions."[13] Notwithstanding the supposed weight of realpolitik within a neorealist structure, Hedley Bull's emphasis on an international society points to the power of international legal values even during the prolonged antagonisms of the Cold War.[14] For Risse and Sikkink, global society relies upon the creation of international law and organizations as " the primary vehicles for stating community norms and for collective legitimization."[15] As they observe:

> Human rights norms have a special status because they both prescribe rules for appropriate behavior and help to define identities of liberal states. Human rights norms have constitutive effects because good human rights performance is one crucial signal to others to identify a member of the community of liberal states.[16] Far from disputing such assertions, the evolving human rights regime in the Americas is very much indebted to the ongoing development of international law within the context of the Organization of American States (OAS). Although the process has not moved as rapidly or in such an entrenched manner as that of Europe, progress

---

13. Ibid., 17.
14. Bull, *The Anarchical Society*.
15. Risse and Sikkink, "The Socialization of International Human Rights Norms," 8.
16. Ibid.

has been made despite a number of circumstances that have proven especially resistant to the institutionalization and internalization of human rights.

American Hegemony and
Cold War Anticommunism

In the Americas, patterns of U.S. dominance in the hemisphere, especially throughout the late nineteenth and early twentieth centuries, combined with the bureaucratic and cultural legacies of Iberian rule, helped to create an almost obsessive concern that held the preservation of sovereignty as one of the most basic rules of statecraft. Authoritarian political traditions, the centrality of the military, centralization of economic resources within oligarchies and tiny insular elites, and small, poorly developed middle classes also conspired against the creation of pluralistic domestic political systems capable of limiting the executive branch's control and dispersing governmental powers among legislative and judicial institutions (never especially important in the civil law traditions). Limited institutional accountability and poorly developed political party systems continued to dilute executive accountability

The legacy of gunboat diplomacy further conditioned states to protect sovereign prerogatives. Indeed, periodic U.S. invasions of Central America and the Caribbean following the Spanish-American War and the establishment of clearly delimited spheres of influence were repeatedly invoked by such philosophically divergent presidents as William McKinley, Theodore Roosevelt, and Woodrow Wilson. The United States proclaimed its dominance in a series of unambiguous doctrinal statements, barely masking the American desire to establish claims to an American Empire in the Caribbean and Central America. The Roosevelt Corollary and the Platt Amendment are especially vivid twentieth-century reminders.

Following Allied victory and the establishment of a global collective security system in the United Nations (U.N.), the U.S. became preoccupied with the establishment of a regional security system, particularly as antagonisms between the U.S. and the USSR began to solidify in 1946–47. As the hemisphere's oldest functioning democracy, human rights were seen as a fitting concern of the Organization of American States, as it was globally in the United Nations system. The Universal Declaration of Human Rights was one of the central founding documents of the system. Thus, while the hemisphere-wide protection of human rights was supported by the United States as it was globally, U.S. concern with fighting communism was also a major policy goal. Indeed, the intensity and scope of U.S. support for regional multipurpose organizations was intensified following the articulation of the Truman Doctrine 1947 and the Marshall Plan's broad-brush economic stabilization program for Europe. In establishing the OAS, the countries of Central America, the Caribbean, and South America entered not a regional trading association, but a collective security organization emanating from a framework of overarching U.S. dominance in the context of growing Cold War antagonisms.

The U.S. emphasis on strengthening regional security and economic cooperation in the Western Hemisphere, Europe, and elsewhere around the globe laid the basis for processes of "instrumental adaptation and strategic bargaining," as defined by Risse and Sikkink, that would bear fruit in an expanded role for human rights decades later. The creation of regional societies, no less than international societies, is a complex and dynamic process fueled by incremental developments, chance, and the recognition of common interests, values, goals, and objectives. As institutions are formed, the passage of time and the changing patterns of world politics create new opportunities for institutional growth and transformation. This is in many ways the story of the development of human rights in the Americas even amid the Cold War objectives of the American foreign policy and the intense preoccupation with protecting sovereignty among the countries of the New World.

The institutional development of the OAS was a major milestone in protecting human rights in the region decades later.[17] The founding documents also speak eloquently about the significance of human rights. Such aspirations go a long way in establishing the basis for "moral consciousness raising" as a process that would link individuals, international intergovernmental organizations, non-state actors, and states in an evolving transnational human rights regime.[18]

The OAS's interest in human rights was articulated first at the 1938 meeting of the Eighth Conference of American States, which adopted a resolution condemning the racial or religious persecution of individuals or groups while "at the same time denying…the right of any racial or religious group to claim the status of a minority."[19] The formal emphasis on human rights began with the adoption of the American Declaration of the Rights and Duties of Man, approved at the Ninth International Conference of American States held in Bogota, Colombia, in 1948, which established the OAS.[20] The declaration

---

17. Risse and Sikkink, "The Socialization of International Human Rights Norms," 11.

18. Ibid.

19. Gerhard Von Glahn, *Law Among Nations: An Introduction to Public International Law* (New York: Macmillan, 1992), 194.

20. OAS, *Basic Documents Pertaining to Human Rights in the Inter-American System* (updated to 1992), 6.

sought to build a hemispheric system for the protection of human rights and projected that the system would be strengthened over time. The third paragraph of the declaration acknowledges the limited field at the time: "The affirmation of essential human rights by the American States together with the guarantees given by the internal regimes of states establish the initial system of protection considered by the American states as being suited to the present social and juridical conditions, not without a recognition on their part that they should increasingly strengthen that system in the international field as conditions become more favorable."[21]

The OAS Charter itself proclaims the "fundamental rights of man" as one of the founding principles of the organization. The Bogota conference also adopted separate conventions that are relevant to the development of the hemispheric protection of human rights in three areas: the political rights of women, a resolution on the economic status of working women, and the Inter-American Charter of Social Guarantees for the protection of all workers.[22]

The preamble of the American Declaration conceptualized a normative order conducive to human rights transcending national sovereignty by declaring that "the essential rights of man are not derived from the fact that he is a national of a certain state, but are based upon attributes of his human personality."[23] The philosophical inheritance of the Enlightenment fused with a realistic understanding of the power of sovereignty in the Americas to create at least an aspiration to bypass state power as a means of protecting human rights. This perspective provides an important foundation for the ongoing development of institutions with such aspirations. The seeds of a transnational vision creating legal institutions capable of blurring the lines of sovereignty were thus created early in the development of human rights institution building in the new world. "Thus, the American states recognize that when the state legislates in this field, it does not create or concede rights but rather recognizes rights that existed prior to the formation of the state, rights that have their origins in the very nature of the individual."[24] Moreover, the American Declaration introduced a commitment to protect human rights in a flexible and forward-looking manner that philosophically and pragmatically supported the protection of new human rights based on changing conditions. So conceived, the Declaration enabled further institutional developments in the form of the Inter-American Commission on Human Rights (1959) and the

---

21. Ibid.
22. Ibid., 5.
23. Ibid., 6.
24. Ibid.

Inter-American Court of Human Rights (1980), later to vigorously oppose horrific violations of humans right by state or parastate forces that reached epidemic proportions in Latin America during the 1970s and 1980s. No other international human rights tribunal had previously declared the practice of disappearance to be a violation of human rights, but the language and spirit of the American Declaration laid the groundwork for the Court's holding that the forced disappearance of a person, even absent the physical evidence of the victim's remains, creates the presumption that the disappeared person had in fact been murdered.[25]

The American Declaration did not, however, establish a framework through which human rights could be monitored and enforced. "Like its U.N. counterpart [the Universal Declaration of Human Rights], which it predated and to which it is similar in many respects, the American Declaration was a simple conference resolution of the organization and was not intended to be legally binding *per se* nor by incorporation into the Charter system." [26] Despite these rather modest beginnings, the American Declaration eventually "acquired the status of an authoritative interpretation" concerning human rights in the OAS system.[27] The declaration's authoritative status was enhanced by the development of the Inter-American Commission and the Inter-American Court.[28] The Commission's growing prominence under the OAS Charter was based on its unrelenting attempts to protect human rights.[29]

The Inter-American Commission: Instrumental Adaptation and Strategic Bargaining

The Commission preceded the establishment of the Court by twenty years. Its work contributes to Risse and Sikkink's first stage in the development of human rights regimes, characterized by instrumental bargains struck by the Commission on behalf of human rights among sovereign territorial state governments. The Commission thus became the pioneering

---

25. *Velasquez Rodriguez Case*, Judgment of July 29, 1988, Series C, No. 4.
26. Scott Davidson, *Human Rights* (Buckingham: Open University Press, 1993), 128.
27. Ibid.
28. Ibid.
29. Handbook of Existing Rules, 16. In order for the Court to have jurisdiction Articles 48–50 must be satisfied, e.g., the Commission must determine the admissibility of a complaint (Art. 48), the friendly settlement of a dispute (Art. 49), and the reporting of cases not settled (Art. 50).

agent of change given its transnational character and motivated by its determination to confront state-sponsored abuses of human rights in the Western Hemisphere. The OAS's Permanent Council adopted a resolution establishing the Inter-American Commission on Human Rights in 1959.[30] The seven-member Commission was established as an "autonomous entity" of the OAS in 1960. "This appeared to mean that, being a creature of resolution, the Commission had no precise legal status as an institution under the Charter."[31]

Events could not have been less promising, for the Commission's establishment coincided with the Cuban Revolution and the strengthening of a Marxist-Leninist regime, formally allied with the Soviet Union, less than 100 miles from the Florida Keys. Cuba's domestic and foreign policy agendas directly challenged the central tenets of American Cold War foreign policy and U.S. nineteenth- and twentieth-century internationalism in the Caribbean and in Central and South America generally. Here geopolitics seemingly would trump the initiation of a major, if yet to be fully defined, human rights initiative under the auspices of a regional collective security organization.

Constructing a regional human rights regime is a multi-layered process dependent on robust transnational support as well as a growing consciousness of the importance of protecting human rights as noted by Risse and Sikkink. Given the traditional importance of geopolitics in the Caribbean and Central America as well as the growing international influence of Cuba as among the Non-aligned Movement, one might have expected the Commission to become a casualty of hemispheric geopolitical crosscurrents. The Commission's steady development and growing credibility was, in part, based on its skillful ability to publicize human rights violations through its Annual Reports. The reports provided the Commission with the power to publicize human rights abuses and highlight non-cooperative states. This was important because the Commission placed "norm violating" states on an international (first, regional) agenda that would become increasingly powerful as human rights activism increased region-wide and internationally in the latter decades of the twentieth century. The Commission's reports became an invaluable baseline to assess human rights violations throughout the Hemisphere. While initially lacking legal authority, over time the professionalism and careful investigations conducted by the Commission gained respect and credibility. This is an essential dimension of moral consciousness raising and provided the Commission with

---

30. Ibid., 129.
31. Ibid.

greater levels of persuasion. The foundations laid by the Commission were effectively utilized by the Inter-American Court's advisory and contentious jurisprudence.

The Commission became a critical vehicle in building transnational linkages with domestic opposition groups in some of the world's most repressive societies. The Commission's site visits were a powerful investigatory tool as well as a key networking vehicle outside of the state's geographical borders.[32] These networks only deepened over the years as the Commission's influence broadened. Here the Commission's presence has been seminal. It served as a vital link to oppressed individuals and groups as well as other intergovernmental and private human rights organizations. Initially, the Commission was confined to a recommendatory and advisory role, but "through a process of auto-interpretation of its constituent instrument" it asserted the right to make "specific recommendations on human rights violations to member states and to undertake studies and make reports on human rights situations in states where large scale violations were alleged to have taken place."[33] These new powers constituted a major breakthrough for the Commission when formal means of dispute resolution had failed between the Commission and a state.

In 1965 the Commission was empowered to receive information from individuals asserting specific violations of due process rights and to make recommendations to states as a consequence.[34] This was an innovation of enormous significance because it provided individuals with recourse to an international fact-finding bureaucracy that transcended parochial, self-interested state concerns. The Commission carved out a singular role within the hemisphere as an international human rights organization that received petitions directly from individuals, groups, and states alleging human rights violations by any of the thirty-five members of the Organization of American States. Moreover, the Commission's site visits were of inestimable value in building a viable hemispheric human rights regime by strengthening both ties to the OAS's intergovernmental system and to human rights advocacy groups within the hemisphere and across the globe.

The right of individuals to petition the Commission is a guarantee **extended to citizens of all OAS member states,**[35] and "the provisions governing private access to the Inter-American system afford greater possibility for filing peti-

---

32. Risse and Sikkink, "The Socialization of International Human Rights Norms," 5.
33. Ibid.
34. Ibid.
35. Dinah Shelton, "Improving Human Rights Protections: Recommendations for Enhancing the Effectiveness of the Inter-American Commission and the Inter-American Court

tions than in any other international human rights system and give the Commission great flexibility in implementing its procedures."[36] Petitions must be filed within the Commission's statute of limitations (six months), all domestic legal remedies must be exhausted, and the case cannot have been brought before another international tribunal before the Commission takes it up.[37] Once an investigation of an individual case is concluded, the Commission prepares a final decision that reports facts, conclusions, and recommendations for state action with the only sanction being the publication of an unfavorable report on a particular state.[38] In spite of the limitations imposed by state sovereignty, the glare of publicity resulting from the Commission's on-site investigations and detailed country profiles has resulted in notable successes for several victims of human rights abuses and their affected societies.[39] As Dinah Shelton noted, "In the course of making its reports, the Commission has discovered torture chambers and disappeared persons. The Commission also succeeded in obtaining the repeal of objectionable laws through its reports. In one instance, the strength of the Commission's report resulted in a resolution of the OAS calling for the overthrow of the Country's government [Nicaragua's Antonio Somoza]."[40]

The OAS resolution calling for Somoza's overthrow helped to delegitimize the Nicaraguan government. "The 1979 resolution on Nicaragua found that the inhumane conduct of the dictatorial regime governing the country, as evidenced by the report of the Inter-American Commission on Human Rights, was the fundamental cause of the dramatic situation facing the Nicaraguan people. The Resolution declared that the solution to problems of Nicaragua should be based upon immediate and definitive replacement of the Somoza regime."[41]

The Commission's ongoing work in Suriname throughout much of the 1980s and 1990s brought hemispheric attention to the nation's large-scale violation of human rights. Domestic mobilization in favor of greater protection of human rights was, in part, aided by the Commission's ongoing presence in Suriname, and ultimately assisted the Commission in its preparation of two

---

of Human Rights," 3 *American University Journal of International Law and Policy* (1988), 327.

36. Ibid.
37. Regulations of the Inter-American Commission, Art. 42.
38. Ibid, 235.
39. Ibid.
40. Shelton, "Improving Human Rights Protections," 377.
41. Ibid.

major human rights cases processed by the Commission that were ultimately submitted to and adjudicated by the Inter-American Court of Human Rights.[42]

The Inter-American Court: Constructing Human Rights

The establishment of the Inter-American Court for Human Rights placed the protection of human rights in a new juridical context. This is essential for the creation of a viable human rights regime aiming at expanded protection and greater legitimacy. In this sense the founding of the Court built on the success of the Commission and earlier aspirations epitomized by the American Declaration. The Court created an institutional context for the protection of human rights without precedent in the new world. Drawing on Risse and Sikkink's typology, the Court gave substance to form, serving as an engine articulating norms and values that raise moral consciousness, assist in the creation of dialogue, and foster argumentation. These developments are essential to the creation of a human rights regime. Indeed, the Court's jurisprudence has been central to the growth of human rights in the Americas. In November 1969, the OAS adopted the American Convention on Human Rights, which contained a detailed provision for the Inter-American Court of Human Rights modeled on the European Court of Human Rights.[43] The attempt to create a coherent structure for the protection of human rights in the Americas occurred in a political climate in which preservation of the sovereignty of states, absent successful economic integration, was the central governing principle. The establishment of a human rights court in the Americas conforms to Risse and Sikkink's critical third stage of development—the establishment of processes of institutionalization and habitualization.

The Statute and Regulations of the Inter-American Commission and the Statutes and Rules of Procedure of the Inter-American Court were approved in 1979 and 1980, respectively,[44] as the push for democratization, though somewhat uneven during the Carter years, was beginning to bear fruit. More than thirty years lapsed between the signing of the American Convention and

---

42. David J. Padilla and Elizabeth A. Houppert, "The OAS and Human Rights in the Caribbean," in Ivelaw L. Griffith and Betty N. Sedoc-Dahlberg (eds.), *Democracy and Human Rights in the Caribbean* (Boulder, CO: Westview, 1997), 38–39.

43. Von Glahn, *Law Among Nations*, 192.

44. OAS, *Basic Documents Pertaining to Human Rights*, 12, 15.

the Commission's ability to act in conjunction with a Court expressly empowered to hear complaints of violations of human rights. Even with the passing of Cold War anticommunism, the 103rd United States Congress refused, as had previous Cold War congresses, to cede national sovereignty to a supranational, albeit hemispheric, regional Court. Congressional reticence continued despite an unprecedented degree of judicial supranationalism resulting from the dispute resolution mechanisms embedded in both the North American Free Trade Association (NAFTA) and the General Agreement on Tariffs and Trade/World Trade Organization (GATT/WTO).

The Court's legitimacy was even more restricted than the Commission's because its contentious jurisdiction arises only from states that have ratified not only the OAS charter but also the American Convention.[45] The U.S. has steadfastly rejected the latter. The Court is, nonetheless, empowered to issue advisory opinions reaching all OAS member states and OAS organs.[46] The institutional structure of the Commission also constitutes something of an obstacle to the establishment of a legitimate and effective Court. The Commission is an established player in the inter-American system and has attained the status of an important transnational actor dealing directly with individuals and groups throughout the hemisphere. Thus the Commission has developed its own organizational persona, which at times conflicts directly with the prerogatives of the Court as supreme arbiter of human rights in the inter-American system. Like the Commission, the Court is composed of seven members. But unlike the Commission, judges are nominated and elected only by those states that have accepted the binding jurisdiction of the Court (twenty in 1999). [47] The Court's jurisdiction is, therefore, far more narrow than the Commission's broad action-oriented warrant. Only the Commission and states that have accepted the compulsory jurisdiction of the Court may submit a case to the Court.[48] There is no individual right of petition to it, and the Commission alone is empowered to receive petitions from individuals. The Court has issued sixteen opinions under its advisory jurisdiction and it has issued 34 binding decisions under its contentious jurisdiction. Considerations of issues concerning reparations and compensatory damages bring the number of cases considered under the courts binding jurisdiction to 49 decisions rendered.

---

45. Shelton, "Improving Human Rights Protections," 329.
46. Ibid.
47. 1999 Annual Report of Inter-American Court of Human Rights, OEA/SerL/V/III.47, doc. 6 (2000).
48. American Convention on Human Rights, Art. 61(1).

Advisory Jurisdiction

The Court's advisory jurisdiction is available to any OAS member state, whether or not it has accepted the Court's contentious jurisdiction. OAS members may also ask the Court to evaluate the compatibility of a member state's domestic laws with OAS agreements protecting human rights. The principal organs of the OAS "in their spheres of competence" may also consult the Court.[49] This broad-based advisory jurisdiction within the inter-American system provides the Court with an "integrationist potential."[50] Throughout the last two decades, the Court has self-consciously sought to build conceptual and jurisprudential linkages among the growing body of human rights scholarship, treaties, conventions, and case law. The Court's advisory jurisdiction is similar to the preliminary ruling mechanism of the European Court of Justice. As the Court established in *The Effect of Reservations* advisory opinion, the Commission will always be able to show as a matter of principle that it is acting within its "sphere of competence" and that it has a legitimate institutional interest in seeking the Court's advisory jurisdiction.[51]

Table 7.1   Advisory Case Law: Evolving Institutionalization

"Other Treaties" Subject to the Advisory Jurisdiction of the Court (Art. 64 American Convention on Human Rights), Advisory Opinion OC-1/82, September 24,1982, Inter-Am. Ct. H.R. (Ser. A) No. 1 (1982).

The Effect of Reservations on the Entry into Force of the American Convention on Human Rights, Advisory Opinion OC-2/82, September 24, 1982, Inter-Am. Ct. H.R. (Ser. A) No. 2 (1982).

Restrictions to the Death Penalty (Arts. 4.2 and 4.4 American Convention on Human Rights), Advisory Opinion OC-3/83, September 8, 1983, Inter-Am. Ct. H.R. (Ser. A) No. 3 (1983).

Proposed Amendments to the Naturalization Provisions of the Constitution of Costa Rica, Advisory Opinion OC-4/84, January 19, 1984, Inter-Am. Ct. H.R. (Ser. A) No. 4 (1984).

Compulsory Membership in an Association Prescribed by Law for the Practice of Journalism (Arts. 13 and 29 American Convention on Human Rights), Advisory Opinion OC-5/85, November 13, 1985, Inter-Am. Ct. H.R. (Ser. A) No. 5 (1985).

---

49. Ibid., Art. 64(1).
50. Davidson, Human Rights, 146.
51. Ibid.

Enforceability of the Right to Reply or Correction (Arts. 14.1, 1.1, and 2 American Convention on Human Rights), Advisory Opinion OC-7/86, August 29, 1986, Inter-Am. Ct. H.R. (Ser. A) No. 7 (1986).

The Word "Laws" in Article 30 of the American Convention on Human Rights, Advisory Opinion OC-6/86, May 9,1986, Inter-Am. Ct. H.R. (Ser. A) No. 6 (1986).

Habeas Corpus in Emergency Situations (Arts. 27.2, 25.1, and 7.6 American Convention on Human Rights), Advisory Opinion OC-8/87, January 30, 1987, Inter-Am. Ct. H.R. (Ser. A) No. 8 (1987).

Judicial Guarantees in States of Emergency (Arts. 27.2, 25, and 8 American Convention on Human Rights), Advisory Opinion OC-9/87, October 6,1987, Inter-Am. Ct. H.R. (Ser. A) No. 9 (1987).

Interpretation of the American Declaration of the Rights and Duties of Man Within the Framework of Article 64 of the American Convention on Human Rights, Advisory Opinion OC-10/89, July 14, 1989, Inter-Am. Ct. H.R. (Ser. A) No. 10 (1989).

Exceptions to the Exhaustion of Domestic Remedies (Arts. 46.1, 46.2.a, and 46.2.b American Convention on Human Rights, Advisory Opinion OC-11/90, August 10, 1990, Inter-Am. Ct. H.R. (Ser. A) No. 11 (1990).

Compatibility of Draft Legislation with Article 8.2.h of the American Convention on Human Rights, Advisory Opinion OC-12/91, December 6, 1991, Inter-Am. Ct. H.R. (Ser. A) No. 12 (1991).

Certain Attributes of the Inter-American Commission On Human Rights (Arts. 41, 42, 44, 46, 47, 50, and 51 American Convention on Human Rights), Advisory Opinion OC-13/93, July 16, 1993, Inter-Am. Ct. H.R. (Ser. A) No. 13 (1993).

International Responsibility for the Promulgation and Enforcement of Laws in Violation of the Convention (Arts. 1 and 2 American Convention on Human Rights), Advisory Opinion OC-14/94, December 9, 1994, Inter-Am. Ct. H.R. (Ser. A) No. 14 (1994).

Reports of the American Convention on Human Rights, Advisory Opinion OC-15/97, November 14, 1997, Inter-Am. Ct. H.R. (Ser. A) No. 15 (1997).

The Right to Information on Consular Assistance in the Framework of the Guarantees of the Due Process of Law, Advisory Opinion OC-16/99, October 1, 1999, Inter-Am. Ct. H.R. (Ser. A) No. 16 (1999).

Juridical status and human rights of the child, Advisory Opinion OC-17/02, August 28, 2002, Inter-Am. Ct. H.R. (Ser. A) No. 17 (2002).

Juridical Condition and Rights of the Undocumented Migrants, Advisory Opinion OC-18, September 17, 2003, Inter-Am. Ct. H.R. (Ser. A) No. 18/03 (2003).

Source: Inter-American Court of Human Rights: Series A.
<http://www1.umn/humanrts/iarch/series_A.html>.

In its advisory opinion, *"Other Treaties" Subject to the Advisory Jurisdiction of the Court,* the Court defined its jurisdiction in expansive terms, conferring on OAS member states the ability to consult the Court regarding the interpretation of any international treaty or convention pertaining to the protection of human rights if it touches the inter-American system in any way.[52] The Court explained that the purpose of the Convention—to protect human rights—mandated such wide jurisdiction.[53]

Although non-binding, the sixteen advisory opinions that the Court has issued clearly aim at the explication of issues that will contribute to the evolving common law of human rights for the inter-American system and, indeed, the growing body of international human rights jurisprudence. In this sense, given the relative dearth of cases invoking the Court's contentious jurisdiction in its first decade, the Court's activism in the realm of advisory opinions constitutes the foundation of an emerging jurisprudence that defines and interprets the provisions of the American Convention for both state and organizational members of the OAS. This collection of opinions is also central to the foundation of the hemispheric human rights regime.

The Court held in the *Exceptions to the Exhaustion of Domestic Remedies* case that "the failure to exhaust domestic legal remedies because of indigence or fear of domestic reprisal in criminal proceedings could not be used by states as a way of blocking the Court's review (failure to exhaust local remedies) under Articles 8 and 46(2)(b) of the convention."[54] The Court further held that states asserting nonexhaustion of local remedies have an affirmative obligation (the burden shifts to the state) to demonstrate that remedies exist and that the petitioner failed to exhaust them under Article 46(1)(a) of the Convention.[55]

---

52. *"Other Treaties" Subject to the Advisory Jurisdiction of the Court,* (Article 64 American Convention on Human Rights), Advisory Opinion OC-8/87 of September 24, 1982, Series A, No. 9, para. 14.

53. Ibid., para. 25.

54. *Exceptions to the Exhaustion of Domestic Remedies,* (Articles 46.1, 46.2.a and 46.2.b American Convention on Human Rights), Advisory Opinion OC-11/90 of August 10, 1990, Series A, No. 11, para., 25, 26, 32.

55. Ibid., para. 35.

The Court's advisory opinions have also aimed at buttressing the push toward democratization during one of the bleakest times in recent Latin America history, taking on the issue of forced disappearances. In two important cases the Court helped to define the fundamental (inherent) nature of democratic societies in the Americas. In *Habeas Corpus in Emergency Situations,* the Court reasoned that habeas corpus not only protects individuals from illegal detention (disappearance) but also guarantees the right to life (murder) and humane treatment (torture).[56] The companion case, *Judicial Guarantees in States of Emergency,* gave meaning to *amparo*—the procedural right to judicial process under the constitution of a state or under Article 25 of the American Convention—holding that it was a non-derogable right, as was habeas corpus, and could not be waived during a state-declared emergency.[57] The Court, in effect, transformed two procedural rights into substantive ones that inhere in the nature of society.[58] As one observer noted, "The force of the Court's opinions derives from its inherent authority" under the American Convention of Human Rights.[59] "Clearly, if a state were to act in a manner contrary to one of the Court's advisory opinions, it would be difficult to avoid the conclusion that it had, in effect, breached its obligations, as interpreted by the Court, under the convention."[60] Most recently the Court addressed the relationship to the guarantees of due process of law for foreign nationals charged with capital crimes in the United States in *The Right to Information on Consular Assistance in the Framework of the Guarantees of the Due Process of Law.* [61] The request for the advisory opinion was brought by Mexico, with special reference to Mexican nationals charged with felonies carrying the death penalty under U.S. state and/or federal laws. The case transcended the bilateral sphere of Mexican/United States relations, however, as evidenced in the extensive amicus curiae briefs of jurists, transnational human rights organi-

---

56. *Habeas Corpus in Emergency Situations,* (Articles 27.2, 25.1, and 7.6 American Convention on Human Rights), Advisory Opinion OC-8/87 of January 30, 1987, Series A, No. 8, para. 36, 40, 42.

57. *Judicial Guarantees in States of Emergency,* (Article 27.2, 25, and 8, American Convention on Human Rights), Advisory Opinion OC-9/87 of October 6, 1987, Series A, No. 9, para. 32, 34.

58. Christina M. Cerna, "Structure and Functioning of the Inter-American Court of Human Rights," *British Yearbook of International Law* Annual (1992), 190–91.

59. Davidson, *Human Rights,* 147.

60. Ibid.

61. *The Right to Information on Consular Assistance in the Framework of the Guarantees of the Due Process of Law,* Advisory Opinion OC-16/99 of October 1, 1999, Series A, No. 16.

zations, and individuals—including Amnesty International, Human Rights Watch/Americas, and Death Penalty Focus of California—as well as such OAS member states as Costa Rica, El Salvador, Guatemala, Honduras, Paraguay, and the Dominican Republic. The Court unanimously held that foreign detainees had the right to immediately receive information on consular assistance available to them and that the receiving state (the United States) was bound by Article 36 of the Vienna Convention on Consular Relations to provide such information to foreign detainees accused of a crime. The United States had in fact ratified the Vienna Convention. The Court found that such information is "an integral part of the body of international human rights standards; that the expression 'without delay' used in Article 36(1)b of the Vienna Convention means that the state's bounden duty is to inform detainees, at the very moment they are arrested, of the rights they hold under this provision, or in all cases, before they make their first statement to authorities."[62] In interpreting Articles 2, 6, 14, and 50 of the International Covenant of Civil and Political Rights as applied to the protection of human rights in the Americas under Article 36(1)b of the Vienna Convention, the Court held that the individual right to information from consular officials encompassed the effective practice of due process of law as guaranteed under Article 14 of the International Covenant on Civil and Political Rights. As a consequence, OAS member states whether federal or unitary in structure were bound by the guarantees of the Vienna Convention to inform detainees of their right to consult with consular officials at the time of their arrest and before any statements were made.[63]

This body of jurisprudence is important not only as a necessary predicate for the exercise of the Court's contentious jurisdiction but also as a means of reinforcing norms, identities, and beliefs integral to judicial review of state behavior in the area of human rights. Taken as a whole, the Court's advisory jurisprudence makes a vital contribution to the realization of Risse and Sikkink's second stage—that encompassing not only consciousness raising but also the framing of persuasive arguments and the creation of dialogue.[64] The Court's explicit attempt to interpret international legal norms via treaties, conventions, and case law illustrates the dynamic quality to its jurisprudence, perhaps best exemplified in the advisory opinion, *The Right to Information on Consular Assistance.*

---

62. Ibid., para, 84, 87, 97, 106.
63. Ibid., para 124.
64. Risse and Sikkink, "The Socialization of International Human Rights Norms," 5, 11.

Contentious Jurisdiction

The Court's first case based on its contentious jurisdiction, *In the Matter of Viviana Gallardo et al.*, underscored two aspects of the Court's approach to human rights in the Americas. On one hand, the Court reached broadly in defining one of the most egregious violations of human rights which had reached near-epidemic dimensions in the 1980s—the forced disappearance of people by state and para-state authorities, absent the victims' remains. On the other hand, the institutional tensions between the Court and the Commission became apparent as the Court asserted its authoritative prerogative to decide what the law was in the area of human rights among those countries accepting its compulsory jurisdiction. In this regard, the Court's contentious jurisdiction illustrates the movement to the stage of institutionalization and habitualization as defined by Risse and Sikkink. This is a critical transitional movement to the establishment of regional human rights regimes even if only partially realized.

Viviana Gallardo was a suspected terrorist who was killed and her two cell-mates wounded while they were held in the custody of the Costa Rican Civil Guard in 1981.[65] Costa Rica apparently tried to advance the work of the Court (and circumvent the Commission) by submitting the case directly to the Court.[66] Although the case had already been disposed of domestically,[67] Costa Rica asked the Court to determine whether the death and injuries suffered constituted a violation by Costa Rican authorities of human rights guaranteed by the American Convention. The Court followed the prescribed route and referred the case to the Commission, which ruled the case inadmissible because Costa Rica had already tried and sentenced the violator. Notably, "this was the first 'case' presented to the Court and it was presented by the Costa Rican Government against itself."[68] The case was subsequently dismissed by the Court because Costa Rica had acted in "conformity with current legal provisions and punished with full force of law the person responsible for the acts charged" and the grounds that led to the submission of the case no longer existed.[69] The significance of the *Gallardo Case*, however, lies in the manner in which the Court characterized its institutional role vis-a-vis the Commission.[70]

---

65. *Viviana Gallardo Case*, Judgment of July 22, 1981, Series A, para. 2.
66. Cerna, "Structure and Functioning," 145.
67. Ibid., 146.
68. Ibid.
69. *Viviana Gallardo Case*, Judgment of September 8, 1983, para. 3, 4.
70. Cerna, "Structure and Functioning," 147.

In describing that relationship, the Court focused on the quasi-judicial power lodged in the Commission's ability to investigate complaints and to bring about friendly settlements of disputes through its "conciliatory function."[71] Thus the Court expressly sought to narrowly define the Commission's role in cases of no real significance and in situations when states were essentially suing themselves. The Court stated: "If, thereafter, in the course of the judicial proceedings there is a dispute relating to the question of whether the admissibility requirements before the Commission have been complied with, it will be for the Court to decide, which for that purpose it has the power to accept or reject the views of the Commission in the manner analogous to its power to accept or reject the Commission's final report."[72]

In his concurrence with the unanimous decision of the Court, Judge Rodolfo E. Piza went even further than his fellow jurists in expressing his dissatisfaction with the role of the Commission:

> On the other hand, except for the procedure of conciliation, I believe that nothing that the Commission may be able to do, within the procedures set forth in the Convention, in the interest of an effective protection of human rights, the Court itself may not also be able to do during the proceedings; and do it even better, as its intervention would add certainty and authority to the proceedings, and at the same time, would reduce considerably the length of the proceedings, contributing to the fulfillment of the idea of prompt and full justice, the absence of which is one of the most serious and frequent violations of human rights, and source and guardian of almost all the rest.[73]

The most important cases confronted by the Court were brought by the Commission under the Convention's compulsory contentious jurisdiction provisions. In 1986, the Commission submitted three cases to the Court involving the forced disappearance of four individuals in Honduras. The *Velasquez Rodriguez Case*, the *Fairen Garbi and Solis Corrales Case*, and the *Godinez Cruz Case* raised some of the most difficult issues to confront any human rights tribunal. These were the first substantive issues confronted by the Court. Angel Manfredo Velasquez Rodriguez, a student, was abducted on September 12, 1981, by members of the Honduran military and security forces. Members of the Velasquez family subsequently filed a complaint against the government of Honduras before the Inter-American Commission of Human Rights.[74] On

---

71. Ibid.
72. *Viviana Gallardo Case*, Judgment of November 13, 1981, para. 27.
73. Ibid. Explanation of Vote of Judge Piza, Judgment of November 13, 1981, para. 10.
74. *Velasquez Rodriguez Case*, Judgment of July 29, 1988, para. 3.

December 11, 1981, two Costa Rican nationals, Francisco Fairen Garbi and Yolanda Solis Corrales, disappeared while traveling through Honduras on their way to Mexico.[75] The third case to be filed with the Commission alleged that Saul Godinez Cruz, a schoolteacher, disappeared on July 22, 1982, while en route to his job in the Honduran capital. In both the cases of Velasquez Rodriguez and Godinez Cruz, eyewitnesses testified that government agents arrested the missing people.[76] Since Honduras had ratified the American Convention of Human Rights and accepted the binding jurisdiction of the Court, the Commission and Court had jurisdiction to pursue the complaint.[77]

The government of Honduras never disputed the substance of the complaints, namely that members of the armed forces and security forces kidnapped and murdered Angel Manfredo Velasquez Rodriguez and Saul Godinez Cruz. In the disappearances of Fairen Garbi and Solis Corrales, Honduras presented evidence purporting to document that the two had left Honduras on December 12, 1981.[78] Citing the absence of conclusive evidence proving the disappearance of Francisco Fairen Garbi and Yolanda Solis Corrales by Honduras, the Court ultimately dismissed the case.[79] The Court did not face a dearth of evidence in either the Velasquez Rodriguez or Godinez Cruz cases, however. Apparently, Honduras failed to take the Commission's inquiry seriously and sought to avoid investigation of the case by raising one procedural objection after another. The government of Honduras indicted seven people for murder, torture, disappearance, and disobedience to state authority in the case of Velasquez Rodriguez and other disappeared persons. Six of the seven indicted people were acquitted of these charges. Because the seventh accused was out of the country, the government maintained that Honduras's domestic jurisdiction had not been exhausted, which blocked the jurisdiction of the Commission and Court. The Inter-American Commission forwarded the case to the Inter-American Court of Human Rights on April 18, 1986, nearly five years after the disappearance of Velasquez Rodriguez. The Inter-American Court, on July 29,1988, held that Honduras violated its obligations under the American Convention of Human Rights to respect and ensure the right to personal liberty (Article 7), the right to humane treatment (Article 5), and the

75. *Fairen Garbi and Solis Corrales Case,* Judgment of March 15, 1989, Series C, No. 8, para. 3, 4.

76. *Godinez Cruz Case,* Judgment of January 20, 1989, Series C, No. 5, para. 3; *Velasquez Rodriguez Case,* Judgment of July 29, 1988, para. 3.

77. *OAS, Basic Documents Pertaining to Human Rights,* 53.

78. *Fairen Garbi and Solis Corrales Case,* Judgment of March 15, 1989, para. 4.

79. Ibid.

right to life (Article 4).[80] In announcing its judgment of July 29, 1988, the Court held that the government of Honduras violated the evolving international law of human rights through the practice of forced disappearances, and its painstaking analysis illustrated how forced disappearance poses a fundamental threat to the integrity of a state's political and judicial systems.[81]

Central to the Court's decision was "the phenomenon of the forced disappearance of people."[82] The Court stated that the disappearance of persons constituted a central mechanism for the political repression of dissidents throughout Latin America, whether it was used selectively or indiscriminately. The Court noted that several military dictatorships had used the forced disappearance of persons as a means of repression, especially during the 1970s, and that even legitimately established governments had resorted to this practice.[83] Although it is difficult to determine how many people fell victim to this practice, the Court estimated the number to be in the thousands.[84]

The Court was equally emphatic in explaining how the practice of forced disappearance creates fundamental cleavages in the political, social, and professional institutions of a national culture undermining the rule of law. The Court noted that the practice of forced disappearance had already generated a response from the international community in the form of the monitoring of disappearances by intergovernmental organizations. It also noted that the most prestigious transnational nongovernmental organizations had also documented the practice. The Court also pointed to the sustained concern of the Inter-American Commission with the problem posed by forced disappearance as a corrosive and corrupting influence within countries as evidenced by the Commission's annual reports to the General Assembly of the OAS.[85] The General Assembly of the OAS had stated in many resolutions that forced disappearance must end immediately because it constituted a crime against humanity.[86] The Court highlighted the current worldwide concern with the problem and pointed to several resolutions by the General Assembly of the United Nations,[87] which had established a working group to study the problem posed by forced disappearances and to the work of other nongovernmental actors in attempting to establish an international convention defining

---

80. *Valasquez Rodriguez Case*, Judgment of July 29, 1988, para. 148–62.
81. Ibid., para. 156–64.
82. Ibid., para. 150.
83. Ibid., para. 149–51.
84. Ibid.
85. Ibid., para. 153.
86. Ibid., para. 152.
87. Ibid., para. 153.

forced disappearance as a crime against humanity.[88] In so doing, the Court emphasized the significance of its decision within the framework of the evolving international law of human rights inasmuch as no other international tribunal had held that forced disappearance violated a person's human rights. The Court repeatedly emphasized that the crime of forced disappearance posed a frontal assault against the state of law.[89] The Court identified a number of levels of complexity characterizing forced disappearance, including secret structures of decision making and the compartmentalization of agencies and individuals involved in the crime. The result was the progressive breakdown of state institutions, often starting with the delegitimation of the armed forces and national security forces and concluding with the corruption of judicial power.[90]

A year later the Court reconvened to consider the award of compensatory damages to the families of the disappeared because no agreement had been reached between the Commission and Honduran officials. The Court ordered the government of Honduras to pay 750,000 lempiras to the wife and three children of Angel Manfredo Velasquez Rodriguez and 650,000 lempiras to the wife and child of Saul Godinez Cruz.[91] A year after the judgment was to have been paid, the government had made part but not all of the payments.[92] The Court raised the issue of the noncompliance at the meeting of the OAS General Assembly in 1991, but the General Assembly did not act.[93]

In the *Aloeboetoe et al. Case*, the government of Suriname accepted responsibility for the massacre of six civilians by soldiers. The central dimension of the decision was the award of reparations. The Court determined that $453,102 would be held in a trust fund and paid by Suriname to the families of the victims. The Court also ordered the government to reopen a school and establish a medical dispensary in a village where relatives of the deceased lived.[94] Recently, the Court decided another case against Suriname, the *Gangaram Panday Case*, whose importance lies in the visibility of the tensions between the Commission and the Court. The case dealt with the detention and

---

88. Ibid., para. 152.

89. Ibid., para. 154.

90. Ibid., para. 165.

91. *Velasquez Rodriguez Case*, Compensatory Damages, Judgment of July 21, 1989, Series C, No. 7, para. 56–60; *Godinez Cruz Case*, Compensatory Damages, Judgment of July 21, 1989, Series C, No. 6, para. 51–55.

92. Cerna, "Structure and Functioning," 228.

93. Ibid.

94. *Aloeboetoe et al. Case*, Judgment of September 10, 1993, Series C, No. 11, para. 116.

death of Mr. Asok Panday, who was taken into police custody when he arrived at the airport in Suriname. Conflicting evidence was presented as to whether the cause of Panday's death by hanging was suicide or homicide,[95] but the Commission challenged the right of the Court to conduct its own assessment of the facts and requested acceptance only of the evidence offered by the Commission.[96] The Court responded by noting the complementary functions of the Commission but emphatically asserting the primacy of its purpose and its supremacy under the Convention: "The Court exercises full jurisdiction over all issues relevant to a case...[and] in exercising these powers, the Court is not bound by what the Commission may have previously decided; rather, its authority to render judgment is in no way restricted. The Court does not act as a Court of review, or appeal or other similar Court in its dealings with the Commission. Its power to examine and review all actions and decisions of the Commission derives from its character as sole judicial organ concerning the Convention."[97]

In assessing the nature of various proofs offered by the Commission and the government of Suriname, the Court took the Commission to task for vacillating between condemnation and praise of Suriname's human rights record. "That in...reports on the Human Rights Situation in Suriname for...1983 and 1985, the Commission...confirmed that 'a number of fundamental human rights established in the American Declaration of the Rights and Duties of Man continue to be violated by the Government of Suriname;' however, in the Commission's Annual Report for 1987-88, approved at the Commission's 74th Session, it is expressly recognized that 'Suriname has taken significant steps to establish the rule of law and democratic institutions and has assumed international obligations in the Inter-American community...all of which indicate a desire to respect and promote human rights."[98] The Court held that whether death occurred by suicide or murder, Panday was illegally detained by members of the military police, and Suriname had thus violated the right to personal liberty as established in Article 7(2) of the convention. It assessed nominal damages at $10,000 to be paid to the victim's widow and children.[99]

The possibilities and limitations of this evolving body of human rights law were reflected in two more recent decisions, the *Amparo Case*[100] and the *Neira*

---

95. *Gangaram Panday Case*, Judgment of January 21, 1994, Series G, No. 16, para. 1–20.

96. Ibid., para. 39.

97. Ibid., para. 41.

98. Ibid., para. 65.

99. Ibid., para. 63–71.

Alegria Case[101] handed down in January 1995. The Court's legitimacy was ultimately reflected in Venezuela's decision to accept responsibility in the former case for the murder of fourteen individuals by the military and the police in 1988 and its obligation to pay damages and provide compensation to the victims and to the families of the deceased.[102] Venezuela's decision came after several attempts by state courts to exonerate the police and military officers responsible for the murders.[103] In the *Neira Alegria Case* the government of Peru fought the jurisdiction of both the Commission and the Court in much the same manner that Honduras had in the *Velasquez Rodriguez Case*.[104] The case of the disappearance of Victor Neira Alegria and three other "detainees" from Peru's infamous El Fronton prison on June 18, 1986, ultimately reached the Court, which found Peru responsible for violations of the right to life, Article 4(1), and habeas corpus, Article 7(6), under the American Convention and ordered Peru to pay damages (in an as yet undefined amount) to the families of the victims.[105]

The pioneering decisions in the Honduras cases established a benchmark that even unrepentant states cannot now ignore. The glare of publicity and the threat of moral opprobrium may not deter violations of human rights in Latin American countries, but acceptance of the Court's compulsory jurisdiction does assure the Commission's and the Court's reach into what were previously sovereign national prerogatives.

"Promises to Keep": The Quest for Institutionalization and Habitualization in the Inter-American System

The quest to construct an inter-American human rights regime remains very much a work in progress, and the legitimate power of the Commission and the Court constitute crucial forces for change. The inter-American system stands in stark contrast to its European counterpart, lacking as it does the

---

100. *Amparo Case,* Judgment of January 18, 1995, Series C, No. 19.

101. *Neira Alegria et al. Case,* Judgment of January 18, 1996.

102. *Amparo Case,* Judgment of January 18, 1995, para. 17.

103. Ibid., para. 18.

104. *Neira Alegria et al. Case,* Preliminary Objections, Judgment of December 1, 1991, para. 29, 30, 34; *Neira Alegria et al. Case,* Judgment of January 19, 1995, para. 63, 65(a), 75.

105. Ibid., para. 91(1), 91(2), and 91(3).

historical, political, economic, and sociological forces that have propelled a united Europe to the forefront of world politics. The absence of consensus on common core values and common ends, amid national rivalries and fears of U.S. hegemony, impaired the establishment of supranational judicial institutions in the New World. Notwithstanding the unflattering comparisons with Europe, the status of human rights in the Americas is not cause for despair nor the abandonment of the hope that a cohesive inter-American system will eventually develop. The road leading to the creation of an American human rights regime already possesses many milestones suggesting that the glass is more than "half empty."

The 1948 American Declaration of Human Rights constituted a huge achievement. It established an aspirational framework essential for the development of norms and values and it illustrates how both patterns of adaptation and strategic bargaining have constituted necessary stages for the establishment of a viable human rights regime. The refusal of the United States to accept the reach of the Declaration's founding principles represents only one dimension of a complex and multi-layered continuum balancing the strategic interests of states. It represents, of course, the weight of vast geopolitical power, previously unknown in world history, as played out in the bipolar struggles of the Cold War. Another axis of the continuum represents the possibility of adaptation and deference to the rule of law in an increasingly transnational and pluralist framework, as the work of Risse and Sikkink suggests.

In 1959, barely eleven years after the proclamation of the American Declaration, a hemispheric entity emerged with a broad, if yet to be defined, purpose to protect human rights in the Americas. Initially ignored and marginalized by the strategic bargaining of states within the OAS, the Inter-American Commission established an agenda that by 1971 was well focused and challenging, notwithstanding the refusal of many states to take its powers or its mandate seriously. As a consciousness-raising entity, the Commission relentlessly pursued objectives that reinforced the importance of the rule of law, the fundamental precept of due process for every individual member of the hemisphere, and a driving belief that governments were accountable for violations of human rights as defined explicitly and broadly by the American Declaration. The Commission's warrant included the entire hemisphere and that framework would become incredibly important as levels of interdependence in transportation and travel, communication networks, and economic and cultural linkages increased furiously in the 1970s and 1980s. The power of these globalizing forces, alongside proliferating transnational organizations and actors of all stripes, helped to empower the Commission. The Commission itself became a powerful hub, linking isolated individuals and groups with other like-minded people and organizations in other countries and regions in ever-more-complex transnational relationships. States sought to reduce and/or eliminate the Commission's objectives, but not even the strategic bargaining of states in the explicitly intergovernmental context of the OAS could succeed in discrediting the work of the Commission. States regularly refused cooperation with the Commission and denied its accusations. But the Commission's last resort—publication of its findings—became with time a potent weapon. As a consequence, requests for help and documentation of appalling human rights violations flowed into the Commission from around the hemisphere.

The growing power of Amnesty International and Americas Watch, two of the best-known transnational human rights organizations, also played a key role in forging incremental networks outside of the formal intergovernmental framework of the Commission, linking isolated individuals with external sources of potential support and political activism. These organizations also constituted a vital source of expertise needed to strengthen support for the rule of law and frameworks that could demand heightened levels of political accountability for governmental powers during periods of democratization. Heightened technological networks—telephones, fax machines, travel, commerce, and now the internet—provided additional wherewithal to help protect and promote human rights during periods of repression followed by cycles of liberalization.

The establishment of the Court in 1979, twenty years after the establishment of the Commission and twenty-nine years after the proclamation of the American Declaration, was a critical milestone in furthering a more ambitious human rights agenda. As the authoritative institution promoting human rights for countries accepting its compulsory jurisdiction and as a critical transnational vehicle advocating a strengthening of the hemisphere's normative framework, the Court's jurisprudence has sought to link human rights to treaties, conventions, case law, and other customary sources of international law. In so doing, the Court has raised the bar regarding the institutionalization of human rights to levels that were simply inconceivable just twenty years before. This does not mean that the habitualization of human rights norms and values, as defined by Risse and Sikkink, have yet largely taken hold among states. But it does suggest that the Court speaks with a moral authority that no other hemispheric institution can muster—embracing the rule of law, fundamental due process concerns, and the steadfast conviction that state power must be held accountable to open democratic institutions.

The Honduran cases of forced disappearance posed many of the toughest problems confronted by any human rights court in the world. But the Inter-

Figure 7.1   Decisions Invoking Contentious Jurisdiction: Incremental Institutionalization and Habitualization of Judicial Authority, 1987–2003

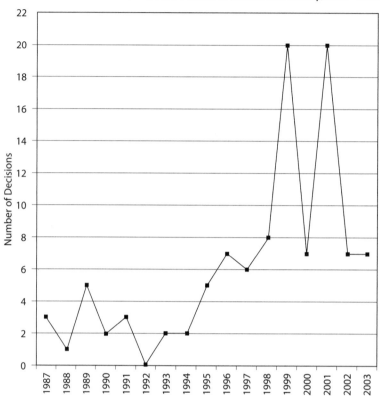

Source: Inter-American Court of Human Rights: Series C, Decisions and Judgment,
1987–2003. <www.1.umn.edu/humanrts/iachr/series_C.html>.

American Court's judgments against sovereign nations were accepted. In these
cases the Court established precedents that invigorated the protection of
human rights across the Americas. More important, the Court's well-reasoned
holdings reinforced the importance of the rule of law at precisely the moment
when the push to establish democratic institutions was gaining momentum.

The work of the Court and the Commission illustrates how the importance
of a transnational human rights regime may increase during a period of democratization. These two entities have explicitly challenged state repression, and
their accomplishments have stirred the conscience and imagination of the peoples of Latin America—an essential dimension of inventing and constructing
broader, deeper human rights regimes ultimately aiming at constraining state

power. This is a major contribution because the Court embodies the fundamental importance of the rule of law in the face of state claims based on national security/national emergency concerns. The Court's forthrightness and moral courage has garnered a measure of moral legitimacy, as one observer noted, "the Court did not shy away from confronting gross, systematic violations of human rights and produced some of its more creative reasoning in these first judgments."[106]

At its best, the Court underscored the importance of the rule of law at a supranational level during a time when the push to democratization was beginning to yield dividends. The Court's decisions must also be analyzed in light of the thousands upon thousands of deaths that have resulted historically from state terrorism in Latin America. In this respect, the cases that have finally reached conclusion illustrate the very long road that the peoples and countries of Latin America must travel before the protection of human rights in the inter-American system becomes institutionalized and habitual. The Court's decisions are nonetheless significant because they represent an expansive reading of the relevant documents establishing the inter-American system in light of ongoing efforts to create an international law of human rights. The decisions' significance may be seen as a contribution to the slow and difficult process of creating a regional common law of human rights in the New World.

Despite the optimism of many that political and economic reforms in Latin America will result in the establishment of a firm foundation supporting democratic states, the end point of the current push toward democratization remains in doubt. Since the 1930s, many countries have experienced shifts from democratic to authoritarian forms of government.[107] As James Malloy explains, "The predominant pattern is cyclical, with alternating democratic and authoritarian 'moments.'"[108] Indeed, one of the most influential students of Latin American corporatism and bureaucratic authoritarianism has questioned the inevitability of democratization in both Latin America and Eastern Europe.[109] Guillermo O'Donnell believes that high levels of territorial and cultural heterogeneity in Peru, Bolivia, Ecuador,

---

106. Cerna, "Structure and Functioning," 229.

107. James M. Malloy, "Politics of Transition in Latin America," in James A. Malloy and Mitchell A. Seligson (eds.), *Authoritarians and Democrats: Regime Transitions in Latin America* (Pittsburgh: University of Pittsburgh Press, 1987), 236.

108. Ibid., 1.

109. Guillermo O'Donnell, "The State, Democratization, and Some Conceptual Problems," in William C. Smith, Carlos H. Acuna, and Eduardo A. Gamarra (eds.), *Latin American Political Economy in the Age of Neoliberal Reform: Theoretical and Comparative Perspectives for the 1990s* (New Brunswick: Transaction Press, 1994), 161.

Brazil, and Mexico make the establishment of democratic institutions very difficulty.[110] Even Venezuela and Colombia, which have long-standing democratic traditions, are, he adds, likely to have difficulty building viable democratic institutions.[111]

Finally, while the organizational rivalries between the Commission and the Court have been important in determining the kinds of cases presented to the Court and, consequently, a smaller body of case law has evolved compared to the enormity of the human rights violations in Latin America, too much can be made of the tensions between the two. These institutional rivalries will likely continue until the different interests of the Commission and the Court are settled definitively. The Court is very young by the standards of other supranational courts. At some point the institutional differences will likely be solved, either by amalgamation of the Commission into the Court, the extension of standing before the Court to individuals, or some combination of the two. From the perspective of the inter-American system, however, the legitimacy and effectiveness of both the Commission and the Court will likely be built over time. The emerging case law has pushed both institutions to the forefront of the struggle to protect human rights throughout the world.

In the Americas, however, history, politics, and culture have been far less amenable to the growth of supranational institutions protecting human rights than in Western Europe. The development of a viable supranational judicial system is by no means certain. Absent the political and economic infrastructure supporting regional integration and a border with a hostile bloc, both of which helped to forge a distinctive sense of European identity after two world wars, the Inter-American Commission on Human Rights and the Inter-American Court of Human Rights have evolved haltingly and unevenly, reflecting in large measure the political, economic, and judicial climate of the 1970s, 1980s, and 1990s.

Significant differences also exist within the inter-American system itself. The prominence of human rights is a fairly recent development. The activism of the U.S. Congress beginning in the early 1970s was, in part, a reaction to the fear of a Nixon/Kissinger imperial presidency in foreign affairs, but it raised consciousness of human rights to an unprecedented level within the United States. As one leading scholar concluded, "despite the flaws of the system, Congress has made an important contribution to U.S. foreign policy by putting human rights back on the agenda and by pressuring the executive

---

110. Ibid.
111. Ibid.

branch to pay serious attention to human rights, and not just in communist countries."[112] Human rights reappeared again on the American agenda in the early 1980s, when the Reagan administration emphasized the primacy of civil and political rights[113] and the need to pursue free market strategies to speed economic development in Latin America and other developing areas.[114] The collapse of communism in the former USSR and Eastern Europe was seen as an important milestone in the push for the development of a democratic hemispheric human rights agenda.

Political and socioeconomic conditions in the region for the past twenty-five years have been perhaps the greatest obstacle to building a solid foundation for viable supranational institutions protecting human rights in the Americas. Authoritarian political systems and rampant poverty and lack of education, claims Scott Davidson, "coupled with widespread fear of challenging the state have made human rights petitioning under an individual system neither easy nor an attractive proposition if one valued longevity."[115] Human rights abuses by Latin American states were distinctive features of the domestic politics of several countries. "Chile, Argentina, Uruguay, Guatemala and El Salvador are countries in which some of the worst excesses of the last decade have been perpetrated by governments against their own civilian populations using military units and death squads. Disappearances, torture, arbitrary detention and extrajudicial executions have been the hallmarks of certain American regimes."[116]

The overwhelming preoccupation of states in the inter-American system with the protection of national sovereignty mirrored an environment deeply hostile to international judicial organizations likely to oppose state security policies that violated human rights. Despite the Inter-American Commission's success in publicizing the gross abuse of human rights throughout the hemisphere during the 1970s and 1980s and the emergence of the Inter-American Court's expansive, courageous, and thoughtful body of case law, only a small number of states accepted the Court's compulsory jurisdiction.

---

112. David P. Forsythe, *Human Rights in International Relations* (Cambridge: Cambridge University Press, 2000), 171.

113. Ibid., 93.

114. Eduardo A. Gamarra, "Market-Oriented Reforms and Democratization in Latin America," in William C. Smith, Carlos H. Acuna, and Eduardo A. Gamarra (eds.), *Latin American Political Economy in the Age of Neoliberal Reform: Theoretical and Comparative Perspectives for the 1990s* (New Brunswick: Transaction Press, 1994), 3.

115. Davidson, *Human Rights*, 126–27.

116. Ibid.

Most recently, the seemingly reinvigorated democratic processes in a number of South American states have heightened the moral legitimacy of the Commission and the Court. "The strengthening of democratic institutions based on respect for human rights and the rule of law," one scholar argued, "has become a priority of newly elected regimes as a means of reinforcing their democratic bases."[117] Increasing democratization in the Americas needs to be evaluated cautiously, however. The establishment of regional judicial supremacy depends in large measure on high degrees of legitimacy domestically. This means that state elites must be able to accept and comply with decisions of a supranational court promoting human rights. The willingness to obey such decisions, in turn, depends on the degree to which the tide of democratization has swept away personalistic, military-backed authoritarian regimes, replacing them with broad-based democratic participations.[118] Such a development presupposes as well the ability of states to complete the transition to democracy and overcome the upheavals attendant in the progressive integration of relatively undeveloped domestic economies into a far-from-stable, increasingly globalized world economy. Latin American states, therefore, confront "two seemingly contradictory objectives simultaneously: to institutionalize competitive politics with expanded political participation and to respond to international financial institutions and foreign governments bent on proving the superiority of marketplace logic."[119] The pursuit of human rights at the regional level is intimately connected to the political development of states and the progressive integration of those societies into the world economy. The challenges to democratization and human rights in the inter-American system are mammoth. The OAS remains far from achieving the "internationalization of norms, identities, interests and behaviors" characteristic of a developed human rights regime, as illustrated in the case of Europe. Despite the uneven development of a human rights regime across Latin America, the miles traveled do matter and the accomplishments of the Commission and Court are notable, as are the distances yet to be achieved.

---

117. Ibid., 127.
118. O'Donnell, "The State, Democratization, and Some Conceptual Problems," 159.
119. Gamarra, "Market-Oriented Reforms," 3.

CHAPTER 8

DISPUTE RESOLUTION UNDER NAFTA AND THE EMERGENCE OF TRANSNATIONAL QUASI-COURTS

David M. O'Brien

Throughout the second half of the twentieth century, the forces of international economics—the so-called "regionalization" and "globalization" of the world economy—along with increasing demands for collective security and human rights, have pushed in the direction of greater economic and political cooperation. Those forces have grown in part from the 1948 General Agreement on Tariffs and Trade (GATT) to the creation and expansion of the World Trade Organization (WTO).[1] But they have also pushed toward "regional integration" around the world, particularly with the creation of free trade areas.[2] The development and continued enlargement of the European Union (EU)—from six member states in 1957 to 15 in 1995, and another ten countries in Central and Eastern Europe admitted in 2004—is, of course, the most prominent and far-reaching example of regional integration.[3] However, there are other, even if less tightly interwoven, systems of economic and political integration: the Association of South East Asian Nations (ASEAN), founded in 1967 by nine Asian nations, for instance, has grown to Ten-Plus-Three (in-

---

1. See Bernard Hoekman and Michel Kostecki, *The Political Economy of the World Trading System: From GATT to WTO* (New York: Oxford University Press, 2001); and John H. Jackson, *The Jurisprudence of GATT and the WTO* (Cambridge: Cambridge University Press, 2000).

2. See, for example, Gustavo Vega-Canovas, "NAFTA and the EU: Toward Convergence?", in Jeffrey J. Anderson (ed.), *Regional Integration and Democracy* (Lanham: Rowman and Littlefield, 1999).

3. See Alec Stone Sweet, Wayne Sandholtz, and Neil Fligstein, *The Institutionalization of Europe* (Oxford: Oxford University Press, 2001); and Stephen George and Ian Bache, *Politics in the European Union* (Oxford: Oxford University Press, 2001).

cluding China, Japan, and South Korea); nineteen nations in the Pacific Basis now comprise the Asia-Pacific Economic Cooperation (APEC); Latin American countries established the Organization of American States (OAS) and since 1995 a number of them have joined the Southern Common Market Treaty, the Merado Comun del Cono Sur (MERCOSUR);[4] and in the 1990s the United States, Canada, and Mexico moved toward removing trade barriers and establishing a free trade zone under the North American Free Trade Agreement (NAFTA).

Along with these new forms of regional and international integration have emerged supranational or transnational courts and quasi-judicial tribunals for resolving disputes. The EU's European Court of Justice (ECJ) is, perhaps, the leading example of the "judicialization of politics"[5] and the role of courts in resolving economic disputes and the development of economic common markets.[6] Still, there are other increasingly important transnational courts, such as the World Court,[7] the European Court of Human Rights,[8] and the OAS's Inter-American Court of Human Rights,[9] among numerous other regional tribunals and transnational quasi-courts.

---

4. José Augusto Guilhon Albuquerque, "MERCOSUR: Democratic Stability and Economic Integration in South America," in Jeffrey J. Anderson (ed.), *Regional Integration and Democracy* (Lanham: Rowman and Littlefield, 1999), 261.

5. See C. Neil Tate and Torbjorn Vallinder (eds.), *The Global Expansion of Judicial Power* (New York: New York University Press, 1995).

6. See, for example, Alec Stone Sweet, *Governing with Judges: Constitutional Politics in Europe* (Oxford: Oxford University Press, 2000); Anthony Arnull, *The European Union and its Court of Justice* (Oxford: Oxford University Press, 1999); Renaud Dehousse, *The European Court of Justice: The Politics of Judicial Integration* (New York: St, Martin's Press, 1998); Miguel Poiares Maduro, *We, the Court—The European Court of Justice and the European Economic Constitution* (Oxford: Hart Publishing, 1998); Karen Alter, *Establishing the Supremacy of European Law* (Oxford: Oxford University Press, 2001); and Anne-Marie Slaughter, Alec Stone Sweet, and J.H.H. Weiler (eds.), *The European Court and National Courts—Doctrine and Jurisprudence: Legal Change in Its Social Context* (Oxford: Hart Publishing, 1998).

7. See Shabtai Rosenne, *The World Court* (Boston: Martinus Nijhoff, 1995); and Karel Wellens, *Economic Conflicts and Disputes before the World Court* (Boston: Khuwer Law International, 1996).

8. See Mary Volcansek (ed.), *Law Above Nations: Supranational Courts and the Legalization of Politics* (Gainesville, FL: University Press of Florida, 1997); and R.A. Lawson and H.G. Schermers (eds.), *Leading Cases of the European Court of Human Rights* (Leiden: Ars Aequi Lilbi, 1997).

9. See Scott Davidson, *The Inter-American Court of Human Rights* (Brookfield: Ashgate, 1992).

This chapter examines one of the less well-known transnational—or, more precisely, binational—forums for the resolution of trade disputes, specifically the use and operation of binational panels or tribunals under the NAFTA's Chapter 19. This essay's first section provides a brief overview of the NAFTA's dispute resolution system before turning, in section two, to the NAFTA's Chapter 19 provisions for establishing binational panels and their processes for dispute resolution. The third section then offers an analysis of the nature of the disputes and of the decisions handed down by these binational panels. Section four concludes with some final observations on the NAFTA's binational panel process and the controversy over whether NAFTA and its dispute resolution process blur the lines of national sovereignty, if not seriously undermining the NAFTA's member states' sovereignty.

An Overview of NAFTA's Dispute Resolution System

Undeniably, the NAFTA has proven as economically significant as it has been politically controversial. In spite of continuing concerns about inequalities among the three member states' laws on labor standards and environmental protection as well as over the alleged infringement on national sovereignty, the NAFTA created the world's largest geographical free trade area, linking 406 million people who produce more than 11 trillion dollars worth of goods and services. Since it took effect on January 1, 1994, the volume of trade between member states expanded from $297 billion to $676 billion in 2000, an increase of 128 percent.[10]

The principal institution of the NAFTA is the Free Trade Commission (FTC). It consists of the member states' trade ministers, meets at least once a year, and oversees implementation of the NAFTA, including its further elaboration and the resolution of disputes over its interpretation and application. The FTC's decisions are made by consensus, based on working groups, and with the assistance of the NAFTA Secretariat. The NAFTA Secretariat is composed of national delegations of the three countries and supports the binational dispute resolution panels, along with publishing and archiving their decisions.

Prior to the NAFTA's going into effect there was no established forum or generally accepted process for resolving trade-related disputes between Canada, Mexico, and the United States. As already noted, unlike the Euro-

---

10. U.S. Department of Treasury, "NAFTA at 7" (2001). <www.ustr.gov/naftareport/nafta-brouchure-eng.pdf>.

pean Union's creation of permanent supranational courts with the ECJ and the Court of First Instance, or the Dispute Settlement Body (DSB) that evolved under the World Trade Organization,[11] NAFTA's member states opted for a variety of dispute resolution processes and a system of ad hoc binational panels tribunals.

The NAFTA, along with two "parallel" side agreements—the North American Agreement on Environmental Cooperation (NAAEC) and the North American Agreement on Labor Cooperation (NAALC)—provides for several dispute resolution mechanisms. They depend on and are triggered by the subject matter of an economic dispute and whether it relates to the interpretation or the application of NAFTA provisions in particular cases. The main mechanisms and dispute resolution procedures (as outlined in specific chapters of the NAFTA) relate to:

1. investment disputes between foreign investors and member states (in Chapter 11);

2. disputes over financial services (in Chapter 14);

3. challenges to and appeals of antidumping and countervailing duty determinations and decisions by member states' designated administrative authorities (in Chapter 19);

4. disputes among member states over the interpretation and application of the NAFTA generally (in Chapter 20);

5. alleged failure of a member state to enforce national environmental laws (as required by the North American Agreement on Environmental Cooperation); and

6. alleged failure of a member state to enforce national labor laws (as required by the North American Agreement on Labor Cooperation).

The next section focuses on only one set of these dispute resolution processes, namely those under Chapter 19 of the NAFTA. These govern challenges to member states' agency regulations and decisions on antidumping (AD) and imposing countervailing duties (CVD) on goods. This focus appears

---

11. See, for example, Azar M. Khansari, "Searching for the Perfect Solution: International Dispute Resolution and the New Trade Organization," 20 *Hastings International and Comparative Law Review* (1996), 183; David Palmeter and Petros C. Mavroidi, "The WTO Legal System: Sources of Law," 92 *American Journal of International Law* (1998), 398; Edwin Vermulst and Bart Driessen, "An Overview of the WTO Dispute Settlement System and its Relationship with the Uruguay Round Agreements," *Journal of World Trade* (1995), 131; and C. O'Neil Taylor, "The Limits of Economic Power: Section 301 and the World Trade Dispute Settlement System," 30 *Vanderbilt Journal of Transnational Law* (1997), 209.

appropriate in part because these disputes are illustrative of NAFTA's dispute resolution mechanism. Moreover, they also represent the most numerous kinds of cases brought under NAFTA. And they are as well, arguably, the most controversial and common "unfair" trade practices recognized by international trade agreements.

Before proceeding, though, something more should be said about these trade practices and the national institutions and administrative agencies that determine them. "Dumping" refers to the practice of one country producing goods that are then sold in another country below "normal value," so that their price in the foreign market and importing country is below that in the market of the producing and exporting country; thus, domestic producers in the importing country are undercut and injured. By contrast, "countervailing duties" are imposed on goods by governments in order to offset another government's subsidies for producers that result in lower prices and cause injury to producers of similar goods in the importing country.

Finally, the regulations and decisions on antidumping regulations and countervailing duties, along with associated injuries, are determined by designated administrative agencies (also referred to under the NAFTA as "investigating authorities") in each country: in Canada by the Revenue Canada and, more commonly, the Canadian International Trade Tribunal (CITT); in Mexico by the Secretaria de Comercio y Fomento Industrial (SECOFI); and in the U.S. by the Department of Commerce and the U.S. International Trade Commission (USITC).

Quasi-Courts and Dispute Resolution under Chapter 19 of NAFTA

Instead of relying on the member states' national courts—the U.S. Court of International Trade (CIT) and the Court of Appeals for the Federal Circuit, for instance, or the Mexican Federal Tax Court (Tribunal Fiscal)—a binational panel hears appeals from and challenges to decisions and determinations of the CITT, SECOFI, and the USITC. Although inviting the criticism that in this regard NAFTA undercuts member states' sovereignty by superimposing binational tribunals over each nation's courts, this transnational dispute resolution mechanism was agreed to for several reasons: the costs and delays of antidumping and countervailing duty appeals in U.S. courts; Canadian and Mexican concerns that U.S. courts were and would be too deferential to the USITC; and the refusal of the U.S. to agree to an exemption for Canada from

U.S. antidumping and countervailing duty laws.[12] In addition, essentially the same kind of mechanism had been agreed to and was in place under the Canadian-U.S. Free Trade Agreement of 1988.

Jurisdiction

When exercising jurisdiction over disputes under Chapter 19, Article 1904 requires the binational tribunals to apply the substantive antidumping and countervailing duty laws of the nation challenged in the appeal, including "the relevant statutes, legislative history, regulations, administrative practice and judicial precedents...that a court of the importing party would rely on...in reviewing a final determination of the competent investigating authority [that is, CITT, SECOFI, or USITC]." Significantly, they also must apply the standard of judicial review and the general legal principles "that a court of the importing party otherwise would apply to a review of a determination of" the CITT, SECOFI, or USITC. In other words, these binational panels apply the relevant domestic law of Canada, Mexico, and the U.S. They, therefore, do not directly apply international law, such as the provisions of the WTO Agreement on the Interpretation of Article VI of GATT, except to the extent that international trading laws have been incorporated into the applicable national law in each case. However, the Canadian government and some scholars maintain, contrariwise, that the NAFTA has basically internationalized national domestic trade laws.

Moreover, the tribunals do not have explicit authority to reverse or dismiss a determination or decision of the CITT, SECOFI, or USITC. Rather, they may technically only either "uphold a final determination [on dumping or subsidies] or remand it for action not inconsistent with the panel's decision." Yet, in spite of that restraint and as further discussed below, panels have reversed member states' agency determinations.[13] More typically, though, the tribunals vacate (and, thereby, effectively reverse) parts of, or the basis for, the decision below and remand the case for further action not inconsistent with the tribunal's decision.

Notably, when accepting jurisdiction over a dispute the five-member tribunals operate in all proceedings and decision making on the basis of majority vote and must be "based on the votes of all members of the panel." Panelists may not recuse themselves or abstain from voting. Consequently,

---

12. U.S. General Accounting Office, U.S.-Canada Free Trade Agreement, *Factors Contributing to Controversy in Appeals of Trade Remedy Cases to Binational Panels* (Washington, D.C.: U.S. General Accounting Office, June 1995).

13. See, for example, *Mexican Antidumping Investigation into Imports of Cut-to-Length Plate Products from the United States,* MEX-94-1904-02 (August 30, 1995).

if a panelist fails to vote or does not vote in a timely fashion, then "proceedings of the panel shall be suspended pending the selection of a substitute panelist."

Finally, a NAFTA tribunal panel's decision is deemed final and without the possibility of appeal except in cases alleging gross misconduct, bias, serious conflict of interests, disregard of fundamental rules of procedure, or for exceeding its authority and jurisdiction. In such an instance, an "Extraordinary Challenge Procedure" permits an appeal to a special three-person review panel or Extraordinary Challenge Committee (ECC). But only a NAFTA member state, not a private party to the dispute or any other "interested parties," may initiate such appeals. Furthermore, Article 1904 of the NAFTA specifically forbids member states from enacting any legislation providing "for an appeal from a panel decision to its domestic courts." At the same time, because of criticisms and the controversy over whether the NAFTA diminishes national sovereignty, the decisions of a NAFTA binational panel do not have the force of law and, as discussed further below, it is left to the appropriate national executive or legislative authorities to decide how to respond under domestic law to an adverse ruling of a NAFTA panel.

Selection and Composition of Binational Panels

Closely related to the controversy over the substitution of the NAFTA tribunals for member states' national courts is that over the process for composing the binational panels. The tribunals function as five-member panels chosen by the parties in a dispute from a standing roster of 75 experts designated by the member states' national NAFTA Secretariat. Members serve part time, with nominal per diem pay, for three-year terms and are eligible for reappointment.

The selection and composition of the tribunal panelists has invited a number of criticisms and court challenges. While panelists may not be "affiliated" with a NAFTA government and are subject to a detailed code of conduct—governing conflicts of interest—preference is given to the appointment of judges and former judges. Yet few jurists have served on the binational panels. The overwhelming majority of the panelists have been attorneys, law school professors, and even non-lawyer trade specialists.[14]

---

14. For the views of some former panelists, see David A. Gantz, "Resolution of Trade Disputes under NAFTA's Chapter 19: The Lessons of Extending the Binational Panel Process to Mexico," 29 *Law and Policy in International Business* (1998), 297; Robert E. Lutz, "Law, Procedure and Culture in Mexico under the NAFTA: The Perspective of a NAFTA Panelist," 3 *Southwestern Journal of Law and Trade in the Americas* (1996), 391; and Harry B. Ends-

As a result, lawsuits filed in U.S. courts have challenged, albeit unsuccessfully, the appointment process for and structure of the binational panels on the ground that provisions of the U.S. Constitution are thereby violated. It has been argued, for example, that the panels include foreign nationals and that the panelists are not appointed either in accordance with the provisions of Article I of the U.S. Constitution, which provides for the creation of "legislative courts" such as the defunct U.S. Commerce Court, the U.S. Court of Military Appeals, and Territorial Courts; or with the "advice and consent" of the U.S. Senate, as required for the appointment of federal judges under Article II. In addition, it has been argued that since most of the panelists lack judicial experience and are unaccountable, their appointments violate the stipulation in Article III that judges "shall hold their Offices during good Behaviour."[15]

Dispute Resolution Process

While the NAFTA permits each nation to maintain its own antidumping and countervailing duty laws and, as already noted, panel decisions do not carry the force of domestic law, Canada, Mexico, and the U.S. are required to adapt their laws and regulations to provisions of the NAFTA, as well as to notify other member nations of any amendments to their laws. Chapter 19 also provides for the formal binational panel process for resolving disputes over (1) amendments to AD and CVD laws, and (2) final AD and CVD determinations on their interpretation and application by the designated national authorities (CITT, SECOFI, and USITC). In other words, a member state's statutory amendments to AD and CVD laws and final agency determinations are the two bases for triggering the NAFTA Chapter 19 dispute resolution process.

More specifically, amendments to a nation's AD and CVD laws may be reviewed by a binational panel when another country alleges that they violate the WTO Antidumping Agreement or Chapter 19 of the NAFTA. The five-member binational panel is selected by the two disputing parties, with each nominating two candidates within thirty days of the filing of a complaint, along with proposed alternative candidates in the event that the other disputing party exercises it right to four preemptory challenges within forty-five days

---

ley, "Dispute Settlement Under the CFTA and NAFTA: From Eleventh Hour Innovation to Accepted Institution," 18 *Hastings International and Comparative Law Review* (1995), 659.

15. See, for example, *American Coalition for Competitive Trade v. United States* (D.C. Cir., 1997), 128 F.3d 761 (dismissed for lack of standing).

after the request to establish the panel was filed. In the event that those dead-lines are not met, the missing panelist is chosen by lot from the roster of po-tential panelists maintained by the NAFTA Secretariat. The fifth panelist must then be chosen within fifty-five days of the request for a panel; and if no agreement is reached, a drawing of lots determines which of the disputing par-ties may select the fifth panelist.

As previously noted, the binational panels operate on the basis of majority vote with respect to selecting a chair, establishing rules of procedure, and all final reports and decisions. Although the panels' deliberations are confidential, based on hearings and submissions from the disputing parties, the panels are required to issue an "initial written declaratory opinion containing findings of fact and its determinations" within ninety days. That report may uphold the amendments to a nation's AD or CVD laws, or recommend modifications if it finds them to violate the NAFTA. The disputing parties, then, have fourteen days to object to the panel's report; otherwise it is final. If a report is challenged, the panel has thirty days to reconsider the matter, after which it must issue its "final opinion" and any dissenting or concurring opinions.

Notably, the panel's report is not binding, only declaratory. Still, if a panel makes recommendations the disputing parties must immediately start con-sultations aimed at arriving at a "mutually satisfactory solution" within ninety days. If within nine months following the end of the consultations no changes in the amendment of a nation's laws is made or another agreement has been reached, then the complaining party may resort to "self help" via enacting "comparable legislation or equivalent executive action," or even, in the most extreme case, terminate the NAFTA with the violating country.

With respect to challenges to AD or CVD agency determinations under a country's laws, the dispute resolution process is similar but the panel's deci-sions are binding. Briefly stated, the party challenging an agency determina-tion has thirty days to request the establishment of a panel. The panel is se-lected as already indicated and operates in all respects by majority rule. Moreover, Chapter 19 imposes a rather tight time schedule on the proceed-ings in order to attain a final decision with 315 days of the request for a panel. See Table 8.1. After hearings, reviewing submissions, and other proceedings, the binational panel determines whether the imposition of a countervailing duty, for example, was permissible under the national law of the importing country, based on "the standard of review…and the legal principles that a court of the importing party otherwise would apply."

In such cases, the panel's report must be issued within ninety days of com-pleting oral arguments and must either (a) affirm the determination of the

Table 8.1   Procedural Stages and Proposed Timeline
for NAFTA Chapter 19 Dispute Resolution Panels

Rule	Stage	Timetable
34	Request for review filed	Day 1
39	Complaints to be filed	Within 30 days
40	Notices of appearance filed	Within 45 days after request for review
Annex 1912(3)	Panel section by parties completed	Day 55
41	Final agency determination, reasons,	15 days after and administrative record filed notice of appearance
Annex 19012(3)	If parties unable to agree, the 5th Panelist to be selected	Day 61
57(1)	Briefs filed	60 days after administrative record filed
57(2)	Briefs by investigating authority	60 days after and participants in support filed complainants' briefs
57(3)	Reply briefs filed	15 days after authority's brief
57(4)	Appendix to briefs filed	10 days after reply briefs
67(1)	Oral arguments to begin	30 days after reply briefs
Article 1904.14	Panel decision due	Day 315

designated national agency authority or (b) remand the case for reconsideration in light of its findings and conclusions. The panel may not change the amount of the duty imposed, for instance, or otherwise alter a national agency's determination. However, the disputing parties are bound by whatever the panel decides. In the event that the agency determination is not affirmed and the case is remanded, the panel is required to "establish as brief a time as is reasonable for compliance with it." The same panel will subsequently review the action taken by the national agency on remand, and "shall normally issue a final decision within 90 days…after such remand action is submitted to it." Consequently, cases brought over AD and CVD agency determinations may result in two or more panel decisions.

Appeals: The Extraordinary Challenge Procedure

Under very limited circumstances the "final" decisions of the binational panels may be appealed, as already noted, according to an "Extraordinary Challenge Procedure." These appeals are filed with the NAFTA Secretariat and are heard by an Extraordinary Challenge Committee. The NAFTA did not provide for regular or routine appeals because they were deemed inconsistent with the main objective of achieving an expeditious process for settling AD and CVD disputes.

Under Chapter 19, appeals must fall within one of three narrowly defined categories alleging (1) the personal failure of a panel member, (2) a serious disregard by the binational panel of a principal procedural provision, or (3) an obvious misuse of the panel's jurisdiction and powers. Furthermore, under Article 1904 it is also necessary for the complaining party to show that any of these actions "materially affected the panel's decision and threatens the integrity of the binational panel review process."

Once an appeal of a binational panel's decision has been filed, the parties have 15 days to select a three-person EEC. The EEC members must be "judges or former judges," in contrast to members of the binational panels, and are selected from a pre-established roster of 15 potential members maintained by the NAFTA Secretariat. Similar to the process for selecting members of the binational panels, each of the disputing parties nominates one committee member, and a drawing of lots determines which party selects the third member.

On appeal, the ECC is empowered to review and analyze all of the factual and legal aspects of the initial case as well as the binational panel's findings and conclusions. Ultimately, the ECC decides whether the extraordinary challenge is justified. If it is not, the ECC dismisses the challenge and, thereby, upholds the original decision of the binational panel. If the appeal is deemed to be justified, the ECC may vacate and remand the case to another binational panel—a panel composed of new members, which in turn reinvestigates the dispute and begins the proceedings anew.

Disputes and Decisions under
Chapter 19 of NAFTA

In the first eight years after the NAFTA went into effect, there were 74 challenges under Chapter 19 to national AD and CVD laws and agency determinations on dumping and countervailing duties by the CITT, USITC, and the SECOFI. Although the NAFTA requires member states to harmonize their laws on dumping and countervailing duties, and thus the number of disputes might be expected to decline over time, there is no indication that has happened. Slightly more requests for reviews were filed between 1998 and 2001 than during the first four years after the NAFTA's taking effect.

Also noteworthy, as indicated in Table 8.2,[16] almost a third (21) of the 74 disputes were terminated by the parties' agreement prior to a decision. Slightly more than a third (27) remain active and unresolved, even though in a couple of cases preliminary decisions of binational panels have been handed down. In three cases, binational panels have issued two decisions and in two there were three decisions. In these cases, the initial panel decision is remanded back to the appropriate administrative agency for reconsideration, before a "final" decision is issued by the panel. Nonetheless, the decisions are indicative of the work and operation of the binational panels. In almost 60 percent of cases, the binational panels handed down decisions within a year of the filing of the complaints, as required by the NAFTA and illustrated in Table 8.1.

Still, about 41 percent of the decisions came down more than a year after the request for review was filed. For example, in *Import of Flat Coated Steel Products from the United States*,[17] the request for review was filed on September 1, 1994, but the initial panel decision did not come down for over two

---

16. Data here and in subsequent tables are based on decisions reported and located at the NAFTA Secretariat's web site (URL www.nafta-sec-alena.org). Three reports by panels under NAFTA Chapter 20 are excluded, along with one decision, *Imports of High-Fructose Corn Syrup Originating in the United States of America*, MEX-USA-98-1904-01 (August 3, 2001), for the link to the decision was dead (as accessed on September 20, 2001). These decisions were cross checked with those reported in Lexis/Nexus Library, International Law (INTLAW), NAFTA decisions (NAFDEC), which included only 35 decisions and of which two were omitted here because they dealt with the Canadian-United States Free Trade Agreement. Note also that several challenges to agency determinations and decisions resulted in two or more binational tribunal decisions and they are counted separately here.

17. *Import of Flat Coated Steel Products from the United States*, MEX-94-1904-01 (September 27, 1996).

Table 8.2   Complaints Filed, Terminations, and Decisions

Year of complaint	Number filed	Terminated by parties	Decision* within a year	Decision* in more than a year	Remains active
1994	9	1	7	4	
1995	11	4	7		
1996 •	4	2	2	1	
1997	11	5	3	7	
1998	8		2	3	5
1999	8	5			3
2000	17	3			14
2001**	6	1			5
Total	74	21	21	15	27

* In several cases there were two or three decisions handed down; they are counted separately here.
** Data through November 2001.

years (756 days), on September 27, 1996. In *Polystyrene and Impact Crystal from the United States*,[18] the request was filed on September 1, 1994, yet the initial panel decision was issued over two years later, on September 12, 1996. Moreover, the case of *Import of Flat Coated Steel Products from the United States*[19] was twice remanded and still not completed until April 1998, more than three years and eight months later.

18. *Polystyrene and Impact Crystal from the United States*, MEX-94-1904-3 (September 12, 1996).
19. *Import of Flat Coated Steel Products from the United States*, MEX-94-1904-1 (April 13, 1998).

The subject matter of the disputes under Chapter 19 have been rather wide ranging—from trade regulations and determinations on baby food; broom corn brooms, fresh cut flowers, sugar, live swine, color picture tubes, malt beverages, porcelain-on-steel cookware, pipe fittings, synthetic baler twin with a knot strength of 200 pounds or less, and to various kinds of steel products. There also appear to have been several repeat players in each country that bring Chapter 19 challenges: U.S. Steel and Bethlehem Steel Corporation, for instance, were involved in no less than eight cases; Stelco, Inc., a Canadian steel producer in five; and Grey Portland Cement and Clinker, a company in Mexico, in three cases.   •

As shown in Table 8.3, challenges to importing nations' antidumping laws and agency decisions greatly outnumber (with 52 cases) injury claims (14) and requests for review of countervailing duty determinations (8). As the largest of the three trading partners, perhaps not surprisingly, the United States has encountered over twice as many Chapter 19 challenges to its regulations and agency decisions than Canada, and over four times as many as those filed against Mexico.

In terms of the 36 decisions rendered by the five-member binational panels, there have been 26 (72 percent) unanimous decisions and 10 (27 percent) non-unanimous decisions. In the non-unanimous decisions, panelists filed seven concurring opinions, six separate opinions dissenting in part from the majority's decision and opinion, and two dissenting opinions, for a total of 15 separate individual opinions.

Recall that, as discussed in section two, the binational panels may technically only either "uphold a final determination [on dumping and countervailing duties] or remand it for action not inconsistent with the panel's decision." Yet analysis of the decisions of the binational panels reveals that only about half (18) affirmed agencies' determinations, another three affirmed in part and remanded, and nine remanded the case back to agencies for reconsideration.

Notably, as Table 8.4 shows, in 6 cases (or 16 percent of the time) the binational panels explicitly reversed in whole or in part the basis for and reasoning in support of an agency determination on dumping or countervailing duties. In other words, like courts elsewhere, the binational panels exhibit a degree of so-called "judicial activism," even though they are temporary, ad hoc, and quasi-judicial tribunals.

One of the first binational panel decisions, *Imports of Cut-to-Length Plate Products from the United States of America*,[20] an antidumping case against Mex-

---

20. *Imports of Cut-to-Length Plate Products from the United States of America*, MEX-94-1904-02 (August 30, 1995).

Table 8.3   Types of Challenges under Chapter 19 of the NAFTA

Country	Number of cases filed	Terminated prior to decision	Decisions	Undecided
Canada				
Injury claim	12	1	9	3
Dumping	7	3	3	2
Countervailing duty				
Mexico				
Injury claim				
Dumping	9	2	8	2
Countervailing duty	1	1		
U.S.				
Injury claim	2	2		
Dumping	36	9	14	17
Countervailing duty	7	3	2	3
Total	74	21	36	27

ico, illustrates the NAFTA panels' "judicial activism." In this case, the complainants challenged the jurisdiction and competence of the SECOFI to make an antidumping determination. They contended that there was no proper delegation of legal authority to the SECOFI and attacked the SECOFI's calculation of the amount of dumping involved, and hence the extent of injury to the Mexican domestic steel industry. The binational panel, as required by the NAFTA, had to review the SECOFI's decisions under the standards of Mexican law, specifically Article 238 of the Mexican Codigo Fiscal de la Federacion

Table 8.4   Outcomes of the Binational Panel Decisions
on Agencies' Determinations

Outcomes	Number	Percentage
Affirmed	18	(50)
Affirmed in part and remanded	3	(8.3)
Reversed	1	(2.7)
Reversed and affirmed in part	2	(5.5)
Reversed in part and remanded	3	(8.3)
Remanded	9	(25)
Total	36	(99.7)

(the Mexican Federal Fiscal Code). Under that standard, an administrative decision or determination may be declared illegal and overturned if one of the following grounds are demonstrated:

1. Lack of competence of the official who issued, ordered, or carried out the proceeding from which said resolution is derived.

2. Omission of the formal requirements provided by law, which affects an individual's defenses and impacts the result of the challenged resolution, including the lack of legal foundation or reasoning, as the case may be.

3. Procedural errors that affect an individual's defenses and impact the result of the challenged resolution.

4. If the facts that underlie the resolution do not exist, are different or were erroneously weighed, or if the resolution was issued in violation of applicable legal provisions or if the correct provisions were not applied.

5. When an administrative determination issued in an exercise of discretionary powers does not correspond with the purposes for which the law confers said powers.

Under that standard, the Mexican Federal Tax Court—and, thus, the binational panel which must apply and exercise review under Mexican law—may declare an administrative authority incompetent or to have failed to establish the basis for rendering the challenged determination.

Accordingly, a majority of the binational panel, including one Mexican and two U.S. panelists, accepted the U.S. companies' argument that the Mexican administrative agency was not a properly delegated authority to render a determination in the case. In the majority's view, the agency's determination imposing antidumping duties was "derived" from improper delegations of authority and the panel concluded that it was bound under Article 238(I) to effectively declare the agency's final determination null and void. In the words of the majority's opinion: "SECOFI, in carrying out this administrative proceeding, failed to comply with basic [Mexican] constitutional and other applicable legal principles." Although, as earlier noted, under the NAFTA standard of review the binational panels may only affirm an administrative agency or remand a matter for reconsideration in light of its opinion, here the majority of the panel asserted the power to dismiss the agency determination outright. It reasoned that because under Mexican law the Mexican Tax Court, which here the binational panel replaced, may reverse and invalidate administrative agency decisions and determinations, then the panel had the authority and power to do so as well.

Two panelists, one Mexican and one from the U.S., dissented, however. They advanced a very different interpretation of the delegation of authority within the SECOFI and concluded that the officials who conducted the investigation into the charge of dumping were competent to do so. Rather than declaring the agency's action null and void, they would have simply remanded the matter to the SECOFI with instructions to recalculate certain aspects of the dumping analysis and to issue a re-determination of the injury.

More generally, a number of trends and features of the binational panels' decisions and opinions are striking. First, in terms of what Martin Shapiro has called "the proto-type of courts"—that is, a triadic relationship between disputing parties and a third-party dispute resolution forum—the NAFTA binational panels, although constituted as quasi-courts, appear to strive to function and to appear like courts.[21] That is so not only in the conduct of their quasi-judicial proceedings, as previously discussed, but also in the opinions handed down justifying or rationalizing their final decisions.

---

21. See Martin Shapiro, *Courts: A Comparative and Political Analysis* (Chicago: University of Chicago Press, 1981), chap. 1; and Stone Sweet, *Governing with Judges*, chap. 1.

Second, with one or two exceptions, the panels' opinions are highly detailed and lengthy, often running between 100 and 300 pages. They also read very much like U.S. federal district court opinions, providing detailed summaries of the disputing parties' arguments about the law and the facts of dumping and countervailing duties, the standard of judicial review, and an analysis of the respective member state's agency's authority and factual determination.

Precisely because the binational panels are required to apply the domestic law of the importing country in reviewing a trade dispute, substantial portions of the panels' opinions are devoted to the appropriate standard of judicial review. In *Certain Solder Joint Pressure Pipe Fittings and Solder Joint Drainage, Waste and Vent Pipe Fittings*,[22] for instance, 19 pages of the 58-page opinion (or 31 percent) are devoted to analyzing the standard of judicial review that would be applied by the Canadian Supreme Court under the Federal Court Act. Notably, the panel canvassed pertinent Canadian precedents pertaining to whether it should apply the substantive standard of "correctness" or the standard of "patent unreasonableness" and, then, considered the matter of judicial review under "the rules of natural justice and procedural injustice." In short, typically the panels consider the applicable domestic law bearing on substantive judicial review and procedural due process.[23] However, more problematic for some panels than drawing on Canadian and U.S. court rulings is that of looking to standards in Mexican domestic law. For in Mexican law a case holding "may have persuasive value but is not itself, or has not yet become, a *Jurisprudencia* [jurisprudential precedent]. When five [decisions] in a row adopt the identical holding (without intervening contrary authority), the fifth case becomes a *Jurisprudencia*, which is treated as a binding legal precedent."[24]

No less importantly, the binational panel in *Certain Solder Joint Pressure Pipe Fittings* concluded that, under Canadian law and Supreme Court precedents, it should adopt a deferential approach, as would the Canadian judiciary, toward reviewing an administrative agency's interpretation of applicable law and procedures. In justifying its standard of review, the binational panel

---

22. *Certain Solder Joint Pressure Pipe Fittings and Solder Joint Drainage, Waste and Vent Pipe Fittings*, CDA-USA-98-1904-03 (April 3, 2000).

23. See, for example, *Certain Cold-Reduced Flat Rolled Sheet Products of Carbon Steel*, CDA-USA-98-1904-02 (July 19, 2000).

24. *Mexican Antidumping Investigation into Cut-to-Length Plate Products from the United States*, MEX-94-1904-02 (August 30, 1995), 30. See also Robert E. Lutz, "Law, Procedure and Culture in Mexico Under the NAFTA," 400–1, and David A. Gantz, "Resolution of Trade Disputes under NAFTA's Chapter 19," 363.

thus relied on the decision of the Canadian Federal Court of Appeal, in *Stelco Inc. v. British Steel Canada Inc.*,[25] an unreported decision, that observed:

> Given the discretionary nature of the Tribunal's decision-making power under [the relevant statute], it is impossible in the abstract to say that any one of the factors typically considered by the Tribunal in these cases is so intrinsically important that it must always be dealt with in the Tribunal's reasons, whenever it is put in issue by the parties. It is for the Tribunal to determine the significance of any factor in light of its conclusions on other factors.

Turning to the standard for procedural review in *Certain Solder Joint Pressure Pipe Fittings*, the binational panel also relied on and quoted from a recent Canadian Supreme Court decision, *Baker v. Canada*,[26] holding that,

> The analysis of what procedures the duty of fairness requires should also take into account and respect the choices of procedures made by the agency itself, particularly when the statute leaves to the decision-maker the ability to choose its own procedures, or when the agency has an expertise in determining what procedures are appropriate in the circumstances.

Likewise, NAFTA binational panels reviewing antidumping and counter-vailing duty disputes brought against the United States tend to adopt a deferential approach—though a slightly less deferential approach than Canadian courts and, presumably, binational panels applying Canadian law—to administrative agencies' interpretations and decisions. They rely primarily on the U.S. Supreme Court's decision in *Chevron v. Natural Resources Defense Council*.[27] Under the so-called *Chevron* doctrine and subsequent federal court decisions,[28] if a statute is "silent or ambiguous with respect to the specific issue, the question for the Court [and hence lower federal courts and binational panels applying U.S. law] is whether the agency's answer is based on a permissible construction of the statute."

---

25. *Stelco Inc. v. British Steel Canada, Inc.* (January 25, 2000), A-365-98 (F.C.A.).

26. *Baker v. Canada* (1997), 2 S.C.R. 817.

27. *Chevron v. Natural Resources Defense Council* (1984), 467 U.S. 837.

28. See also *Rust v. Sullivan*, (1991), 500 U.S. 173; and *Food and Drug Administration v. Brown and Williamson* (2000), 529 U.S. 120. But note that some lower federal courts and legal scholars have criticized the *Chevron* doctrine. See Cass Sunstein, "Law and Administration After *Chevron*," 90 *Colorado Law Review* (1990), 2071; and Thomas W. Merrill, "Judicial Deference to Executive Precedent," 101 *Yale Law Journal* (1992), 969.

Accordingly, the binational panel in *The Matter of Porcelain-on-Steel Cookware from Mexico*,[29] for instance, while noting that it "must satisfy itself that an agency determination is supported by the administrative record as a whole" and "must conduct a meaningful review," concluded in language worth quoting at length as a further indication of the binational panels' deference to administrative agencies and of the opinions they hand down:[30]

> Like a reviewing court, a binational panel must extend deference to reasonable agency interpretations of a statute that the agency administers. *National R.R. Passenger Corp. v. Boston & Me. Corp.*, 503 U.S. 407, 417 (1992). But when a statute remains silent or ambiguous with respect to a particular issue, "the question for the Court is whether the agency's answer is based on a permissible construction of the statute." Id. (quoting *Chevron, U.S.A. v. Natural Resources Defense Council*, 467 U.S. 837, 843 (1984)). So long as the agency's methodology and procedures constitute a reasonable means of effectuating the statutory purpose, a panel can neither substitute its judgment for that of the agency nor impose its own standards with respect to the sufficiency of the agency's investigation or methods. *Texas Crushed Stone Co. v. United States*, 35 F.3d 1535, 1540 (Fed. Cir. 1994); *Budd Co., Wheel & Brake Div. V. United States*, 773 F. Supp. 1549, 1553 (Ct. Int'l Trade 1991).

As a result, the binational panels are generally highly deferential in adopting standards of review, and therefore inclined to affirm (as earlier shown in Table 8.4) the decisions of a NAFTA member state's administrative agencies, or alternatively to remand for reconsideration in light of their findings. In other words, panel decisions reversing agency interpretations and determinations tend to be due to reaching rival conclusions about the agency's factual analysis, methods of causation analysis, and its quantification of the impact and injuries resulting from dumping, or antidumping determinations, and the imposition of countervailing duties.

Finally, but notably, the binational panels are not bound to the relevant decisions of other panels and panel decisions are not technically considered as

---

29. *The Matter of Porcelain-on-Steel Cookware from Mexico*, USA-95-1904-01 (April 30, 1996). See also *In the Matter of Grey Portland Cement and Clinker from Mexico*, U.S.-97-1904-01 (June 19, 1999), 1999 FTAPD LEXIS 4, 29-30; and *In the Matter of Live Swine from Canada*, USA-94-1904-01 (May 30, 1995), 1995 FTAPD LEXIS 12, 7–9.

30. *The Matter of Porcelain-on-Steel Cookware from Mexico*, USA-95-1904-01 (April 30, 1996), 1996 FTAPD LEXIS 3, 8–9.

precedent. Indeed, the NAFTA specifically provides in Chapter 19 that "the decision of a panel under this article [1904] shall be binding on the involved Parties with respect to the particular matter that is before the panel." Nonetheless, recent panel opinions have relied on prior panel decisions interpreting domestic standards of judicial review and applicable law.[31] Their recognition of and reliance on previous panel decisions is significant in at least two respects. First, the growing practice underscores the NAFTA quasi-judicial panels' apparent aspiration to function and to appear like common law courts, and thereby solidify their legitimacy and the legitimacy of the NAFTA dispute resolution process. Second, the binational panels' reliance on and respect for treating prior panel decisions as precedents in part compensates for the absence of an appellate process, except for (as earlier noted) challenges to their decisions under the extremely narrow criteria for Extraordinary Challenge Committee actions over initial panel decisions.

Conclusion

The NAFTA was controversial when it was negotiated, and it remains so. Recall that in 1990, at the time negotiations over the NAFTA were beginning, when running for the Republican Party's presidential nomination Patrick Buchanan seized on the NAFTA and opposed its adoption on the ground that it infringed on national sovereignty. Recall also, as a further measure of the controversy sparked by the NAFTA, that it was not approved by a two-thirds vote of the Senate, as required under the Treaty Clause of Article II of the U.S. Constitution. Instead, it was approved as "fast track" legislation, requiring the approval of simple majorities in both the House of Representatives and the Senate. And the NAFTA Implementation Act was ultimately approved on December 8, 1993 by a bitterly divided vote in the House of 234 to 200, and a 61 to 38 vote in the Senate.[32]

Opponents—including an odd mix of some conservatives, labor unions, and environmental interest groups—continue to challenge the constitutionality of the NAFTA, and in particular its method of adoption as well as its dis-

---

31. See, for example, *Certain Solder Joint Pressure Pipe Fittings*, 18; *Certain Cold-Reduced Flat Rolled Steel Products of Carbon Steel*, 18; and *Mexican Antidumping Investigation into Imports of Cut-to-Length Plate Products from the United States*, 1995 FTAPD LEXIS 11, 46-47.

32. See 138 *Congressional Record* H10,048 (daily ed., November 17, 1993); and 139 *Congressional Record* S16,712-713 (daily ed., November 20, 1993).

pute resolution provisions. Most of the lawsuits, as noted earlier, have been dismissed because federal courts have denied standing to the parties to bring the suits.[33] However, federal district court Judge Robert B. Propst in a lengthy opinion did conclude that the passage of the NAFTA as "fast track" legislation was a constitutional exercise of Congress's power under the Commerce Clause of Article I and did not have to be ratified under the Treaty Clause by a two-thirds majority of the Senate.[34] Moreover, Judge Propst proceeded to consider and reject the plaintiffs' arguments that the NAFTA and its provisions for dispute resolution by binational panels infringed on national sovereignty. Nonetheless, in due course in 2001, a panel of the U.S. Court of Appeals for the Eleventh Circuit reversed Judge Propst's ruling upon concluding that the challenge to the NAFTA's constitutionality presented a "nonjusticiable political question."[35]

It seems fair to conclude that the prospects for a definitive judicial ruling on the constitutionality of the NAFTA are not very good and, in any event, would not likely allay the fears of critics who charge that the NAFTA undermines national sovereignty. Admittedly, some legal scholars and defenders of the NAFTA counter that, "Viewed in traditional public international law terms, adherence to these international treaties [including the NAFTA] is, by its very nature, an affirmation of sovereignty and not a denial or limitation of it."[36] Such arguments, to be sure, are undoubtedly unpersuasive and not reassuring for the most strident of the NAFTA's critics.[37] But, the fact remains that, politically, the seventeenth-century concept of national sovereignty has been, and continues to undergo, a fundamental transformation as a result of the pressures of greater economic "regionalization" and "globalization." The NAFTA binational panels, no less than the ECJ and other supranational courts and tribunals, reflect the inexorable movement toward overlapping public and private spheres of governance—and hence dispute resolution processes—that transcend national territories, boundaries, and old doctrines of national sovereignty.

---

33. See, for example, *American Coalition for Competitive Trade v. United States.*

34. *Made in the USA Foundation, United Steel Workers of America, Local 12L United Steel Workers v. United States* (1999), 56 F. Supp. 2s 1226.

35. *Made in the USA Foundation, United Steel Workers of America, Local 12L United Steel Workers v. United States* (11th Cir., 2001), 242 F.3d 1300.

36. Lawrence L. Herman, "Sovereignty Revisited: Settlement of International Trade Disputes—Challenge to Sovereignty—A Canadian Perspective," 24 *Canada-United States Law Review* (1998), 122.

37. See, for example, Anthony DePalma, "NAFTA's Powerful Little Secret: Obscure Tribunals Settle Disputes, but Go Too Fat, Critics Say," *New York Times* (March 11, 2001), C1.

CHAPTER 9

SOVEREIGNTY, TRANSNATIONAL CONSTRAINTS, AND UNIVERSAL CRIMINAL JURISDICTION

Donald W. Jackson

Sovereignty is a much-abused concept. It is often invoked in the hope that it will serve as an impenetrable shield against intrusions upon state preroga-tives, even while it is denigrated by others—even in the same context—as an artifice for avoiding accountability for misdeeds both of states and their lead-ers. The short lesson of this paper is that sovereignty has always had various and inconstant meanings. It is a fickle word whose meanings most often have been socially constructed for instrumental purposes.[1] In the first decade of the twenty-first century, the efficacy of sovereignty as a shield is clearly in decline, except, of course, for those nations whose economic or military powers con-tinue to fortify its potency. But then it is power, rather than the concept of sovereignty, that wins. The United States is the most conspicuous of such na-tions, and its opposition to the proposed International Criminal Court (ICC) is an excellent example of its interest in preserving its "sovereignty" against the constraints even of international law. The Rome Statute for the ICC provides for an international tribunal to try war crimes, crimes against humanity, and genocide. The Court was ratified on April 11, 2002 with 60 state signatories. It entered into force on July 1, 2002.

Two sorts of constraints on the prerogatives of sovereignty are considered in this paper. The first are transnational and regional, those contained in agreements, such as the European Convention on Human Rights.[2] The sec-

---

1. See, for example, a book with an insightful title: Thomas J. Biersteker and Cynthia Weber (eds.), *State Sovereignty as Social Construct* (Cambridge: Cambridge University Press, 1996).

2. Council of Europe, *The European Convention for the Protection of Human Rights and*

ond sort of constraint, the concept of universal criminal *jurisdiction*, may rest either on *jus cogens*[3] under customary international law, or on obligations undertaken under (potentially) global conventions (such as the Rome Statute for the ICC).

Meanings of Sovereignty

The inconstant meanings of sovereignty are well illustrated by a two-part article written in the latter days of World War II, when the Allies were seeking a "new world order" for that time, an article with the suggestive title, "On Relative Sovereignty."[4] Hans Aufricht wrote that many students of sovereignty had previously and recently argued against it as an absolute concept, insisting that it should be relative. The simple notion was the supremacy of law could be accorded domestic or international norms, but not both. Thus an *absolute* sovereign state would be one that is independent of any superior entity and simultaneously independent of any superior law. However, under *relative* sovereignty, an independent or sovereign state might be independent of any superior entity, but it might still be dependent on international law. Indeed, it was international law that first defined the requisites and prerogatives of independent or sovereign states.[5]

While it may have been the case that in 1944-45 the preponderance of relationships between independent states and superior international law were

---

Fundamental Freedoms (ECHR, 1950).

3. *Jus cogens* [*Latin, lit.: compelling right. English: peremptory norm*]: The norms recognized under *jus cogens* are supposed to be absolutely binding on all states in the world, at all times. Norms against genocide, slavery, and torture are examples. See H. Victor Condé, *A Handbook of International Rights Terminology* (Lincoln, NE: University of Nebraska Press, 1999). According to one authority, the phrase first appeared in modern positive international law in the 1969 Vienna Convention on the Law of Treaties, Art. 53, which defined *jus cogens* as a "peremptory norm of general international law . . . recognized by the international community of states as a whole from which no derogation is permitted." See Alfred P. Rubin, "*Actio Popularis, Jus Cogens* and Offenses *Erga Omnes*?", 35 (2) *New England Law Review* (2001), 271.

4. Hans Aufricht, "On Relative Sovereignty," parts I and II, 30 *Cornell Law Quarterly* (1944–45), 137–59, 318–49.

5. According to the Restatement (Third), *Foreign Relations Law of the United States* (New York: American Law Institute, 1987), Section 201, "Under international law, a state is an entity that has a defined territory and a permanent population, under the control of its own government, and that engages in, or has the capacity to engage in, formal relations with other such entities."

found in treaties, such as in adherence to the jurisdiction of the Permanent Court of International Justice (as it then was), even then, customary international law sometimes had universal application, as in the rules concerning the privileges and immunities of diplomatic representatives.

It was also the case that the claims of absolute sovereignty were then besmirched by the extravagant and offensive claims of the Third Reich. Thus in 1944, Aufricht noted the fundamental claim of Nazi jurisprudence that, "Law is what is advantageous to the national community" (*Recht ist was der Volksgemeinschaft nützt*), so that "the German Reich is justified in disregarding any legal obligation which is incompatible with the real or alleged advantage of the German nation."[6] The Western Allies were then strongly arrayed against such claims and the Nuremberg trials directly contradicted absolute sovereignty.[7]

Thus, it is instructive to note that on December 7, 2001, the U.S. Senate voted 78-21 in favor of a provision, the American Service Members Protection Act (ASPA) first proposed by Senator Jesses Helms (R., NC), which would bar U.S. cooperation with the prospective International Criminal Court. It also provided for the president to use "all means necessary and appropriate" to free any American detained under the authority of the ICC, and would limit U.S. involvement in U.N. peacekeeping missions unless the U.N. specifically exempts American forces from prosecution before the ICC. The provision also would restrict foreign aid to any country that fails to sign an agreement protecting American troops within their borders from ICC jurisdiction.[8] On December 20, 2001, the ASPA provision was dropped from the Department of Defense Appropriations Bill, but anti-ICC members of Congress promise to revive it. The contrast between the U.S. views on sovereignty at the end of World War II and the present anti-ICC movement, with strong bipartisan support, represents a stark tidal change.

Aufricht duly noted in 1945 that "international law comprises rules addressed to states, private individuals and supranational [agencies],"[9] while the U.S. now essentially takes the World War II German position of being immune to such rules, albeit for different reasons. Aufricht recognized that the tide at

---

6. Aufricht, "On Relative Sovereignty," 4, 145.

7. Unless one discounts the Nuremberg precedent as simply "victors' justice," as indeed some do.

8. Alan Fram, "Senate Votes Against International Criminal Court," Associated Press (December 7, 2001). Listserv icc-info@yahoo.groups.com, consulted on December 10, 2001.

9. Aufricht, "On Relative Sovereignty," 4, 325.

the end of World War II, including the U.S., ran toward international protection of human rights.[10]

Of course, the contrary premise that sovereignty must be absolute has a long and strong lineage. Jean Bodin wrote in 1576 that "Sovereignty is the absolute and perpetual power of a commonwealth,"[11] but his definition was based on the premise that only "sovereign princes" could be the repositories of sovereignty:

> For the prerogatives of sovereignty have to be of such a sort that they apply only to a sovereign prince. If, on the contrary, they can be shared with subjects, one cannot say that they are the marks of sovereignty. For just as a crown no longer has that name if it is breached, or if its rosettes are torn away, so sovereign majesty loses its greatness if someone makes a breach in it and encroaches on a party of its domain.[12]

According to Bodin the prerogatives of sovereign princes include the Powers (1) to make law, (2) to declare war or make peace, (3) to establish the principal officers of the state, (4) to judge controversies (in the last instance), and (5) to grant pardons and remissions from the rigid application of the law. Unfortunately, his description became, "a convenient supplementary secular slogan for the various absolute monarchies of the time".[13] Even though Bodin's conception does not rest on the divine right of kings, clearly his is not a foundation for sovereignty that fits comfortably with U.S. constitutional traditions, or indeed with those of modern European democracies.[14]

It was the Peace of Westphalia, the political settlement of the Thirty Years War signed at Munster in 1648, that gave us the modern state-based system of sovereignty. A major consequence of the Peace was the rise of new political en-

---

10. Hans Aufricht cites the report by Quincy Wright, *Human Rights and the World Order* (New York: Commission to Study the Organization of Peace, 1943). This report argued that the enforcement of a universal bill of human rights [note: the Universal Declaration of Human Rights was adopted by the U.N. General Assembly five years later in 1948] eventually might rely on an international political council or on an international court that "might be vested with authority to render preventive or remedial judgments whenever a state invoked its authority, in case impairments of the bill of human rights were anticipated or alleged" (29).

11. Jean Bodin, *On Sovereignty: Four Chapters from the Six Books on the Commonwealth*, translated and edited by Julian H. Franklin (Cambridge: Cambridge University Press, 1992), 1.

12. Ibid., 10.

13. W. Michael Reisman, "Sovereignty and Human Rights in Contemporary International Law," 84 *The American Journal of International Law* (1990), 866–76.

14. Various commentators note that Bodin's description of sovereign authority was also consistent with the authoritarian tone of Calvin Hobbes's *Leviathan*.

tities (states) and the decline, relatively, of the Holy Roman Empire and of the Catholic Church. One scholar describes the elements of this system as:

> a set of norms, mutually agreed upon by polities who are members of the society, that define the holders of authority and the prerogatives, specifically in answer to three questions: Who are these legitimate polities? What are the rules for becoming one of these polities? And what are the basic prerogatives of these polities?[15]

The keys to the emergence of this system required state-based institutions with discernible and enforceable geographic boundaries and the elimination of those authorities that would interfere effectively from outside.[16] But the question remained: whether such state-based sovereignty must be supreme and absolute within its boundaries. The answer usually depends on who is asking that question and for what purposes. For Bodin, all authority must be lodged in one *sovereign*. However, absolute *state* sovereignty was the ideal of the Peace of Westphalia, just as it still is the putative last refuge of some nation-states today. Still, many constitutional systems developed over the past three centuries commonly have involved both the geographic division of powers within a polity (federalism) as well as the institutional separation of powers. Likewise, rights documents have long purported to limit the powers of governments over their citizens through entrenched provisions.

The idea that state sovereignty includes the principle of non-intervention, which has been called the "key prerogative of modern states" and which also may be understood as the foundation of state independence, did not arise as an important idea until the eighteenth century.[17] But non-intervention as a fundamental attribute on state independence does not necessarily mean that states are empowered to do whatever they will to their citizens—or to others within their boundaries. Indeed, non-intervention is enshrined in Article 2.7 of the United Nations Charter, *provided* that state policies are "essentially within [their] domestic jurisdiction," while Article 2.4 requires U.N. members to "refrain in their international relations from the threat or use of force against the territorial integrity or political independence of any state." Yet indeed, these provisions have been invoked by states that have been accused of human rights violations. They claim that interference in such affairs violates matters within their exclusive domestic jurisdiction, but the contemporary an-

---

15. Daniel Philpott, "Westphalia, Authority and International Society," 47 *Political Studies* (1999), 567.

16. Ibid., 569.

17. Ibid., 582.

swer (or the one that is in the process of becoming) is this: No state has the right to violate human rights as part of its sovereign domestic jurisdiction. The steps in this process of becoming represent the balance of this paper.

Transnational Constraints: The British Experience

The European states that are members of the Council of Europe (and thereby are adherents to the European Convention on Human Rights) have obligated themselves to abide by the decisions of the European Court of Human Rights, which sits at Strasbourg. That court, whose judges were first elected in 1959, is the oldest and, by the experience of actual cases, the most solidly established regional human rights forum.[18] For example, the salience of the court may be reflected in the filing of a case there in late December 2001 against the Netherlands on behalf of Slobodan Milosevic, claiming that his arrest, detention at The Hague, and pending trial before the International Criminal Tribunal for the Former Yugoslavia violated the European Convention on Human Rights.[19]

The European Convention for the Protection of Human Rights and Fundamental Freedoms (ECHR), which has been amended or supplemented by eleven protocols, first went into effect in September 1953. The most important changes respecting the structure and process of its enforcement institutions since its creation are found in Protocol 11, which entered into force respecting the then-41 contracting European state parties on November 1, 1998. This Protocol established a full-time court, replacing the part-time European Commission and Court of Human Rights.[20]

One of the best illustrations of the potential impact of the European Court of Human Rights on its member states can be found in its cases from the United Kingdom. During the first 30 years of the Court's existence (1959-89),[21] the U.K. was found to be in violation of the ECHR 23 times; it was the

---

18. The Inter-American Court on Human Rights was established in 1979, but rendered its first decisions on contentious cases in the late 1980s.

19. "World Briefing/Europe: Yugoslavia: Milosevic Challenges His Arrest," *New York Times*, December 22, 2001 (accessed through http://nytimes.qpass.com).

20. This section draws on my essay on the European Commission and Court of Human Rights in the forthcoming book: Herbert Kritzer (ed.), *Legal Systems of the World: A Political, Social and Cultural Encyclopedia* (Santa Barbara, CA: ABC-CLIO).

21. For an excellent overview of the European human rights system prior to the recent reforms, see R. St. J. Macdonald, F. Matscher, and H. Petzold (eds.), *The European System for the Protection of Human Rights* (Boston: Martinus Nijhoff, 1993).

country most frequently before the court, measured both by the number of complaints filed and by the number of violations found. My own study of these violations focused on violations arising from the "prevention of terrorism" in Northern Ireland, the operation of U.K. prisons, freedom of expression (especially freedom of the press), and immigration and citizenship policy.[22] Since the end of 1989 through published case reports for March 2002,[23] the United Kingdom has been found guilty of violations in another 44 cases.[24] The preponderance of these violations have concerned issues concerning detention and hearing/due process issues (Articles 5 and 6), although it is interesting to note that since June 1996, six violations of Article 3 (inhuman or degrading treatment),[25] eight violations of Article 8 (respect for privacy and family life),[26] and three violations of Article 10 (freedom of expression)[27] have been found.

---

22. Donald W. Jackson, *The United Kingdom Confronts the European Convention on Human Rights* (Gainesville, FL: University Press of Florida, 1997).

23. In the *European Human Rights Reports* (London: Sweet & Maxwell).

24. My book covered the 41 violations found through case reports for June 1996.

25. *Chahal v. U.K.*, 23 Eur. Court H.R. 413 (May 1997, Chahal, a Sikh separatist, whose deportation posed a risk of torture); *D v. U.K.*, 24 Eur. Court H.R. 423 (November 1997, D, drug courier with AIDS, whose deportation to St. Kitts would constitute inhuman treatment given his condition); *A v. U.K.*, 27 Eur. Court H.R. 611 (June 1999, a child who had been severely beaten by this father had not been sufficiently protected under U.K. law); *Hilal v. U.K.*, 33 Eur. Court H.R. 31 (July 2001, Hilal's deportation to Zanzibar offered the prospect of inhuman treatment); *Keenan v. U.K.*, 33 Eur. Court H.R. 913 (April 2001, Keenan, an inmate of Exeter prison who committed suicide, had been insufficiently protected by prison authorities); and *Z and Others v. U.K.*, 34 Eur. Court H.R. 97 (January 2002, failure of local authority to protect child from severe neglect and abuse).

26. *Halford v. U.K.*, 24 Eur. Court H.R. 523 (December 1997, Halford, a former assistant chief constable whose home and office calls had been intercepted); *McLeod v. U.K.*, 27 Eur. Court H.R. 493 (May 1999, police entry into home); *Smith and Grady v. U.K.*, 29 Eur. Court H.R. 493 (May 2000, Ministry of Defense investigation of sexual orientation of serving members of the Royal Navy); *Lustig-Prean and Beckett v. U.K.*, 29 Eur. Court H.R. 548 (September 1999, as in *Smith and Grady*); *Adt v. U.K.*, 31 Eur. Court H.R. 803 (May 2001, laws prohibiting male homosexual conduct in private); *Khan v. U.K.*, 31 Eur. Court H.R. 1016 (June 2001, eavesdropping); *Hatton and Others v. U.K.*, 34 Eur. Court H.R. 1 (January 2002, noise levels from airport); and *TP and KM v. U.K.*, 34 Eur. Court H.R. 42 (January 2002, wrongful removal of child into care by local authority).

27. *Bowman v. U.K.*, 26 Eur. Court H.R. 1 (July 1998, limits on expenditures for distribution of literature in an election); *Steel and Others v. U.K.*, 28 Eur. Court H.R. 603 (December 1999, activists protesting the sale of fighter aircraft); and *Hashman and Harrup v. U.K.*, 30 Eur. Court H.R. 241 (September 2000, animal rights anti-hunt activists).

Among the several reasons suggested for the frequency of ECHR violations by the U.K. was that it had no entrenched rights document and that the provisions of the ECHR had not been made directly applicable in U.K. courts, as they had in most other adherent countries. Other possible factors in the frequency of U.K. cases are the availability of advocates willing to take such cases and the activity of human rights non-governmental organizations (NGOs).[28] Whatever the contributing causes, the frequency of violations produced reactions in the U.K. ranging from severe embarrassment to anger and denunciation of the European Court of Human Rights.

Proponents of reform have long urged that the U.K. adopt its own rights document, but in the U.K. that runs up against the doctrine of parliamentary supremacy, which holds that the elected representatives of the people ought to be able to legislate on any subject and that one Parliament should not be able to bind its successors by entrenching a rights document against subsequent legislation. Moreover, along with parliamentary sovereignty as a remedy for the abuses of power, skepticism about entrenched rights has been a long tradition in the U.K.,[29] as represented by this quote from Dicey, which appears in a recent human rights text:

> [M]ost foreign constitution makers have begun with declarations of rights. For this they have often been in no way to blame.…On the other hand, there remains through the English constitution that inseparable connection between enforcing a right and the right to be enforced which is the strength of judicial legislation. The law…means that the Englishmen whose labours gradually framed the completed set of laws and institutions which we call the Constitution, fixed their minds more intently on providing the remedies for the enforcement of particular rights…than upon any Declaration of the Rights of Man or of Englishmen.[30]

However, everyone understands that certain decisions in fact and deed are not reversible by Parliament. Membership in the European Union is one such

---

28. Probably the best recent book on the key role of NGOs in supporting rights litigation is Charles Epp, *The Rights Revolution: Lawyers, Activists, and Supreme Courts in Comparative Perspective* (Chicago: University of Chicago Press, 1998).

29. For a good review of individual rights in the U.K. prior to the Human Rights Act 1998, see Christopher McCrudden and Gerald Chambers (eds.), *Individual Rights and the Law in Britain* (Oxford: Clarendon Press, 1994).

30. A. Dicey, *An Introduction to the Study of the Law and the Constitution* (London: Macmillan, 1965), 198–99, as quoted in Richard Clayton and Hugh Tomlinson, *The Law of Human Rights* (Oxford: Oxford University Press, 2000), 25.

decision. Through that membership the policies of the Union and the decisions of its Court of Justice have binding authority over U.K. governments and over Parliament; the U.K. exit from the Union is unthinkable except perhaps for the dreams of the most anti-European members of the Conservative Party. Indeed, Leslie Goldstein's recent book, *Constituting Federal Sovereignty*, concludes that resistance of member states to central European Union authority and policies have been rare compared to the other federations she studied.[31] Even though Euro-skeptics have been more influential in the U.K. than in most European countries, there is no practical path back from Europe and even more enhanced federalism is on the horizon.

Rather than attempting to withdraw into an island kingdom, the practical solution for the many violations of the ECHR by the U.K. was the adoption of the Human Rights Act 1998.[32] In addition to giving the provisions of the ECHR full effect in U.K. domestic law (giving U.K. courts the opportunity to enforce the ECHR, rather than having such cases decided in the first instance at Strasbourg), that act provides in Section 3 that in U.K. cases involving a possible conflict between a U.K. statute and the provisions of the ECHR: "So far as it is possible to do so,…legislation must be read and given effect in a way that is compatible with Convention rights." However, under Section 4, when a U.K. court is "satisfied that [a] provision is incompatible with a Convention right, it may make a declaration of that incompatibility."[33] Finally, Section 10 provides that in the event of such incompatibility, appropriate (and accelerated) steps may be taken to amend the law to remove the incompatibility. That leaves Parliament (nominally at least) with the last say. That is about as close to granting to U.K. courts the right to annul acts of Parliament as we are likely to see.

It is now clear that membership in the Council of Europe and adherence to the ECHR has made sovereign authority in the United Kingdom subject to the decisions of a transnational human rights court, while the European Union and its Court of Justice seem well advanced on the road toward a federated Europe.[34]

---

31. Leslie Friedman Goldstein, *Constituting Federal Sovereignty: The European Union in Comparative Context* (Baltimore: The Johns Hopkins University Press, 2001), 150. These were the United States, the Dutch Republic, and the Swiss Federation.

32. Christopher Baker (ed.), *Human Rights Act 1998: A Practitioner's Guide* (London: Sweet and Maxwell, 1998).

33. Section 4(6) says that such a declaration does not void the statute.

34. Goldstein, *Constituting Federal Sovereignty*, 31, 17–18. Neil MacCormick argues that "the United Kingdom and its European partners are 'post sovereign states' as members of the European Community." Neil MacCormick, *Questioning Sovereignty: Law State and Nation in the European Commonwealth* (Oxford: Oxford University Press, 1999), 73, 131 et seq.

Universal Criminal Jurisdiction

Broadly defined, universal jurisdiction is the authority of state courts or international tribunals with criminal jurisdiction to prosecute certain crimes recognized under international law, no matter where the offense occurred or regardless of the nationality of either the victim or the perpetrator. Universal jurisdiction currently is a hot topic among international lawyers and human rights NGOs,[35] although it has reached the consciousness of few others, excepting international law professors, especially in the U.S.[36] It also is viewed in a much more friendly manner—by those who follow such developments —in Europe than in the United States (at least when it has the potential of actually applying to the conduct of the U.S. government or its military, rather than to atrocities committed by the "genocidal" leaders of "rogue" states, for example, those within the former Yugoslavia). While human rights NGOs have their own statements on universal jurisdiction,[37] perhaps the most notable recent explication of universal jurisdiction is that contained in the Princeton Principles on Universal Jurisdiction.[38] That is where this essay will end, but it is useful first to review some of the steps leading up to such a statement of principles.

---

35. Note, for example, two recent conferences in Europe. The first, "Shifting Boundaries: A Conference on Moving from a Culture of Impunity to a Culture of Accountability," was convened by the Netherlands Institute for Human Rights (SIM), Utrecht University, and the United Nations University (Tokyo) in Utrecht in late November, 2001. The second, "Combating Impunity: Stakes and Perspectives," was convened in Brussels in March 2002 by the NGO Coalition for the International Criminal Court and the Belgian Ministry of Foreign Affairs.

36. Notable exceptions in the United States include a Symposium on "Universal Jurisdiction: Myths, Realities and Prospects," held in Boston in November, 2000, its papers being presented in Volume 35, no. 2 of the *New England Law Review* (Winter 2001), and a conference on "International Justice, War Crimes and Terrorism: The U.S. Record," held in New York City at the New School University in April 2002.

37. Amnesty International, for example, has a statement containing fourteen principles. See <www.amnesty.org>, under universal jurisdiction, for various documents on the subject. Also see Amnesty International, *Universal Jurisdiction: The Duty of States to Enact and Implement Legislation* (available on CD-ROM, AI Index: IOR 53/002-018/2001.)

38. Princeton Project on Universal Jurisdiction, "The Princeton Principles on Universal Jurisdiction" (2001). <www.princeton.edu/~lapa/univ_jur.pdf>, consulted on December 14, 2001.

Precedents from the Past Relative to Universal Jurisdiction

Most scholars cite Hugo Grotius' *De Jure Belli ac Paci Libri Tres* (1625)[39] as the first overview of positive public international law, most of it covering the law of war as applied to states, and not with criminal responsibility.

Piracy and Slavery

Some scholars argue that piracy[40] was the first subject of universal jurisdiction in favor of any state that would enforce a prohibition against such acts. However, Alfred Rubin, an authority of the law of piracy, concludes that "there has never been a successful prosecution in any country for piracy without the prosecuting state's jurisdiction being based on nationality: of the offender,… the victims,…the ship, or the territory where the act occurred."[41] These days the 1982 *Convention on the Law of the Sea*[42] provides in Article 105 that "*every State* may seize a pirate ship or aircraft, or a ship taken by piracy and under the control of pirates, and arrest the persons and seize the property on board." The courts of the State that accomplished the seizure have jurisdiction to try and punish pirates who are seized.[43]

The *Brussels Act* (1890) was the first "comprehensive treaty" on the slave trade. Through that act the major trading nations, excepting France, agreed to outlaw the slave trade on the high seas and to arrest anyone engaged in transporting slaves (Anti-Slavery International, 2001). This Act was followed by the *Slavery Convention* of 1926 and then by the U.N. *Supplementary Convention on the Abolition of Slavery, the Slave Trade and Institutions and Practices Similar to Slavery* (1956), which has 118 participating State Parties.[44] The 1957 Convention provides in Article 3 that trading in slaves "shall be a crim-

---

39. Hugo Grotius, *De Jure Belli Ac Pacis Libri Tres* (Oxford: Oxford University Press, 1925 ed.).

40. Defined as any authorized act of violence committed by a private vessel on the open sea against another vessel with intent to plunder.

41. Michael P. Scharf and Thomas P. Fisher, "Forward," in "Symposium: Universal Jurisdiction: Myths, Realities, and Prospects," 35 (2) *New England Law Review* (2001), 228.

42. This Convention carries forward provisions from the 1958 Geneva Convention on the High Seas.

43. Gerhard Von Glahn, *Law Among Nations: An Introduction to Public International Law* (New York: Macmillan, 1992), 327.

44. Human Rights Library, University of Minnesota, "Supplementary Convention on the Abolition of Slavery, the Slave Trade and Institutions and Practices Similar to Slavery"

inal offense" under the laws of the State Parties that adhere to the treaty. It was crime on the high seas that gave both piracy and the transporting of slaves their relatively early criminal status under international law.

Nuremberg

A commission was created by the Allies at the end of World War I with a key issue being the prosecution of Kaiser Wilhelm and other German "war criminals" for "crimes against the laws of humanity." Eventually Article 227 of the Treaty of Versailles called for an ad hoc tribunal to prosecute the Kaiser for a "supreme offense against international morality and the sanctity of treaties."[45] The Kaiser's escape to the Netherlands and that country's refusal to extradite him effectively ended that prospect. Only a few German officials were prosecuted and only token sentences were imposed.

So it was the Nuremberg Charter[46] and the ensuing prosecutions that were the principal twentieth-century precedents for universal jurisdiction. The Charter created the International Military Tribunal to consist of four judges (one from each of the four powers), and the jurisdiction of the tribunal was defined to include the following crimes:[47]

> Crimes against Peace. Art. 6(a): Planning, preparation, initiation or waging of a war of aggression, or a war in violation of international treaties or agreements.
> War Crimes. Art 6(b): Violations of the laws or customs of war, to include murder, ill-treatment or deportation to slave labor...of civilian population of an occupied territory, ill-treatment of prisoners of war or persons on the seas, killing of hostages, plunder of public or private property, wanton destruction of cities, or devastation not justified by military necessity.
> Crimes Against Humanity. Art. 6(c): Murder, extermination, enslavement, deportation and other inhuman acts committed against any civilian population, or persecutions on political, racial or religious grounds in execution of or in connection with any crime within

---

(2001). <www1.umnedu/humanrts/instree/f3scas.htm, consulted on December 17, 2001>.

45. Von Glahn, *Law Among Nations*, 41, 878.

46. Also known as the London Charter for the Prosecution and Punishment of Major War Criminals of the European Axis (August 1945).

47. Genocide will be considered separately below.

the jurisdiction of the Tribunal, whether or not in violation of the domestic law of the country where perpetrated.

The war crimes specified in Article 6(b) of the London Charter in turn were based in part on customary international law as set out in the 1899[48] and 1907 Hague Conventions and the 1929 Geneva Convention Relative to Treatment of Prisoners of War.[49] The London Charter and the Nuremberg Precedent were affirmed in 1946 by the General Assembly of the United Nations in Resolution 95(I). Three features of the Charter particularly sustained universal jurisdiction. The first was in Article 6(c), which established crimes against humanity regardless of their criminality under the jurisdiction of the country where perpetrated. The second was in Article 7, which provided that there should be no immunity for heads of state or high government officials. The third, in Article 8, denied the defense of superior orders to a defendant, while allowing consideration of such in mitigation of punishment.

Genocide

In December 1946, the General Assembly of the U.N. adopted Resolution 96(I), which expressly made genocide (derived from the London Charter's definition of crimes against humanity) a crime under international law. Two years later the General Assembly adopted the Convention on the Prevention and Punishment of the Crime of Genocide (1948). Genocide was defined in Article 2 as acts committed with the intent to destroy, in whole or in part, a national, ethnical, racial, or religious group. The listed acts included murder, causing serious bodily injury or mental harm, restricting births within a group, or forcibly transferring children from one group to another group. Such crimes could be prosecuted in the territory where the acts were committed or in an international criminal tribunal created by the parties to the Convention. Genocide could not be treated as a political crime under the Convention for the purpose of denying extradition and the contracting parties pledged to grant requests for extradition in accordance with their laws or treaties in force (Article 7). In 1951, the International Court of Justice issued an advisory opinion holding that the crime of genocide is *jus cogens* and not

---

48. 1899 Convention on the Law and Customs of War on Land.

49. M. Cherif Bassiouni, "From Versailles to Rwanda in Seventy-five Years: The Need to Establish a Permanent International Criminal Court," 10 *Harvard Human Rights Law Journal* (1997), 11–62.

subject to derogation.[50] The Restatement (Third) Foreign Relations Law of the United States (1987) treats genocide as an offense for which all states have universal jurisdiction under *jus cogens*. Grave breaches of the Geneva Conventions are also subject to prosecution by all nations.

Geneva Conventions of 1949

The International Committee of the Red Cross, working with the Swiss government, convened a conference in 1949 on the protection of the victims of war that eventually led to four conventions.[51] Convention IV, on the protection of civilians in time of war, is the one most directly involved in defining crimes against humanity. Under Article 146 states have a duty to prosecute perpetrators, "*regardless of their own nationality*," for grave breaches of the Convention. Those states that are unwilling to prosecute under Convention IV have a duty to extradite to a country that is willing.[52]

It is important to note that in *Demjanjuk v. Petrovsky* (1985), a federal circuit court said with respect to war crimes, "The underlying assumption is that the crimes are offenses against the law of nations or against humanity and the prosecuting nation is acting for all nations."[53]

The Eichmann Case[54]

The Decision of the District Court of Jerusalem of 1961 and of the Supreme Court of Israel of 1962 upholding the conviction of Adolf Eichmann for mass murder was based on the "universal character of the crimes committed and on the crime of genocide as recognized by the Genocide Convention two years before,"[55] even under the circumstances of Eichmann's abduction from Ar-

---

50. *Advisory Opinion*, I.C.J., May 28, 1951.

51. Convention I dealt with treatment of the wounded and sick of armed forces in the field; II dealt with armed conflict at sea; III dealt with prisoners of war. President George W. Bush's recent Executive Order authorizing trials before military tribunals for foreign nationals engaged in acts of terrorism against the United States may violate several provisions of Convention III. See *New York Times* (December 26, 2001), B6.

52. Von Glahn, *Law Among Nations*, 41, 889.

53. *Demjanjuk*, 777 F2d 571 (6th Cir. 1985), 582, cited by Henry T. King, Jr., "Universal Jurisdiction: Myths, Realities, Prospects, War Crimes and Crimes Against Humanity: The Nuremberg Precedent," 35 *New England Law Review* (2001), 285.

54. A fascinating account of the Eichmann abduction can be found in Peter Z. Malkin and Harry Stein, *Eichmann in My Hands* (New York: Warner Books, 1990).

55. Henry J. Steiner and Philip Alston, *International Human Rights in Context: Law, Politics, Morals* (Oxford: Oxford University Press, 2000), 1034–36.

gentina and his trial in the courts of a state that did not exist when his crimes were committed.[56]

Torture

In 1984, the U.N. General Assembly adopted the Convention Against Torture and Other Cruel, Inhuman or Degrading Treatment or Punishment. That Convention entered into force in 1987. The Convention, by itself, may have had little direct effect through the Committee Against Torture (CAT) established by the Convention, however torture now is also recognized as *jus cogens* and subject to universal jurisdiction under customary international law.[57] The case against General Pinochet in Spain and Britain (considered below) was on torture and conspiracy to torture. Torture represents one of several instances in which U.S. case law expressly sustains universal jurisdiction. (See *Filártiga v. Peña-Irala* (1980), *Committee of U.S. Citizens Living in Nicaragua v. Reagan* (1988), and *Kadic v. Karadzic* (1995).)[58]

Contemporary Developments

Contemporary, in the sense of this section, begins with the vote of the U.N. Security Council on February 22, 1993 to create an ad hoc International Criminal Tribunal for the former Yugoslavia,[59] but key events have accelerated in frequency since 1998, beginning with the U.N. Conference in Rome in July

---

56. Such abduction is, under international law, regarded as an act against the state in which the person abducted resides, and does not support the denial of criminal jurisdiction because of the abduction. In this instance Israel apologized and Argentina did not press the issue. See Von Glann, *Law Among Nations,* 41, 314–15.

57. Malcolm D. Evans and Rod Morgan, *Preventing Torture: A Study of the European Convention for the Prevention of Torture and Inhuman or Degrading Treatment or Punishment* (Oxford: Oxford University Press, 1999), 62.

58. Under the Alien Tort Claims Act (1789), federal courts have "jurisdiction for suits alleging torts committed anywhere in the world against aliens in violation of the law of nations." *Kadic v. Karadzic* (2d Cir., 1995), 70 F.3d 232. Liability may thus be found for genocide, war crimes, and crimes against humanity. See also *Filártiga v. Peña-Irala* (2d Cir., 1980), 630 F2d 876; and *Committee of U.S. Citizens Living in Nicaragua v. Reagan* (D.C. Cir., 1988), 859 F2d 929.

59. For an excellent review of war crimes litigation, with a focus on the prosecutions from the former Yugoslavia, see Aryeh Neier, *War Crimes: Brutality, Genocide, Terror and the Struggle for Justice* (New York: Times Books, 1998). On the politics of war crimes tribunals, see Gary Jonathan Bass, *Stay the Hand of Vengeance: The Politics of War Crimes Tribunals* (Princeton: Princeton University Press, 2000).

1998 on the creation of a permanent International Criminal Court and the arrest of General Pinochet in London in October 1998.

The precedents reviewed in this section all illustrate current trends in criminal accountability through the application of universal jurisdiction. Most, but not all, are positive outcomes. Those reviewed here are exemplary.

Ad Hoc Tribunals

The International Criminal Tribunal for the Former Yugoslavia (ICTY) was created by a Security Council resolution in 1993 and held its first session at The Hague on November 17, 1993. The International Criminal Tribunal for Rwanda (ICTR) was created by Security Council vote of November 8, 1994, and currently sits in Arusha, Tanzania. The Security Council's referral to these tribunals empowers them to adjudicate the commission of crimes against humanity in both situations and, in principle, the Security Council's authority to refer cases to ad hoc tribunals could lead to the adjudication of such crimes anywhere in the world. That, of course, is one reason why the U.S., with its Security Council veto, prefers that such criminal prosecutions be under Security Council authorization. Probably the efficacy of the ICTY will be measured by the trial of Slobodan Milosevic, at least unless and until Franjo Tudjman (Croatia) and Radovan Karadzic and General Ratko Mladzic (Bosnian Serbs) are brought before the court.

The Pinochet Case[60]

The Pinochet precedent is an important step forward, for, at a minimum, it affirms the basis for prosecution of human rights violations of notorious public officials in the courts of nation-states, in this instance through the courts of the United Kingdom and Spain. The Spanish prosecution of Augusto Pinochet Ugarte began in May 1996 in a complaint that accused him and others of the deaths of Chileans and others of "diverse nationalities" through murder, torture, kidnapping, and disappearances from Chile and other countries during the years 1976-83. A request for Pinochet's arrest in the United King-

---

60. The background and documents in the Pinochet case are contained in Reed Brody and Michael Ratner (eds.), *The Pinochet Papers: The Case of Augusto Pinochet in Spain and Britain* (The Hague: Kluwer Law International, 2000). The information recited here is all drawn from that source.

dom was issued on October 16, 1998, and the first provisional warrant was issued that same day. The key final decision of the House of Lords, where the central question was whether Pinochet was entitled to state immunity from extradition, was rendered on March 24, 1999.[61]

The opinion of Lord Browne-Wilkinson in *Pinochet III* acknowledged universal jurisdiction over the international crime of torture, but turned on the question of whether international law grants immunity to heads of state respecting such crimes, and, if so, when such immunity ceases. If the organization of torture by General Pinochet could be seen to be part of his official functions as head of state, the immunity might continue even after he left office. So the case came down to the issue of whether the implementation of torture can be a state function.[62] The House of Lords found that it could not. The Torture Convention defines torture as pain and suffering "inflicted by or at the instigation of or with the consent or acquiescence of a *public official*," and requires each State Party to ensure that all acts of torture are offenses under its criminal law (which the U.K. did through the Criminal Justice Act 1989). The United Kingdom's ratification of the U.N. Torture Convention was effective from December 8, 1988, while Chile's ratification was in October 1988. Thus as of December 8, 1988, at the latest, the United Kingdom had the duty either to prosecute or extradite Pinochet. Thus Browne-Wilkinson's opinion rested on a treaty obligation, while others, including two judges in *Pinochet III* and the majority in *Pinochet I*, concluded that immunity should have been barred under customary international law.[63]

The Hissène Habré Case

The fragility even of partial victories like that in the Pinochet case is illustrated by a recent case from Senegal. Hissèn Habré is the former head of state of Chad, serving from 1982-90. His dictatorship was believed to be responsible for many serious human rights violations, but no actions against him were taken in Chad. Criminal proceedings for complicity in torture were brought against him in Senegal in February 2000 when a judge in Dakar indicted him

---

61. The decision of the House of Lords of November 25, 1998 (*Pinochet I*) was set aside on December 17, 1998 (*Pinochet II*) due to the appearance of a conflict of interest of Lord Hoffman in *Pinochet I*. The dispositive ruling was in *Pinochet III*, March 24, 1999.

62. Brody and Ratner, *The Pinochet Papers*, 58, 271.

63. Pinochet's de facto extradition to Spain and his eventual prosecution either in Spain or Chile turned on the question of his mental and/or physical capacity to stand trial, rather than on universal jurisdiction, and is beyond the scope of this paper

and ordered an investigation for other crimes against humanity. However, the prosecution was dismissed because the U.N. Torture Convention had not been implemented into Senegalese law, as required by the Convention. Since the crimes had not taken place in Senegal, the dismissal was confirmed by the Senegalese court of last resort (*Cour de cassation*) in March 2001.[64] This outcome stands in stark contrast with recent developments in Europe, of which Belgium may be the best example. Belgium stands out because following the negative decision in Senegal, a complaint was filed against Habré in Belgium. In September 2001, President Déby said in an interview that he was ready for "Habré to leave to a country 'capable of organizing a fair trial.' "[65] Since neither Senegal nor Chad opposes such a prosecution, there appears to be no jurisdictional obstacle to a trial in Belgium.

The Belgian Example

Belgium adopted several statutes that enabled the prosecution of international crimes within its courts. The Geneva Conventions have had application in Belgian courts since 1952 and the Additional Protocols I and II[66] since 1986. A 1993 law detailed the circumstances under which grave breaches of the Geneva Conventions could be tried and punished in Belgium. In 1999, Belgium added genocide and crimes against humanity to those over which its courts can exercise universal jurisdiction, and it provided that no immunity based on official capacity shall apply. Several cases were brought against Rwandans in 1995. In 1998, six Chileans living in Belgium filed a complaint against General Pinochet under the 1993 Belgian statute. Belgian Judge Vandermeersch determined in a preliminary hearing in November 1998 that, since the 1999 statute was not yet in effect, customary international law, specifically *jus cogens*, would sustain universal jurisdiction and Pinochet's prosecution in Belgian courts.[67] The problem, of course, remained that of bringing Pinochet within Belgian jurisdiction. Belgium did intervene in the pending extradition proceeding in the United Kingdom, but on March 2, 2000, U.K. Home Sec-

---

64. Matthias Ruggert, "Pinochet Follow Up: The End of Sovereign Immunity," 48 *Netherlands International Law Review* (2001), 171–95.

65. Amnesty International, "Chad: The Habré Legacy" (2001). URL web.amnesty.org, consulted on December 20, 2001.

66. These Protocols (1977) expand the rules of the 1949 Conventions and add some new protections.

67. Redress, "Universal Jurisdiction in Europe. Annex: Law and Cases in Ten European Countries." <www.redress.org/annex.html>, consulted on December 20, 2001.

retary Jack Straw determined not to extradite Pinochet to Spain due to his incapacity to stand trial. Later that day a Chilean Air Force airplane flew Pinochet home.[68]

Despite Pinochet's flight, a greater impediment to such prosecutions in Belgium came in the recent decision of the International Court of Justice in *Democratic Republic of the Congo* [DRC] *v. Belgium* (2002).[69] The case brought by the DRC in the ICJ involved a dispute concerning an "international arrest warrant" issued by a Belgian examining magistrate on April 11, 2000, against Abdulaye Yerodia Ndombasi, who was Minister of Foreign Affairs of the DRC when his alleged crimes were committed. Belgium sought the arrest of Yerodia for grave breaches of the Geneva Conventions and additional protocols and for crimes against humanity. Specifically, Yerodia was accused of "having made various speeches inciting racial hatred" in August 1998, which allegedly contributed to the slaughter of Tutsis.[70] On April 15, 2001, Yerodia ceased to be a member of the government of the DRC, but the DRC nonetheless asserted immunity of office on his behalf. Among other arguments, Belgium asserted that immunity affords no protection for the commission of crimes against humanity.[71] The DRC's response was that while there may be exceptions to immunity for duly convened international tribunals that undertake the prosecution of war crimes or crimes against humanity, such exceptions do not apply for prosecutions in national courts. This was the argument accepted by the majority of a badly divided ICJ,[72] which noted, however, that immunity before courts of other nations does not bar (1) prosecution for crimes against international law in their own country, (2) prosecution when immunity is waived by the state of the national alleged to have committed a crime under international law, (3) prosecution of a state official for acts committed before or after his or her period of office, or for acts committed in a purely private capacity while in office, or (4) prosecution before an international tri-

---

68. Brody and Ratner, *The Pinochet Papers*, 58, 20.

69. Decision of February 14, 2002, General List No. 121. Available on the ICJ website: <www.icj-cij.org>.

70. *Democratic Republic of the Congo v. Belgium*, Eur. Court H.R. (February 14, 2002), 8.

71. Ibid., 20 et seq.

72. The joint separate opinion of Judges Higgins, Kooijmans, and Buergenthal was more encouraging. That opinion found that the allegations against Mr. Yerodia were for the sort of crimes under which the exercise of universal jurisdiction is not precluded under international law (16) and that immunity should have shielded him only for "official acts" (20) and only so long as he remained in office (21). Consistent with the Law Lords decision in the Pinochet case, this separate opinion also found that serious breaches of international law cannot be held to be official acts of a government official.

bunal with jurisdiction over the alleged crimes.[73] Even so, the decision may seriously impede other prosecutions pending before Belgian courts,[74] or other national courts, and makes the creation of a permanent international criminal court even more significant.

Equally problematic has been the political pressure exerted on Belgium for its aggressive use of universal jurisdiction. In March 2003, the United States warned Belgium that its laws might mean that the senior officials would refuse to visit Brussels, the venue of NATO headquarters.[75]

In July 2003, Belgium amended its law respective universal jurisdiction due to pressures, especially from the United States and Israel. The Belgian law gives the senior prosecutor in Belgium the authority to refer a complaint filed in Belgium to the country charged if the crimes charged had no tangible link to Belgium. This might have the effect of transferring a case brought against Ariel Sharon (due to his alleged role in the Sabra and Shatila refugee camp massacres) from Belgium to Israel. The Belgian judiciary were also authorized to refer complaints to the International Criminal Court. Moreover, Belgian courts would exercise universal jurisdiction only when complaints were brought by Belgian citizens or residents. Complaints against foreigners would be possible only under very narrow and strict conditions. On September 25, 2003, a Belgian court dismissed war crimes complaints brought against President George H. W. Bush (arising out of the Persian Gulf War) and Prime Minister Ariel Sharon of Israel.[76]

Prospects: The International Criminal Court

The Rome Statute for the International Criminal Court covers a long list of crimes: genocide, war crimes, and crimes against humanity, and, for the first time, it provides for express jurisdiction over sexual crimes (rape, forced pregnancy, forced sterilization, etc.).[77] However, the statute does not rely on universal jurisdiction. Rather, the crimes covered by the Statute must have been

---

73. Ibid., 22.

74. For example, the prosecution of Israeli Prime Minister, Ariel Sharon, in connection with the massacre of Palestinians in Lebanese refugees camps in 1982, while he was Israeli Defense Minister.

75. "US warns Belgium on war crimes cases," *Reuters*, March 8, 2003. <www.alertnet. org/thenews/newsdesk/N18324994>, consulted on March 18, 2003.

76. "Belgian parliament scraps genocide law," *Reuters*, July 30, 2003. <http://news.bbc. co.uk/hi/Europe/3108633,.stm>, consulted on July 30, 2003.

77. For an overview of the Rome Statute see Mauro Politi and Guiseppi Nesi (eds.), *The Rome Statute of the International Criminal Court* (Burlington, VT: Ashgate, 2001).

committed either in a state that has ratified the Statute or by an accused national from a state that has ratified (in either instance the state of commission or of the accused may consent to ad hoc jurisdiction). The only other route to prosecution is through the Security Council of the U.N., which is also given the power to suspend prosecutions. Moreover, the principal of "complimentarily" is contained in the Statute, so that a case can come before the International Criminal Court only when a state is unable or unwilling to prosecute in its own courts. With such restrictions it is perplexing, especially to Europeans, that the United States is so strongly opposed to the Statute and that it has consistently worked against it since it was adopted by a vote of 120-7 in Rome in the summer of 1998.[78] The problem, of course, is that a member of the U.S. military might be accused of a treaty crime while serving in a country that has ratified the Rome Statute. Even then the U.S. could take jurisdiction by bringing an action using its own procedures under military law. On July 1, 2002, the Rome Statute for the International Criminal Court entered into force. In March 2003, the first judges of the Court and the chief prosecutor were elected.[79] Even so, the global coverage of the court is problematic; the best example is that many Asian countries have not ratified the Rome Statute.[80] Whether it can be effective absent huge geographic areas of non-ratification, or in the face of continuing U.S. opposition, is a question that is unanswerable at present. Even more problematic is the reality that the nation-states that now seem to be the most likely violators of the Rome Statute may also be the most unlikely "ratifiers." That is why the developments in universal jurisdiction reviewed in this paper are important.

Conclusion: Sovereignty, Globalization, and the Princeton Principles

While there has been great attention by many scholars in the last decade to various transformations related to globalization, few American political scientists have paid attention to the global transformations in justice systems that

---

78. Ralph G. Carter and Donald W. Jackson, "The International Criminal Court: Present at the Creation?", in Ralph G. Carter (ed.), *Contemporary Cases in U.S. Foreign Policy: From Terrorism to Trade* (Washington, DC: Congressional Quarterly Books, 2002).

79. As of March 2004 there were 92 ratifications or accessions to the Rome Statute.

80. Including, as of March, 2004, China, Indonesia, Japan, North and South Korea, Malaysia, and Taiwan.

are represented by the developments reviewed in this paper.[81] Indeed, American public law scholars long devoted most of their attention to the Supreme Court of the United States, and when research finally expanded to include lower federal courts and American state court systems, it tended to treat American judicial systems as closed systems (in the sense that rarely was there attention to extra-U.S. institutions or influences). While that may have been a reasonable perspective in the 1960s, or even as late as the 1980s, now it is seriously flawed. Further, even most comparative judicial research has been nation-state focused, except for substantial contributions on transnational developments within Europe.[82] Thus we should note carefully the provisions of *Principle 1—Fundamentals of Universal Jurisdiction*, from the Princeton Principles on Universal Jurisdiction:

> 1. For purposes of these Principles, universal jurisdiction is criminal jurisdiction based solely on the nature of the crime, without regard to where the crime was committed, the nationality of the alleged or convicted perpetrator, the nationality of the victim, or any other connection to the state exercising such jurisdiction.
>
> 2. Universal jurisdiction may be exercised by a competent and ordinary judicial body of any state in order to try a person duly accused of committing serious crimes under international law…, provided the person is present before such judicial body.

Principle 2 lists piracy, slavery, war crimes, crimes against peace, crimes against humanity, genocide, and torture as the serious international crimes that ought to be subject to universal jurisdiction, and *Principle 3* provides that national courts may apply jurisdiction to these crimes even if they are not made criminal under its domestic jurisdiction.

Of course, the Princeton Principles do not have the force of law. They represent the views of scholars and sponsoring organizations, most prominently the Woodrow Wilson School at Princeton and the International Commission of Jurists (but the perspective is broadly shared by Human Rights Watch, Amnesty International, and others as well). Writing in the *Forward* to the Principles, Mary Robinson, the U.N. High Commissioner for Human Rights, said that:

---

81. David Forsythe of the University of Nebraska is a notable exception. See his book, *The Internationalization of Human Rights* (Lexington: Lexington Books, 1991).

82. See, for example, Mary L. Volcansek, *Judicial Politics in Europe* (New York: Peter Lang, 1986) and *Law Above Nations: Supranational Courts and the Legalization of Politics* (Gainesville, FL: University Press of Florida, 1997); Goldstein, *Constituting Federal Sovereignty*, 31; and Alec Stone Sweet, *Governing With Judges: Constitutional Politics in Europe* (Oxford: Oxford University Press, 2000).

While the principle of universal jurisdiction has long existed for [such] crimes…it is rapidly evolving as a result of significant recent developments. I applaud the fact that the Princeton Principles acknowledge that this doctrine continues to develop in law and practice.[83]

And a legal scholar wrote in a recent symposium on universal jurisdiction that:

Further progress seems inevitable as the fundamental values driving the evolution of universal jurisdiction gain even broader acceptance by the international community as a whole. Through this process the duty to prosecute universal jurisdiction crimes, and perhaps even the duty to prevent them, could eventually gain recognition as compelling *jus cogens* norms from which no derogation is permitted.[84]

Obviously, political leaders in the United States in both parties currently take a much different view, but the U.S. case law, as represented by *Kadic v. Karadzic*, reflects the global tendency, unless, of course, the ICJ decision in *DRC v. Belgium* represent the first step of reaction. The time has come for American political scientists to begin to think about the ways in which the public law and judicial systems of nation-states, including U.S. law and courts, may be connected both to regional/transnational institutions and their decisions and to the decisions of courts in other countries that may exercise universal jurisdiction —and even to a permanent International Criminal Court. For example, if the norms and processes of a state-based judicial system traditionally rest on broad cultural consensus about the rule of law and about the legitimacy of courts,[85] what will be the cultural foundations of courts that exercise universal criminal jurisdiction? And what will be the appropriate accountability mechanisms for ensuring that such courts indeed act properly? If courts successfully fulfill the functions of rule adjudication and conflict resolution, they do so because they are viewed as legitimate. The context of legitimacy for courts exercising the universal jurisdiction reviewed in this paper is yet to be explored.

---

83. Mary Robinson, "Introduction," in *The Princeton Principles On Universal Jurisdiction*, 36, 16 <http://www.law.uc.edu/morgan/newsdir/univjuris.html>.

84. Bartram S. Brown, "The Evolving Concept of Universal Jurisdiction," 35 (2) *New England Law Review* (2000), 397.

85. See particularly James L. Gibson, Gregory A. Caldeira, and Vanessa A. Baird, "On the Legitimacy of National High Courts," 92 (2) *American Political Science Review* (June 1998), which concludes that "national high courts vary enormously in the degree to which they have achieved institutional legitimacy," and that while the U.S. Supreme Court is among the "more legitimate institutions," other high courts have achieved legitimacy as well (356).

Chapter 10

Bringing Her Out of the Shadows: An Empirical Analysis of Sentences in Rape Cases before the International Criminal Tribunal for the Former Yugoslavia

Kimi King, James Meernick

Gender justice in the international arena has received heightened attention in the last decade as a result of decisions handed down by the International War Crimes Tribunal for the Former Yugoslavia (ICTY)[1] and the International War Crimes Tribunal for Rwanda (ICTR).[2] While both tribunals had a mandate to bring justice to persons responsible for the Balkan and Rwandan conflicts, the immediate mandate from the U.N. Security Council was to promote general and specific deterrence, to advance peace and reconciliation, and to do justice. The more difficult, long-term goal is to end the culture of impunity that allowed violence to continue occurring. Accomplishing either aim treads, however, on sensitive issues of national sovereignty. The implication is that a

---

1. International Tribunal for the Prosecution of Persons for Serious Violations of International Humanitarian Law Committed in the Territory of the Former Yugoslavia Since 1991. See S.C. Res. 827, U.N. SCOR, 48th Sess., Res. & Dec., at 29, U.N. Doc. S/INF/49 (1993), reprinted in 32 I.L.M. 1203, available at www.icty.org (Basic Legal Documents).

2. International Criminal Tribunal for the Prosecution of Persons Responsible for Genocide and Other Serious Violations of International Humanitarian Law Committed in the Territory of Rwanda and Rwandan Citizens. See S.C. Res. 955, U.N. SCOR, 49th Sess., Res. & Dec., at 15, U.N. Doc. S/RES/955 (1994), reprinted in 33 I.L.M 1598, available at www.ictr.org (Basic Legal Texts).

nation's own judicial system is incapable of dispassionate justice, and that only an international tribunal can be accepted as capable of finding truth. Some of the most basic elements of sovereignty are brushed aside.

Sexual violence during armed conflict is as timeless as war itself. In virtually every extended account of armed struggle there are references to the use of sexual assault by warring entities as a method of control, humiliation, and torture. But while sexual assault has been a constant in violent, political conflicts, the first attempts to outlaw rape as a weapon of war did not appear until the American Civil War. While Frances Lieber's code attempted to limit the use of rape, sexual assault remained an accepted part of armed hostilities throughout the twentieth century, with one notable exception.[3] Afterward, there was at least some recognition on the part of governments that rape was a weapon of war deserving of criminal status and punishment, and international humanitarian laws began to include rape as a category deserving of punishment as a war crime and a crime against humanity.[4]

The champions who support the new international criminal tribunals argue that the prohibition on sexual violence will make government and military leaders liable for actions taken under their command. Supporters argue that the ICTY and the ICTR statutes are landmarks because a civilian tribunal with a global reach has finally meted out justice against persons who allow sexual assault to occur during armed conflict. Even though the military tribunals of Nuremburg and Tokyo prosecuted acts of rape, it was not until judgments from the ICTY and ICTR that commanders, as well as field soldiers, began to be held accountable systematically for sexual violence.[5]

This issue of whether gender justice has been served by the ICTY is part of a larger debate about the effectiveness of the courts given the anarchic nature of the international system, and there are two voices of criticisms that are heard. First, opponents of the tribunals argue that the trials are not fair and

---

3. Ruth Seifert, "The Second Front. The Logic of Sexual Violence in Wars," 19 *Women's Studies International Forum* (1996).

4. For a discussion of the history surrounding mass rape, use Catherine A. MacKinnon, "Rape, Genocide and Women's Human Rights," and Alexandra Stiglmayer, "The Rapes in Bosnia-Herzegovina," both in Alexandra Stiglmayer (ed.), *Mass Rape: The War Against Women in Bosnia-Herzegovina* (Lincoln: University of Nebraska Press, 1994). For a general discussion of rape and society see Susan Brownmiller, *Against Our Will: Men, Women and Rape* (New York: Bantam Books, 1975).

5. The Nuremberg prosecutors did not charge officials with rape. Even those convicted under the Tokyo trials were found guilty only of command and control over their troops that had carried out the rapes.

that any sentence handed down is only a "victors' justice" forced upon the losing party by the winning coalition. Any punishment is, in other words, suspect. Indeed, from the inception of the tribunals, scholars, activists, politicians, and the organs of the U.N. itself have severely criticized the tribunals' work and questioned whether they are useful.[6]

The second source of criticism, perhaps more damning, has come from feminists who support the tribunal, but who argue that the ICTY and the ICTR have not gone far enough in promoting women's rights. When the tribunals were first established, they were thought to be the achievement of a goal that women's advocates worked toward for years—prosecuting gender violence under international humanitarian laws. Until the establishment of the ICTY and ICTR, the idea that rape could be considered a war crime or a crime against humanity was rhetorical, wishful thinking.[7] In theory, humanitarian principles supported the idea that sexual violence could and should be considered as such, but substantive support did not follow for three primary reasons. First, little in the text of humanitarian laws provides for protections from gender-related violence.[8] Second, sparse precedent exists that rape merits prosecution during times of war. Finally, the greatest obstacle—from a feminist standpoint—has been that customary international law depends upon a mostly masculine jurisprudence unwilling to recognize that part of the "spoils" of war were in the form of the feminine personae.[9]

---

6. See D.S. Bloch and E. Weinstein, "Velvet Glove and Iron Fist: A New Paradigm for the Permanent War Crimes Court," 22 *Hastings International and Comparative Law Review* (1998), which states that the creation of the tribunals was a "farce" and "attempts to salve guilty Western consciences." The Tribunal has been scrutinized by the Security Council and the General Assembly regarding length of trials and the limited number of persons that have been put on trial. Report of the Advisory Committee on Administrative and Budgetary Questions, U.N. Doc. A/54/874 (2000) (questioning delays and costs).

7. Kelly D. Askin, *War Crimes Against Women: Prosecution in International War Crimes Tribunals* (Boston: Martinus Nijhoff, 1997).

8. A debate exists about the degree to which the Geneva Conventions protect against rape during war. "Rape" does not appear as an enumerated crime under the Conventions, although the responsibility of protecting civilian women from rape is protected under the Fourth Geneva Convention. Ironically, this might mean that it is copasetic to allow men to be raped, but not women. Fourth Geneva Convention, Art. 27 ("women shall be especially protected against any attack on their honour, in particular against rape, enforced prostitution, or any form of indecent assault").

9. Kelly D. Askin, "Sexual Violence in Decisions and Indictments of the Yugoslav and Rwandan Tribunals: Current Status," 93 *American Journal of International Law* (1999), 32–33; Catherine Niarchos, "Women, War and Rape: Challenges Facing the International

Have the war crimes' tribunals advanced the cause of "doing justice" by aggressively enforcing laws against rape? How should we begin to quantify or qualify "doing justice" for the victims of rape during war? Have the tribunals punished the leaders in command or control positions, and thereby limited state sovereignty as a potential defense when the charges against their troops included rape? This paper unfolds in three sections to begin an answer. First, we analyze the treatment of gender violence in armed conflicts. The second section focuses on violence in the former Yugoslavia, as well as the establishment of the ICTY. We focus on this tribunal, in part, because the ICTR has rendered so few judgments, and in virtually all of the cases the defendants have received life in prison. Therefore, a doctrinal (rather than empirical) analysis is more appropriate for evaluating the Rwandan tribunal.[10] The final section develops a simple model of sentencing outcomes to determine whether ICTY decisions have advanced the cause of retributive justice for rape victims in terms of the sentences given to those found guilty.

We argue that if one measures the "effective delivery of justice" as lengthy sentences to aggressively punish persons alleged to have allowed or to have committed sexual assault or those in command and control authority, then the ICTY has made progress toward the cause of "doing justice." We conclude that the criticisms of the ICTY regarding its ineffectiveness and complaints about gender justice may be misguided from an empirical standpoint.

International Gender Justice for All? Armed Conflict and Mass Rape

Whether there are gender-based differences in views about war and peace,[11] scholars and practitioners have gradually recognized that the study of international relations should include gender-based analyses.[12] Especially because

---

Tribunal for the Former Yugoslavia," 17 *Human Rights Quarterly* (1995); and Catherine A. MacKinnon, "Rape, Genocide and Women's Human Rights."

10. Notably, in the Akayesu case, the ICTR found for the first time in history that acts of rape can be considered forms of genocide. *Prosecutor v. Jean-Paul Akayesu*, Case No. ICTR-96-4-T (Trial Chamber, September 2, 1998), available at www.ictr.org (Cases).

11. Mark Tessler and Ina Warriner, "Gender, Feminism and Attitudes Toward International Conflict: Exploring Relationships with Survey Data from the Middle East," 49 *World Politics* (1994).

12. Craig Murphy, "Seeing Women, Recognizing Gender, Recasting International Relations," 50 *International Organization* (1996); Cynthia Enloe, *The Morning After: Sexual Politics at the End of the Cold War* (Berkeley: University of California Press, 1993); and

of the limited use of humanitarian law to constrain political and military leaders, the interplay of accountability between persons who control the use of force and the victims against whom the force is used remains critical in sending signals that wrongdoing will be penalized. Nowhere is this more important than in mass rapes where commanders and leaders have the ability to commit human rights violations on a magnitude far greater than they could as individuals. As others have argued, ending war crimes and the culture of impunity requires that the international community and affiliate institutions aggressively apply the tools of humanitarian law, especially those regarding rape.[13] Persons accused of rape by virtue of being in command and control are arguably acting in the name of some official group, whether it is a sovereign nation or a rebel entity.

Rape, wherever and whenever it occurs, is inherently tied to the role of women's identities within the cultures and societies where they reside. As feminists have continually noted, "the personal is political."[14] This understanding of violence against women in the global context requires re-conceptualizing the manner in which we study sexual violence.[15] The very act of rape is designed to dehumanize and destroy an important section of the "enemy's" population by targeting women and girls. It is the targeting of women because of their role as guardians of social and cultural traditions that makes rape a powerful weapon of the state or its enemies.[16] Women in any given group hold the key to the group's future reproductive capacities. Women, as the bearers of future generations, are the very humanity upon which the community exists. When rape is used as a weapon of war, the political has become the personal,

---

Onora O'Neill, "Justice, Gender and International Boundaries," 20 *British Journal of Political Science* (1990).

13. Theodor Meron, "War Crimes in Yugoslavia and the Development of International Law," 88 *American Journal of International Law* (1994); Theodor Meron, "The Case of War Crimes Trials in Yugoslavia," 72 *Foreign Affairs* (1993); and Theodor Meron, "Rape as a Crime Under International Humanitarian Law," 87 *American Journal of International Law* (1993).

14. According to MacKinnon this "means that women's distinctive experience as women occurs within that sphere that has been socially lived as the personal—private, emotional, interiorized, particular, individuated, intimate—so that what it is to know the politics of woman's situation is to know women's personal lives." See MacKinnon, "Rape, Genocide and Women's Human Rights."

15. Sally Merry, "International Research on Women and Violence: Rights, Religion and Community Approaches to Violence Against Women in the Context of Globalization," 35 *Law and Society Review* (2001).

16. Darren Anne Nebesar, "Gender-Based Violence as a Weapon of War," 4 *Journal of International Law and Policy* (1998).

and depending upon the state involved, the government may include such a weapon in its arsenal.

Research aimed at breaking the cycle of gender-based violence has focused overwhelmingly on normative principles or doctrinal arguments to support the aggressiveness of international laws and organizations in prosecuting rape.[17] Moreover, the ICTY and the ICTR have been criticized for "not getting it" when it comes to the necessity of aggressively prosecuting persons accused of rape.[18] Consistent skepticism and popular wisdom have been that male-dominated institutions will not provide equal treatment.[19] Until women are part of the dialogue regarding the treatment of gender violence in international law, there can be no justice.[20]

Since the decline of the Cold War, the issue of international justice for rape victims has been on the human rights agenda.[21] This is a result of the recognition and the documentation that—especially during the twentieth century—mass rape has been used as a weapon of war.[22] Some of the accounts of mass rape are better known, such as the Japanese "Rape of Nanking" in China and the sexual enslavement of Korean women before and during World War II.[23] Others are less publicized, such as the French gov-

---

17. Benjamin Ference, "A Prosecutor's Personal Account: From Nuremberg to Rome," 52 *Journal of International Affairs* (1999); Beth Stephens, "Humanitarian Law and Gender Violence: An End to Centuries of Neglect?", 3 *Hofstra Law and Policy Symposium* (1999); Kathleen M. Pratt and Laurel E. Fletcher, "Time for Justice: The Case for International Prosecutions of Rape and Gender-Based Violence in the Former Yugoslavia," 9 *Berkeley Women's Law Journal* (1994), 77; Catherine A. MacKinnon, "Rape, Genocide and Women's Human Rights"; and Danise Ayedlott, "Mass Rape During War: Prosecuting Bosnian Rapists Under International Law," 7 *Emory International Law Review* (1993).

18. Patricia H. Davis, "The Politics of Prosecuting Rape as a War Crime," 34 *International Lawyer* (2000).

19. Niarchos, "Women, War and Rape."

20. Anne M. Hoefgen, "There Will be No Justice Unless Women Are Part of that Justice," 14 *Wisconsin Womens' Law Journal* (1999); and Rhonda Copelon, "Surfacing Gender: Reconceptualizing Crimes Against Women in Time of War," in Alexandra Stiglmayer (ed.), *Mass Rape: The War Against Women in Bosnia-Herzegovina* (Lincoln: Nebraska University Press, 1994).

21. Enloe, *The Morning After.*

22. Askin, "Sexual Violence in Decisions and Indictments"; and Nebesar, "Gender-Based Violence as a Weapon of War."

23. Evidence was admitted at Nuremberg about the treatment of females at concentration camps. The Tokyo Tribunal did note mass rapes, but minimized the widespread sexual enslavement by the Japanese. Japan has slowly accepted responsibility in the last decade. T.R. Reid, "Openly Apologetic, Japan Recalls War's End," *Washington Post* (August 16, 1993), A12.

ernment in 1943 allowing Moroccan mercenaries to rape women found in Italian territory, and the tattooing of rape victims with "Whore for Hitler's Troops."[24]

The use of mass rape has not diminished as an increase of awareness about sexual violence and armed conflict has occurred on the global stage.[25] Nor is mass rape specific to conflicts with international dimensions: witness attacks by the communist members of the Shining Path on Peruvian rural women in 1992[26] and the rapes of women who supported President Jean-Bertrand Aristide after his 1991 overthrow.[27] Rape does not distinguish between the status of the victor and the vanquished, nor does it discriminate based on the underlying political or religious system. Russian troops raped German women to retaliate for the treatment of Soviet women by the Nazis, and Kuwaiti soldiers did the same after Saddam Hussein's invasion had been repelled.[28] Whether it is fascist Nazis raping Jewish and Soviet women, democratic American soldiers raping Vietnamese women, or Taliban members abducting and raping ethnic Tajik and Hazara women, rape is a constant for soldiers.[29]

While the issue of rape as part of war and armed conflict did surface in the military tribunals that followed World War II, it was not until the establishment of the Yugoslavian and Rwandan tribunals that an international judicial body specifically considered the legality of rape in international law. Perhaps what is most striking about these allegations of gender violence is that, for the first time, evidence systematically documented that rape was a weapon to carry out ethnic cleansing and genocide.[30] It was not, however, the first time that laws were established to punish those who rape during armed conflicts.

---

24. Seifert, "The Second Front," and Lance Morrow, "Unspeakable," *Time* (February 22, 1993), 48.

25. United Nations, *United Nations Sub-Commission on Prevention of Discrimination and Protection of Minorities: Preliminary Report of the Special Rapporteur on the Situation of Systematic Rape, Sexual Slavery and Slavery Like Practices during Periods of Armed Conflict.* U.N. Doc. E/Cn. 4/Sub. 2/1996/26 (1996).

26. America's Watch and Women's Rights Project, *Untold Terror: Violence Against Women in Peru's Armed Conflict* (Washington, D.C.: America's Watch, 1992).

27. Janet Reitman, "Political Repression by Rape Increasing in Haiti," *Washington Post* (July 22, 1994), A10.

28. For a discussion of the extent that rape has become the rule in armed conflict, see Judith Gradam and Michelle Jarvic, "Women and Armed Conflict: The International Response to the Beijing Platform for Action," 32 *Columbia Human Rights Law Review* (2000).

29. Brownmiller, *Against Our Will.*

30. Stephen Schwartz, "Rape as a Weapon of War in the Former Yugoslavia," 5 *Hastings Women's Law Journal* (1994).

The first legal limits on troops for sexual assault during armed conflict were the prohibitions provided by the Lieber Code during the American Civil War, through which Union Army members could be charged with rape as a capital offense.[31] While the Hague Conventions of 1907[32] did not explicitly provide protection against rape, there were limits placed on the conduct of war that ultimately gave the International Military Tribunal for Nuremberg[33] and the International Military Tribunal for the Far East (Tokyo Tribunal)[34] the ability to prosecute mass rape.

Significantly, no one was charged with rape under the Nuremberg Charter, but the accounts of mass rapes documented sexual violence as a form of torture and control during war. Rape remained, theoretically, part of the class of crimes against humanity that included "murder, extermination, enslavement, deportation, and other inhumane acts committed against any civilian population." While the Tokyo Charter, like its German counterpart, did not list rape as a specific war crime, it did include it as a violation of "recognized customs and conventions of war" along with mass murder, pillage, brigandage, and torture. Significantly, no commanding officer was held responsible for rapes he personally participated in, but for the first time commanding officers were held accountable for failing their affirmative duty to ensure that rape did not occur.

The subsequent development of international legal doctrine expanded the prohibition on rape. Like the Nuremberg Charter, Control Council Law Number 10 established military tribunals in occupation zones. Crimes against humanity included rape and were:

> Atrocities and offences, including but not limited to murder, extermination, enslavement, deportation, imprisonment, torture, rape, or other inhumane acts committed against any civilian population,

---

31. Francis Lieber, Instructions for the Government of Armies of the United States in the Field, Art. 44. Printed as U.S. War Department, Adjutant General's Office, General Orders, No. 100 (Apr. 24, 1863), cited in Gary D. Solis, "Obedience of Orders and the Law of War: Judicial Application in American Forums," 15 *American University International Law Review* (2000).

32. Convention Respecting the Laws and Customs of War on Land, October 18, 1907, Art. 56, 36 Stat.; Hague Convention Respecting the Laws and Customs of War, 26 Martens (2d) 949, 32 Stat. 1803.

33. Agreement for the Prosecution and Punishment of Major War Criminals of the European Axis (London Agreement), Aug. 8, 1945, 82 U.N.T.S. 279, Art. 6.

34. Charter of the International Military Tribunal for the Far East, January 19, 1946 (General Orders No.1), as amended, General Orders No. 20, April 26, 1946, TIAS No. 1589, 4 Bevans 20.

or persecutions on political, racial or religious grounds whether or
not in violation of domestic laws of country where perpetrated.[35]

The twelve trials that came after the judgments at Nuremberg tried 191 high-
ranking military officials as well as civilians in 12 trials under the Control
Council Law. Like Tokyo, the importance of these trials was not in the prosecution of rapes (none were charged with rape), but for holding commanding officers accountable for their troops' actions.[36] The significance was that it
paved the way for subsequent international conventions and the ICTY statute
because for the first time rape was an independent category of crime and commanding officers were ultimately held accountable, even if it was not explicitly for the charge of sexual violence.

The *Geneva Conventions of 1949 and the Additional Protocols*[37] were the
first post-Nuremberg and Tokyo laws that either implicitly or explicitly prohibited sexual assault during armed conflicts. After the large-scale atrocities
documented by the International Committee of the Red Cross (ICRC), the
"Grave Breach Provisions" limited torture and inhuman treatment, as well
as "willfully causing great suffering or serious injury to body or health." In
1992, the ICRC indicated that the operative phrase of "willfully causing"
could be interpreted to include actions such as rape. "Common Article 3,"
so-called because it is included in all four of the Geneva Conventions, illustrates the "common principle" that is woven into humanitarian law. While
rape is not specifically mentioned, the Convention notes say that the list is
not exclusive. Thus, any actions that are violent—including mutilation,
cruel treatment, torture, and outrages upon personal dignity—can be considered. Finally, Article 27 in the Fourth Convention provides the most explicit authority for punishing gender-based crimes. Women are to be protected from "rape, enforced prostitution, or any form of indecent assault"
[emphasis added].

---

35. Allied Control Council Law No. 10, Punishment of Persons Guilty of War Crimes,
Crimes Against Peace and Against Humanity, Dec. 20, 1945, Official Gazette of the Control Council for Germany, No. 3, Berlin (January 31, 1946).

36. Solis, "Obedience of Orders and the Law of War."

37. Geneva Convention for the Amelioration of the Condition of the Wounded and
Sick in the Armed Forces in the Field, August 12, 1949, 6 U.S.T. 3114, 75 U.N.T.S. 3;
Geneva Convention for the Amelioration of the Condition of the Wounded, Sick and Ship-
wrecked Members of the Armed Forces at Sea, August 12, 1949, 6 U.S.T. 3217, 75 U.N.T.S.
85; Geneva Convention Relative to the Treatment of Prisoners of War, August 12, 1949, 6
U.S.T. 3316, 75 U.N.T.S. 135; Geneva Protection Relative to the Protection of Civilian Persons in Time of War, August 12, 1949, 6 U.S.T. 3518, 75 U.N.T.S. 287.

It is against this backdrop that the ICTY statute was developed. We turn now to the genesis of the mass rapes during the Balkan wars, the establishment of the war crimes tribunal at The Hague, and the prosecution of individuals for rape as a war crime.

Conflict in the Former Yugoslavia: The Establishment of the ICTY Statute and Tribunal

The conflict between Croatians, Serbians, and Muslims dates back hundreds of years,[38] and whether the international community's involvement can ultimately end centuries of ethnic rivalry has been hotly debated.[39] Grievances that were the immediate precipitants of the violence, however, date back to Muslim and Croat cooperation with Hitler under the auspices of the Utashe government during World War II. Following the Nazi downfall and Tito's subsequent control and consolidation of power from 1946 to 1966, ethnic rivalries were suppressed with Serbs, Croats, and Muslims maintaining their ethnic identities even as they inter-married and lived as neighbors. After Tito's death, tensions re-emerged with a vengeance, especially after the fall of the Berlin Wall. Finally, in 1991, the country collapsed into Croatia, Serbia, Montenegro, Slovenia, and Bosnia. Serbia and Montenegro formed the Federal Republic of Yugoslavia, and Croatia and Slovenia obtained autonomous international recognition with the United Nation's grant of member status in May of 1992. Bosnia-Herzegovina remained problematic. With a population that was 43.7% Slavic Muslim, 31.3% Serbian, and 17.3% Croatian, the armed forces inside each regional stronghold declared independence on behalf of the Serbian population, and a state of war was declared in June 1992.

By the time the Dayton Peace Accords[40] were signed on December 14, 1995, establishing a peace agreement of sorts, the same region that had been the site for the onset of World War I in 1914 had become the site of, to date, the worst mass rapes in history. Estimates vary, but anywhere from 20,000 to 50,000 women were raped—in camps, apartments, military units, temporary broth-

---

38. Stiglmayer, "The Rapes in Bosnia-Herzegovina."

39. M. Cherif Bassiouni and Peter Manikas, *The Law of the International Criminal Tribunal for the Former Yugoslavia* (Irvington-on-Hudson: Transnational Publishers, 1996).

40. Dayton Peace Agreement, Paris, France, December 14, 1995; U.S. Department of State Dispatch Supplement, Volume 7, No. 1. <www.state.gov/www/regions/eur/bosnia/bosagree.html>, consulted on March 1, 2002.

els, or anywhere else that armed forces could guarantee that the soldiers would have access to them.[41]

Evidence exists that mass rapes were carried out for innumerable purposes —humiliation or degradation of the enemy, impregnation to destroy ethnic lineage, isolation of women from their families and husbands after the rape, and terrorization of a population to drive them from their homes.[42] Mass rapes were not confined to atrocities by Serbian men; Bosnian and Croatian forces were also accused of gender violence, and human rights organizations documented that rape by all factions occurred regularly.[43] Women were raped regularly and repeatedly; orally and anally raped; gang raped; publicly raped; privately raped; raped in front of their families or other victims; mutilated while they were being raped; and raped to gain information about friends and family members.[44] Women were not the only victims—such atrocities were also committed against men who were targeted because they were leaders. Such tactics served to humiliate the enemy and to render men "inferior" by methods including forced fellatio by other men and family members and the mutilation of sexual organs to reduce prisoners to the status of women.

The impact of these mass rapes may never fully be known. Women in sexual enslavement situations testified that the abuse became so cruel that they did not know whether it was day or night and described themselves as the "walking dead."[45] Injuries were so severe that some women died, and more tragically, others took their own lives to avoid future rapes or the dishonor that would follow public awareness that they were now "unclean."[46]

---

41. Amy E. Ray, "The Shame of It: Gender-Based Terrorism in the Former Yugoslavia and the Failure of International Human Rights Law to Comprehend the Injuries," 46 *American University Law Review* (1997). The United Nations War Crimes Commission Chairman and Rapporteur M. Cherif Bassiouni estimated that there were 12,000 instances of unreported and reported rapes. Final Report of the Commission of Experts Established Pursuant to Security Council Resolution 780 (1992) U.N. SCOR, Addendum Annex IX, at 70–71, U.N. Doc. S/1994/674/Add.2 (Vol. I) (1995). In contrast, MacKinnon, "Rape, Genocide and Women's Human Rights," estimates those numbers to be much higher— 50,000. Interviews with ICTY personnel in March 2001 indicated women were reluctant to testify publicly because of fear of reprisal, condemnation, and abandonment.

42. Ray; "The Shame of It," and Misha Glenny, *The Fall of Yugoslavia: The Third Balkan War* (New York: Viking Press, 1992).

43. Askin, *War Crimes Against Women*; Bassiouni and Manikas, *The Law of the International Criminal Tribunal*; and Schwartz, "Rape as a Weapon of War."

44. Ray, "The Shame of It."

45. Stiglmayer, "The Rapes in Bosnia-Herzegovina."

46. Ibid., and Roy Gutman, *Witness to Genocide: The 1993 Pulitzer Prize-Winning Dispatches on the Ethnic Cleansing of Bosnia* (New York: MacMillan Publishing, 1993).

After accounts of the mass rapes were documented by human rights groups and journalists, the international community responded.[47] The U.N. Security Council expressed "grave alarm" at the atrocities of rape committed during the conflict and acknowledged that the mass rapes merited prosecution.[48] Pursuant to Security Council Resolution 827, the International Criminal Tribunal for the Former Yugoslavia was given authority to prosecute war criminals.[49]

The statute establishes the trial and appellate chambers, as well as the procedures for prosecution. The ICTY has three units: the Chambers (including all of the tribunals' judges), the Office of the Prosecutor (responsible for trying each case), and the Registry (serving as a secretariat for both the other two units). Judges are nominated by the U.N. Security Council from member countries. The jurists are fairly autonomous, with the ability to adopt rules of evidence and procedure without interference by the appointive organ. Cases may be appealed to the five-member Appeals Chamber whose judges are appointed in the same fashion as trial judges. Due process, protection against double jeopardy, and other evidentiary guarantees are provided, although there have been criticisms regarding the appropriate use of various types of evidence and defendants' rights.[50]

The ICTY was delayed initially in hearing cases, but its first trial resulted in Drazen Erdomovic's guilty plea for one count of crimes against humanity. Although many have criticized the ICTY's slow pace, the process has been substantially accelerated, and, in 2001 alone, over 15 defendants received judgments from the tribunal. In all, the Trial Chamber has issued 29 sentences in 32 cases since 1996.

The first real trial of the ICTY's process occurred in the Dusko Tadic case that highlights the deficiencies and difficulties of prosecuting rape cases. The learning curve for the prosecutor was especially steep, since it represented the first time anyone in history had ever been charged with rape as an offense separate and apart from other crimes listed in the indictment. In the Tadic case,

---

47. Gutman, *Witness to Genocide*.

48. Report of the Secretary-General Pursuant to Paragraph 2 of Security Council Resolution 808 (1993), U.N. SCOR, U.N. Doc. S/25704 (1993).

49. S.C. Res 827, U.N. SCOR, 3217th mtg., U.N. Doc. S/Res./827, 32 I.L.M. 1203 (1993), amended by S.C. Res. 1166, U.N. SCOR, 3878th mtg, U.N. Doc. S/Res./1166 (1998), available at www.icty.org (Basic Documents).

50. Patricia M. Wald, "Establish Incredible Events by Credible Evidence: The Use of Affidavit Testimony in Yugoslavia War Crimes Tribunal Proceedings," 42 *Harvard International Law Journal* (2001).

an alleged rape victim (Witness F)—after agreeing to testify—subsequently refused. The only evidence the prosecution presented was eyewitness testimony by another witness who was later found to have been lying. After multiple amendments to the indictment, all charges of rape were ultimately withdrawn. Notably, the ICTY still relied on testimony regarding rape for evaluating the sentences on other substantive charges. Tadic was convicted under other provisions of the ICTY statute for crimes of sexual violence, specifically for participating in the sexual mutilation of a male prisoner and for aiding and abetting persecution by the use of sexual assault against females. He ultimately received a sentence of twenty years on those counts.

In the months that followed, there was much speculation that ICTY would be aggressive in prosecuting crimes against humanity and would be sensitive to allegations of mass rape as a weapon of war. In the Celibici camp case, two of the defendants, Hazim Delic and Zdravko Mucic, were accused of sexual violence against men and sexual assault against women. Mucic was accused of command and control responsibility for allowing rapes to be carried out under his authority. Even though no witness named him as an "active participant" in any of the tortures, rapes, or murders that were committed while he was commander at the camp, he received a sentence of seven years for eleven of the thirteen counts where he was found guilty, including superior authority for allowing rapes to occur. In sharp contrast, Delic—who was a deputy commander, but whom the Trial Chamber referred to as someone who "took a sadistic pleasure in causing the detainees pain and suffering"—received a sentence of twenty years for thirteen of thirty-eight counts where he was found guilty. But in the Delic case, for the first time in history, someone had been found guilty of rape as torture under customary international law. Many wondered whether the ICTY would be aggressive about prosecuting rape when it was not linked to other underlying charges of murder or torture as had been the case for both of the defendants.[51]

By the close of 1998, the ICTY finally tried and convicted someone solely on rape charges. The ICTY found Anton Furundzija guilty of standing by—in violation of the laws and customs of war—while "Witness A" was interro-

---

51. In part this is due to the fact that in the Delis case, he had detained and interrogated the two victims, thus allowing the Tribunal to say that it met the necessary requirements of torture. It remained unclear after the Celebici camp case whether detention and interrogation would always be required for finding of rape as a form of torture in international law. Christin B. Coan, "Rethinking the Spoils of War: Prosecuting Rape as a War Crime in the International Criminal Tribunal for the Former Yugoslavia," 26 *North Carolina Journal of International Law and Commercial Regulation* (2000).

gated, beaten, and ultimately raped by another soldier. Specifically, Furundz-ija, as a member of the Croatian Defence Council, allowed a soldier to rub a knife against Witness A's thighs and lower stomach while she was threatened with the knife being put in her vagina if she did not answer questions truthfully. Furundzija continued questioning Witness A and another male victim while they were beaten with a baton. Ultimately, Witness A was orally and vaginally raped while Furundzija stood by. For this, the defendant was found guilty of torture as violation of the laws and customs of war and given a ten-year sentence. He was also found guilty of aiding and abetting outrages upon personal dignity for rape, for which he received an eight-year sentence.

Over the course of the next four years, the ICTY decided numerous issues that directly affected the outcome of sexual assault cases, including standards for submitting evidence, actions necessary for protecting witnesses, and most recently, establishing the substantive elements and requirements for sexual assault charges to merit conviction. Specifically, in the Kunarac, Kovac, and Vukovic cases (also known as the Foca case or "the rape camp case"), the ICTY convicted defendants for the first time in the ICTY proceedings for rape as a crime against humanity. While earlier trials had found rape to be a war crime or a violation of the grave breach provisions, the ICTY had not convicted anyone of a crime against humanity based on the charge of rape alone. Moreover, it marked for the first time that the continued detention of women for months on end for sexual assault, one as young as twelve years old, was held as a crime against humanity.

What is striking about the rape camp case is that while this was a "first" for the Tribunal, the men responsible were not in command and control positions. The court specifically denied this defense. In all, since 1977, 13 defendants have been tried on charges of rape or sexual assault, and the ICTY has ordered over 226 years of prison time for those persons convicted of rape, with the average sentence being approximately 17 years. Even despite the "firsts" that have occurred over the course of the Tribunal's history to date, criticisms have abounded.

Critics of the ICTY have argued that these victories are minor and point to problems in the treatment of witnesses. Some have argued that the Tribunal has not gone far enough in addressing gender violence crimes,[52] while others claim that the high threshold for establishing rape as a crime against humanity, requiring evidence of mass or systemic rapes, creates difficulty in

---

52. Hoefgen, "There Will be no Justice," and Davis, "The Politics of Prosecuting Rape as a War Crime."

prosecuting sexual assault cases.[53] Paradoxically, even though the ICTY statute explicitly allows for conviction of rape as a crime against humanity and other categories do not explicitly provide for rape, it may be easier to prove rape under sections of the statute that do not specifically address rape, e.g. war crimes or grave breaches. Finally, some have argued that what is so horrific about sexual assault during armed conflict is that it allows superior officers in command to condone victimization en masse against women. This literally means that the act of rape turns women's bodies into battlefields by persons claiming state sovereignty.[54] In order to examine whether these criticisms of the ICTY are accurate, we turn now to a model based on the above discussion. We develop a model to examine whether the ICTY has been effective in "doing justice" to rape victims under the four Articles of the ICTY statute.

Doing Justice: Theory, Data and Method

The U.N. Security Council in the ICTY Preamble stated it was "determined to put an end to such crimes and to take effective measures to bring to justice the persons who are responsible for them". The U.N. was committed to "the process of national reconciliation and to the restoration and maintenance of peace," and "to ensuring that such violations are halted and effectively redressed." The issue of what constitutes the "effective delivery of justice" or "doing justice" has been widely debated. In the last five years alone, over seventy-five law review articles have evaluated or used the concept of "justice" to evaluate some aspect of the war crimes tribunals.

Two theories of justice that continually reoccur in the debates among scholars, practitioners, advocates, and activists—especially in the context of doing justice—focus on either the deterrent effect or the retributive effect of bringing criminals to trial.[55] Each goal is defined differently by scholars, but the core component of each is similar. Under deterrent justice, the function of

---

53. Coan, "Rethinking the Spoils of War."

54. Susan Brownmiller, "Making Female Bodies the Battlefield," in Alexandra Stiglmayer (ed.), *Mass Rape: The War Against Women in Bosnia-Herzegovina* (Lincoln: University of Nebraska Press, 1994); and Ayedlott, "Mass Rape During War.

55. Yves Beigbeder, *Judging War Criminals: The Politics of International Justice* (New York: St. Martin's Press, 1999); and Payam Akhavan, "Justice in The Hague, Peace in the Former Yugoslavia? A Commentary on the United Nations War Crimes Tribunal," 20 *Human Rights Quarterly* (1998).

criminal prosecution is to limit or minimize future behaviors. Deterrence intends to ensure that future atrocities do not occur by other persons or that the accused cannot commit the atrocities again himself.[56] Under principles of retributive justice, the purpose of punishment serves a more individualized rationale. Sanctions or sentences bring closure to the conflict: for the survivors and the "collective memory," for the society that demands order; or for the defendants who are punished appropriately for their behavior in accordance with the principle of *lex talionise*—having the punishment fit the crime.[57]

The goal of deterrence in stopping war criminals is evident from the ICTY Preamble. Such statements do not bind the Tribunal, but it has been cited at the sentencing phase, though inconsistently. For example, in the Celebici case, the judges referred to the importance of deterrence, however in the Foca case, the Tribunal rejected axiomatic applications of the U.N. mandate. It would be "inappropriate to have recourse to that Resolution for guidance of what the general sentencing factors of the International Tribunal should be....It cannot be said that the Security Council intended this passage to serve as a guide on general sentencing factors."[58] In any event, the goal of deterrence may be difficult to quantify because "genocidaires" may not be rational actors,[59] and it may be impossible for any tribunal to halt genocide and mass violence.[60]

Turning to the retributive theory of justice, the judges have cited the importance of retribution when issuing sentences. The victim witness units and protection of witnesses under the statute establish principles that acknowledge the importance of the victim's role and the necessity of ensuring witness protection.[61] This concept of proportionality in punishment also reflects the importance of redressing victims' pain and injuries, even if critics argue that retribution is a euphemism for "vengeance."[62]

---

56. Only one female has been publicly indicted at ICTY to date. *Prosecutor v. Plasvic*, Case No. IT-00-40, available at <www.un.org/icty/ind-e-htm>.

57. Jose E. Alvarez, "Rush to Closure: Lessons of the Tadic Judgment," 96 *Michigan Law Review* (1998).

58. *Prosecutor v. Delalic*, Case No. IT-96-21, P 1202 (Trial Chamber, November 16, 1998); and *Prosecutor v. Kunarac*, Case No. IT-96-23-T (Trial Chamber, February 22, 2001), both available at <www.un.org/icty>.

59. Martha Minow, *Between Vengeance and Forgiveness* (Boston: Beacon Press, 1998).

60. Alvarez, "Rush to Closure," and Aryeh Neier, *War Crimes: Brutality, Genocide, Terror, and the Struggle for Justice* (New York: Times Books, 1998).

61. Endless criticism has focused on the failure of the U.N. to provide adequate victim protections. Undoubtedly, the failure of witnesses to testify is a barrier to prosecution.

62. One scholar has argued that the "principle of proportionality has become the leading guideline for calculating sentence lengths in many countries and it may be considered

Dependent Variable: Sentence

The use of sentencing outcomes in any given defendant's case is appropriate for evaluating the Tribunal because it directly links punishment to accountability and allocates responsibility to individuals rather than to ethnic groups. Ultimately the sentence is the outcome that the court renders as a policymaking body. As the ICTY hands down sentences, it sends signals about the status and treatment of women in international law. This, in turn, may lead to breaking the cycle of violence and the culture of impunity. Examining sentencing outcomes is also useful because it serves the function of measuring the personal responsibility of the defendant while recognizing the impact on the victims:[63]

> A sentence proportional to the degree to which the perpetrator affected a victim's ability to realize his or her value, for example, acts to re-establish the victim's worth. The sentence in a criminal case implicitly contains a judgment about the extent of the victim's rights, about the victim's value, and even about the victim's humanity.[64]

Are defendants accused of violating international humanitarian laws more likely to receive lengthier sentences in sexual assault cases? Are persons in command and control positions more likely to receive lengthier sentences? Does it make a difference whether the assault is prosecuted as a war crime or as a crime against humanity? We analyze sentences handed down by the ICTY to determine the extent to which such punishment reflects the gravity of the crimes committed and the guilty party's responsibility.

The data set and the units of analysis are drawn from completed trials where individual criminals have been sentenced. To date there have been thirty-one trials of first instance—twenty-nine persons have been found guilty and given sentences ranging from two-and-a-half to forty-six years. We have not included cases remanded by the Appeals Chamber because the subsequent sentence imposed by the Trial Chamber may reflect, to a greater degree, ap-

---

the dominant sentencing model in international law." Allison Marston Danner, "Constructing a Hierarchy of Crimes in International Criminal Law Sentencing," 87 *Virginia Law Review* (2001). For one of the few empirical analyses on the Tribunal involving victim perception and justice, see Sanja Kutnjak Ivkovic, "Justice by the International Criminal Tribunal for the Former Yugoslavia," 37 *Stanford Journal of International Law* (2001), which employed a survey conducted in Yugoslavia of survivors and victims and their views on the fairness of the ICTY as compared to the national courts.

63. Copelon, "Surfacing Gender."
64. Danner, "Constructing a Hierarchy."

pellate influence and not determinations about appropriate sanctions. Using OLS regression we use sentence length (measured in months) as the dependent variable for guilty verdicts issued through March 1, 2002.

Command and Control Power

Responsibility for command and control authority over soldiers is one of the earliest principles established under the laws and customs of war.[65] Holding commanding officers accountable was one of the most important accomplishments of the Nuremberg and Tokyo tribunals. The ICTY statute specifically considers the responsibility of commanding officers under Article 7 by both denying inferior officers the ability to claim "I was only following orders" and by holding superior officers responsible for violations that occur under their authority. The ICTY has been criticized for not capturing enough of the "big fish," and judges have indicated that capturing the top-level leadership is important for the Court to be seen as effective.[66]

People who are higher up in the command hierarchy should share a greater burden of responsibility than their subordinate counterparts who have probably not participated in the strategic and tactical decisions that are made during the haze of battle. In the context of rape, the failure of a commanding officer to oppose the use of sexual violence gives carte blanche for mass rapes to occur and for the rest of the troops to reap the spoils of war. The ICTY stated as much in the Foca case when the Tribunal said that the defendant Kunarac used "his bravery in combat to gain the respect of his men, and he maintained it by providing them with women."[67] As such, one would expect that the higher the indictee in the chain of command, the more severe the sentence. To make this determination the Tribunal's descriptions of defendants' positions and responsibilities were examined. We distinguish among low-level war criminals, such as ordinary soldiers and prison camp guards; mid-level officials, such as prison camp commanders, military officers below the rank of colonel, and political figures below cabinet-level status; and high-level officials, including military officials at or above the rank of colonel and political officials of cabinet-level status or higher. An ordinal variable with these three

---

65. Solis, "Obedience of Orders."

66. Patricia M. Wald, "The International Criminal Tribunal for the Former Yugoslavia Comes of Age: Some Observations on Day-to-Day Dilemmas of an International Court," 5 *Washington University Journal of Law and Policy* (2001).

67. *Prosecutor v. Kunarac*, at finding 585.

values measures ascending power and responsibility, dividing the lines according to those listed above.

The ICTY Articles and Rape

The prohibition on rape is a relatively new international legal principle, and prior to the ICTY and ICTR judgments, it was not precisely defined in humanitarian law.[68] The authoritative sections for the prosecution of defendants are contained in four articles that include grave breaches of the 1949 Geneva Conventions,[69] violations of the laws or customs of war,[70] acts of genocide pursuant to the 1948 Convention on the Prevention and Punishment of the Crime of Genocide,[71] and crimes against humanity.[72]

Each substantive provision has a "chapeau" or introductory language that sets a threshold establishing the elements of the offense and justifying jurisdiction. The enumerated crimes that are subsequently listed include a range of acts that are typically criminalized under national jurisdictions.[73] The categories of crimes necessarily overlap, and notably murder or willful killing appears in three of the four Articles. In contrast, rape only appears once—under the crimes against humanity provisions.

However, each of the four Articles can be interpreted to cover rape, and rape need not be specifically enumerated to prosecute the underlying acts associated with the substantive charge. ICTY prosecutors can choose among the universe of crimes available, and indeed allegations of rape have been charged under each of the Articles.[74] The first two Articles tend to apply to armed conflicts with an international character. Under Article 2, persons can be held accountable for "grave breaches." While rape is not specifically enu-

---

68. Even after such judgments there are debates about whether the definitions established by the tribunals are correct, appropriate, or fair.

69. ICTY Statute Art. 2, 35 I.L.M., 1192, available at www.icty.org (Basic Legal Documents).

70. ICTY Statute Art. 3, 35 I.L.M., 1192–93.

71. ICTY Statute Art. 4, 35 I.L.M., 1193.

72. ICTY Statute Art. 5, 35 I.L.M., 1193–94.

73. Danner, "Constructing a Hierarchy," and Beth Van Schaack, "The Definition of Crimes Against Humanity: Resolving the Incoherence," 37 *Columbia Journal of Transnational Law* (1999).

74. Gabrielle Kirk McDonald, "Friedmann Award Address: Crimes of Sexual Violence: The Experience of the International Criminal Tribunal," 39 *Columbia Journal of Transnational Law* (2000); and Patricia Viseur Sellers and Kaoru Okuizumi, "Intentional Prosecution of Sexual Assaults," 7 *Transnational Law and Contemporary Problems* (1997).

merated, the ICTY has interpreted this provision to include rape—implicitly as torture and as an application of customary international law under the Geneva Convention Protocols which do enumerate rape.[75] Second and closely related to the grave breach provisions are Article 3 protections established according to the laws and customs of war. The Article does not enumerate rape, but it prohibits "wanton destruction of cities, towns or villages, or devastation not justified by military necessity; [or] attack, or bombardment, by whatever means, of undefended towns, villages, dwellings, or buildings." This section has been used in the same manner as charges under the grave breach provisions.[76]

The remaining two classes of crimes do not require the armed conflict to be international for the ICTY to take jurisdiction, and there is overlap between the provisions for genocide and crimes against humanity. Genocide "can be regarded as a species and progeny of the broader genus of crimes against humanity."[77] Genocide—the crime of all crimes—is viewed as the "ultimate crime against humanity," and it is the systematic destruction of a group by:

> any of the following acts committed with the intent to destroy, in whole or in part, a national, ethnical, racial or religious group by killing members of the group; causing serious bodily or mental harm to members of the group; deliberately inflicting on the group conditions of life calculated to bring about its physical destruction in whole or in part; imposing measures intended to prevent births within the group; forcibly transferring children of the group to another group.

Crimes against humanity under Article 5 are defined as "inhumane acts: willful killing, torture or rape, committed as part of a widespread or systematic attack against any civilian population on national, political, ethnic, racial or religious grounds." It is here that the statute explicitly acknowledges rape as a crime, and it is here that scholars argue there is the greatest authority for ending the culture of impunity as it relates to rape.[78]

---

75. M. Cherif Bassiouni, *Crimes Against Humanity in International Criminal Law* (Boston: Martinus Nijhoff, 1999); *Prosecutor v. Delalic.*

76. *Prosecutor v. Furundzija*, Case No. IT-95-17 II T (Trial Chamber, December 10, 1998), available at www.un.org/icty.

77. Theodor Meron, "The Humanization of Humanitarian Law," 94 *American Journal of International Law* (1995).

78. Coan, "Rethinking the Spoils of War."

Most advocates for women argue that if justice is to be done, the ICTY must be aggressive in prosecuting the genocide and the crimes against humanity provisions.[79] To that end, scholars and practitioners argue that aggressive sentencing for crimes against humanity sends a signal from the international community that attacks on civilian populations will not be tolerated.

There has been considerable discussion over rape as genocide or at least a genocidal weapon of war.[80] Using rapes to impregnate women and pollute the ethnic lineage or to alienate women from their ethnic identification could be considered genocide, because the intent is to destroy certain ethnic, racial, or religious groups.[81] As evidence provided in the sexual enslavement trial noted, women were frequently taunted by their rapists and told that they would now be forced to carry Serb babies and that no Muslim men would be with them after the assaults.

As for the crimes against humanity provisions, the feminist argument here is that rape is specifically provided for in the statute. As such, the ICTY staff (whether it is the prosecutor or the judges) has authoritative text on the prohibition against rape. The use of positivist law to explicitly prosecute sexual violence may provide a greater sense of justice for victims, clarify the protections for victims of sexual violence, and assist in the establishment of international legal norms that contribute to gender-based protections.[82]

To examine whether there is a relationship between the substantive law associated with each charge and the sentence the defendant received, I examined each count and subsequent judgment on the count. All charges of genocide and crimes against humanity were coded as dichotomous variables. The rape variable is measured according to whether the underlying acts that contribute to a charge under the enumerated provisions are premised on rape or claims of sexual assault in the last amended indictment presented by the Office of Prosecution. Once again, this is measured as a dichotomous variable. If the interests of retributive justice are served, the direction should be positive.

---

79. Beth Stephens, "Humanitarian Law and Gender Violence: An End to Centuries of Neglect?", 3 *Hofstra Law and Policy Symposium* (1999); Brook Sari Moshan, "Women, War and Words: The Gender Component in the Permanent International Criminal Court's Definition of Crimes Against Humanity," 22 *Fordham International Law Journal* (1998); and Theodor Meron, "Rape as a Crime Under International Humanitarian Law," 87 *American Journal of International Law* (1993).

80. Glenny, *The Fall of Yugoslavia.*

81. Askin, *War Crimes Against Women*, and Ray, "The Shame of It."

82. Stephens, "Humanitarian Law and Gender Violence," and Moshan, *Women, War and Words.*

Total Number of Counts Charged

The final variable controls for the number of counts levied against the defendant to measure more accurately the relationship between the length of sentence and substantive variables. Intuitively, the more charges an indictee faces, the greater the likelihood that a lengthy sentence will be imposed if the defendant is found guilty. This effect has long been recognized as "throwing the book" at someone in order to ensure an appropriate sentence. The variable for the count total is a summary of all charges that the defendant stands accused of on the last amended indictment before the judgment regarding sentence is rendered.

Discussion

The results are presented in Table 10.1 and indicate that, contrary to criticisms leveled against the Tribunal, it has been fairly aggressive in handing down sentences against persons in command authority and persons found guilty of crimes against humanity. The results indicate that the overall model performs well ($p > .01$) and that each of the variables is statistically significant with, most notably, the exception of rape. Even though the rape variable is not significant ($p > .12$), it lends support to the Tribunal's defenders' assertions that sexual assault cases are not being marginalized by the sentences given to defendants found guilty of sexual assault.[83] The control variable for the number of counts the defendant is charged with is significant as well, indicating that it was both appropriate and necessary to control for sentences that include multiple counts.

Consistent with doctrinal rulings that have extended judicial authority under the Nuremberg and Tokyo Tribunals, defendants with command and control power are receiving lengthier sentences. A shift in command authority increases the sentence by over 9.8 years. This is consistent with the Tribunals' mandate under the statute to hold high-ranking officials responsible for actions committed on their watch.[84] This should be welcome news to persons advocating retribution for top-level leaders, and it may send a signal that the culture of impunity is becoming unacceptable in international law.[85]

For persons who support the enforcement of human rights laws to combat sexual violence committed en masse, the results may have even more importance. In part, this is because, for the first time in history, commanding offi-

---

83. Askin, "Sexual Violence in Decisions and Indictments."
84. Solis, "Obedience of Orders."
85. Wald, "International Criminal Tribunal," and U.N. SCOR, 49th Sess., 3453d mtg., at 7, 14, U.N. Doc. S/PV.3453 (1994).

Table 10.1   OLS Regression Estimates
Analysis of the ICTY Sentences in Rape Cases

	Coefficient	Standard error	T-statistic
Rape	46.62	(37)	1.23*
Command and control	117.91	(27.8)	4.24**
Crime against humanity	151.46	(52.73)	2.87**
Total counts charged	5.71	(1.88)	3.03**
Intercept	193.13	(75.76)	–

N=29
Model significance probability>F=.001
R-squared=.57
Adj. R-squared=.5**
*p>.05 (one-tailed test)
**p>.01 (one-tailed test)

cers have been held responsible for the actions of the subordinates. In five of the 13 cases involving rape, superior officers stood accused of either standing by while rapes occurred or actively participating in the rapes. If gross violations of command authority result in heavier punishments, perhaps there may be some deterrent value for future commanders. At a minimum, the findings here support a retributive theory of justice that commanders will be held responsible for their actions.

As a preliminary note on the variable for genocide and crimes against humanity, we argued that defendants accused of these categories would be given longer sentences because these are typically actions that are assaults on civilian populations, and hence an attack on all humanity. Aggressive prosecution of such cases is essential, because here is where terror reaches non-combatants.[86] Adequately gauging the effect of genocide as an independent factor

---

86. Copelon, "Surfacing Gender," and Danner, "Constructing a Hierarchy."

is impossible because of the nature of decisions by the Prosecutor's office to seek charges of genocide. Indeed, interviews with Tribunal staff indicated that there is a reluctance to prosecute under those charges because of the difficulty in proving the "intent to destroy" element under the ICTY statute. There are only two defendants who were accused of genocide, Jelisic and Krstic, and in both instances the defendants were also accused of crimes against humanity, although only Krstic was ultimately found guilty of genocide.[87] As a result, only crimes against humanity compared to war crimes and grave beaches are considered.

The findings support the idea that the Tribunal is giving lengthier sentences to persons attacking the civilian population rather than to persons who take actions in the course of war. Persons sentenced for crimes against humanity receive an increased sentence of more than 151 months or more than 12.5 years longer than persons who are accused of war crimes and grave breaches.

Judges on the panels may believe that attacks on civilian populations are especially egregious and merit longer sentences and may also be implicitly adopting a hierarchy among the crimes in the statute, although both the Appeals and the Trial Chambers have rejected that claim. A series of three cases have attempted to establish whether some categories of crimes merit heavier penalties, but the Tribunal ultimately rejected this principle suggesting that only case-by-case analyses are appropriate and indicating that there can be "no distinction between the seriousness of a crime against humanity and that of a war crime."[88] Nonetheless, the findings will trouble those jurists that have argued there are no distinctions among the different substantive laws used to prosecute defendants. Contrary to the decisions in Tadic and Furundzija, there may be a hierarchy among the crimes, and the Tribunal may already be de facto engaging in the ranking of crimes when it renders sentences.[89] Advocates will probably herald these findings because they add legitimacy to the argument that one of the most important functions the Tribunal can serve is to expand the authority over crimes against humanity.[90]

---

87. Therefore, it was impossible to use a model that considered the effects of genocide as separate from crimes against humanity. *Prosecutor v. Krstic,* Case No. IT-98-33 (Trial Chamber, August 2, 2001), available at <www.un.org/icty>.

88. *Prosecutor v. Erdemovic,* Case No. IT-96-22, P 3 (Appeals Chamber, October 7, 1997); *Prosecutor v. Tadic,* Case No. IT-94-1-T (Trial Chamber, November 11, 1999); and *Prosecutor v. Furundzija,* all available at <www.un.org/icty>.

89. Danner, "Constructing a Hierarchy."

90. Meron, "The Humanization of Humanitarian Law."

The argument of some that the aggressive enforcement of crimes against humanity has a secondary effect of enhancing the status of rape victims by providing them with additional protections is strengthened. To the extent that crimes against humanity are aggressively enforced and that rape is only enumerated under the crimes against humanity article of the statute, future generations of jurists may be willing to actively assert the protection of rape victims as a principle of *jus cogens* or a principle of international law that states accept as a norm to be followed and not derogated.

The variable rape findings are, while not significant, interesting because persons accused of sexual assault receive an additional 46 months on their sentences, ceteris paribus. Contrary to critics who argue that the tribunal has not done enough to protect women's rights[91] or that the ICTY has been ineffective in addressing allegations of rape,[92] we do not find support for such a conclusion.

This is particularly true when examining the two comparable categories of crimes that are frequently cited as equally as insidious as rape, murder and torture. Many of the victims who have testified at trial referred to the assaults as being comparable to death or to an extreme torture that continues long after the act. When a model replacing rape with the crime of murder (or willful killing) is used, defendants received sentences that were 48 months less than all other types of crimes ($p > .16$). Similarly, defendants accused of torture received sentences that were 27 months less than all other types of crimes ($p > .54$) (results not shown). This lends support to the conclusion that judges may be issuing heavier sentences in sexual assault cases than in cases involving murder and torture.[93]

Viewing the ICTY rape cases from a qualitative standpoint, it is almost incomprehensible to imagine that any punishment could serve as an appropriate sanction for the violations committed. Research on the plight of the victims has documented extensively the trauma of survivors, and it is doubtful that any judgment from any court of law could ever make the victims of the Balkan atrocities feel whole again.[94] As Judge Wald (2001b) notes:

---

91. Alvarez, "Rush to Closure."

92. Davis, "The Politics of Prosecuting Rape."

93. A model including both the variables of murder and rape indicates that the effects of cases involving both murder and rape dilute the significance of the rape variable (results not shown). While a discussion of murder and sexual assault is beyond the scope of this research, it may be that judges are issuing heavier sentences in cases where there are charges of rape without charges of murder.

94. Vera Folnegovic-Smalc, "Psychiatric Aspects of the Rapes in the War Against the Republics of Croatia and Bosnia-Herzegovina," in Alexandra Stiglmayer (ed.), *Mass Rape:*

It is not possible to recount in any shorthand way their stories: the physical or emotional horrors lived through; the ruination of their lives, families, and communities; and the residues of hate, hopelessness and despair. Most of the witnesses were severely traumatized. Some saw three generations of men in their families killed within a week's time. Many were tortured, and women including twelve and thirteen year-old girls, underwent torture in the form of indiscriminate gang rapes and prolonged sexual enslavement."[95]

The results from the rape variable are not so surprising considering that ICTY judges have said that they are sensitive to sentencing in relation to the plight of victims. Indeed, in most of the sentencing statements issued by the Tribunal, the court will specifically refer to the victims of sexual assault as having dealt with an unfathomable terror. This is because the experiences were horrific and unimaginable, and because the Tribunal has a role in promoting women's rights.[96] The results here indicate that the tribunal has been somewhat forceful in sentencing persons whose underlying charges include rape.

Notably, the findings from the model in Table 1 are insignificant from an empirical standpoint. The results confirm, therefore, what feminist critics have said about the ICTY's lack of effectiveness in levying harsh sentences against persons accused of rape. After all, almost four years elapsed after the first allegations of rape surfaced before defendants were found guilty of crimes against humanity with rape being the sole basis for the counts charged. Feminists may be correct that we cannot minimize the **substantial** problems the Tribunal has experienced as it relates to rape victims. There have been numerous problems regarding the collection of evidence, witness protection, and the physical and emotional aid given to women who testify before the tribunal.[97] The speed at which the trials proceed has hampered the Tribunal's effectiveness, resulting in the "re-victimization" of the victim. Judges of the tribunal have openly acknowledged these problems, but have argued this means only that the Tribunal needs to work harder.[98]

To examine whether there are differences between defendants who commit grave breaches and war crimes, as well as rape, as compared to defendants

---

The War Against Women in Bosnia-Herzegovina (Lincoln: University of Nebraska Press, 1994). For survey research on victim perceptions regarding survival and life after the war, see Ivkovic, "Justice by the International Criminal Tribunal."

95. Wald, "The International Criminal Tribunal."
96. Ibid.
97. Davis, "The Politics of Prosecuting Rape."
98. Wald, "The International Criminal Tribunal."

Table 10.2   OLS Regression Estimates
Analysis of the ICTY Sentences
Rape as a War Crime Compared to Rape as a Crime against Humanity

	Coefficient	Standard error	T-statistic
Rape	-29.04	(70.54)	-.41*
Command and control	77.63	(43.61)	1.78**
Crime against humanity	117.77	(7.8)	3.82**
Total counts charged	4.6	(2.06)	2.24**
Intercept	193.13	(75.76)	−

N=29
Model significance probability>F-.001
R-squared=.48
Adj. R-squared=.42**
*p>.01 (one-tailed test)
**p>.05 (one-tailed test)

who have committed crimes against humanity, as well as rape, another model was developed. Table 10.2 illustrates that there may be support for arguing that even though the Tribunal has been aggressive about punishing rape as an enumerated crime, it is the combination of crimes against humanity, with specific allegations of rape, which leads to lengthier sentences.

The overall fit of the model drops as reflected in the adjusted R-squared (reduced from fifty to forty-two), but the coefficients from command and control, as well as the control variable for total counts charged, continue to perform about the same. Interestingly, when rape and grave breach charges are levied against a defendant, he received a *reduced* sentence by almost twenty-seven months. When there are charges of rape and crimes against humanity, the defendant receives a seventy-seven month *lengthier* sentence as compared to the model in Table 1. In contrast to that model, there is a significant effect for persons accused of both rape and the statute that explicitly enumerates rape. This adds support for the idea that the ICTY has in fact protected victims of sexual violence.

One has the feeling in reading the comments of the Tribunal's critics that the call for aggressive human rights enforcement is almost habitual rather than of empirical substantiation.[99] Perhaps this is because to praise the work of the Tribunal might mean that the organization would rest on its laurels or become lax in its treatment of the victims who have suffered through the trauma that occurred (and continues to occur) in the Balkans. Perhaps advocates are concerned that such findings will result in the reduction of resources for sexual assault cases and investigations. To that end, my findings arguably undermine feminist criticisms of the ICTY for doctrinal and policy reasons.[100]

We would argue exactly the opposite of these criticisms. The findings suggest that judges are sympathetic to crimes of rape and crimes against humanity, and advocates should take advantage of those findings to ensure the greatest degree of international humanitarian protection possible. It is not just the charge of rape, or that rape be charged as a crime against humanity, but the combination of going after those in command and control positions, coupled with aggressive enforcement of rape under all the provisions of the statute, including crimes against humanity, that will help the ICTY to achieve its mission to "do justice."

As for why judges may be more likely to issue heavier sentences in cases where rape is alleged, we would suggest that perhaps it is the concern that somehow the victims have been left as the "walking dead" that encourages judges to issue heavier penalties. There may not be much that the Tribunal can do for the people who did not survive the Balkan wars, but the Tribunal can do much for those who managed to live through them. This, too, would be consistent with a retributive theory of justice. Prosecutors might choose to spend additional rime on cases under investigation where rape is alleged. Moreover, given the complaints that victim-witnesses in gender violence cases are not treated fairly, the ICTY Prosecutor's office should devote more attention and resources to these units because perhaps judges are more sympathetic to the prosecution in rape cases.

Contrary to some normative arguments,[101] the ICTY has attempted to advance the cause of protecting women's rights from gender violence.[102] In interviews with male and female judges at the Tribunals and in the writings of the jurists themselves, the Tribunal continually maintains its sensitivity to is-

99. Davis, "The Politics of Prosecuting Rape."

100. Hoefgen, "There Will Be No Justice"; Stephens, "Humanitarian Law and Gender Violence."

101. Davis, "The Politics of Prosecuting Rape."

102. Askin, "Sexual Violence in Decisions and Indictments."

sues of gender justice.[103] Both at the Tribunal in The Hague and at the U.N. there have been concerted efforts to place women on the bench, and there has been a strong presence of women, especially in rape cases.[104] Under provisions relating to the establishment of the Victims' Assistance Unit (Article 34), the statute requests that qualified personnel, both male and female, be hired. Women have occupied a number of key policymaking positions, including president and chief prosecutor. While some have criticized the Tribunal for being weak when prosecuting persons accused of rape, the judgments rendered in the last five years are remarkable for solidifying principles of international law, for establishing a definition of rape under international law, and for prosecuting gender violence.[105]

Conclusion

Unlike the trials at Nuremberg and Tokyo which marginalized mass rapes, the ICTY judgments seem to be providing for a shift in the doctrine regarding rape.[106] The decisions regarding the prohibition on sexual enslavement, the clarification regarding the definition of rape, and the inclusion of rape as a war crime all support the proposition that a shift is occurring.[107] The Tribunal is more likely to hand down tougher sentences when gender violence forms part of the underlying charges, but there is an important caveat. The inclusion of rape or sexual assault in the charges is not nearly as important as other factors —namely the substantive charge (whether genocide, crimes against humanity, or war crimes) and the command and control authority of the accused.

The debate will continue regarding whether the ICTY has contributed to the next generation of human rights enforcement and limiting the power of persons in command and control. The Tribunal's judgments regarding command and control, following the lead from Tokyo, have expanded the accountability of commanding officers who allow sexual assault to occur on their

---

103. McDonald, "Friedmann Award Address," and Wald, "The International Criminal Tribunal."

104. Coan, "Rethinking the Spoils of War."

105. Askin, "Sexual Violence in Decisions and Indictments."

106. Christopher Scott Maravilla, "Rape as a War Crime: The Implications of the International Criminal Tribunal for the Former Yugoslavia's Decision in *Prosecutor v. Kunarac, Kovac and Vukovic* on International Humanitarian Law," 13 *Florida Journal of International Law* (2001).

107. *Prosecutor v. Kunarac, Kovac, & Vukovic*, Case No. IT-96-23 (Trial Chamber, February 22, 2001), available at <www.un.org/icty>.

watch. And the extension of substantive doctrines surrounding sexual assault may provide tomorrow's jurists with principles that can be used for holding persons found guilty of sexual assault responsible. This in turn may lead to a gradual recognition that command and control responsibility will result in greater levels of punishment for those who treat rape victims as spoils of war to be passed out to the troops. Clearly, moreover, the ICTY has limited national sovereignty by trying both ordinary soldiers and command and control officials at the international bar.

We would argue that the Yugoslavian tribunal has advanced the cause of limiting the culture of impunity that has surrounded mass rape. The cause has been advanced, though, not as much as others have argued should be the case, or even as much as some might have hoped. The work of the Tribunal is, however, far from complete. At the time of writing, forty-four persons are being held in detention, and another twenty-one have arrest warrants issued (excluding those under seal by the ICTY). For advocates of protecting victims of rape, the opportunities have never been greater to advance the cause of international justice. Never before has there been a body of law to break the boundaries that have allowed rape to occur across all cultures and across all conflicts. Never before have people in command positions been held responsible for rapes that occur on their watch. The ICTY has not just rendered important rulings that advance the protection of rape victims; it has opened the door to a discussion about permissibility of rape during armed conflict and the limits of sexual enslavement as crimes against humanity. As a court, it has crossed national borders and set precedents for future crossings. Our results here support that the ICTY has gone even further than just doctrinal statements. It has also been willing to do justice by giving longer sentences to those accused of rape. Just as rape has been used as a weapon of war, perhaps with the next generation of cases, before other international tribunals, the charge of rape can be used as a weapon of retribution.

BIBLIOGRAPHY

Abbott, Frederick M. 2000. "NAFTA and the Legalization of World Politics: A Case Study," 54 *International Organization*.

———. 2000. "The North American Integration Regime and its Implications for the World Trading System." In *The EU, the WTO, and the NAFTA* edited by J.H.H. Weiler. Oxford: Oxford University Press.

Abbott, Kenneth W. and Duncan Snidal. 2000. "Hard and Soft Law in International Governance," 54 *International Organization*.

Abel, Richard L. 1973. "A Comparative Theory of Dispute Institutions in Society," 8 *Law and Society Review*.

Akhavan, Payam. 1998. "Justice in The Hague, Peace in the Former Yugoslavia? A Commentary on the United Nations War Crimes Tribunal," 20 *Human Rights Quarterly*.

Albuquerque, José Augusto Guilhon. 1999. "Mercosur: Democratic Stability and Economic Integration in South America." In *Regional Integration and Democracy* edited by Jeffrey J. Anderson, Lanham: Rowman and Littlefield.

Almond, Gabriel A. 1996. "Political Science: The History of the Discipline." In *A New Handbook of Political Science* edited by Robert E. Goodin and Hans-Dieter Klingemann, Oxford: Oxford University Press.

Alter, Karen. 2001. *Establishing the Supremacy of European Law*, Oxford: Oxford University Press.

Alter, Karen J. 2000. "The European Union's Legal System and Domestic Policy: Spillover or Backlash?", 54 (3) *International Organization*.

Alvarez, José E. 1998. "Rush to Closure: Lessons of the Tadic Judgment," 96 *Michigan Law Review*.

Appadurai, Arjun. 1993. "Disjuncture and Difference in the Global Cultural Economy." In *The Phantom Public Sphere* edited by B. Robbins, Minneapolis: University of Minnesota Press.

Arnull, Anthony. 1999. *The European Union and its Court of Justice*, Oxford: Oxford University Press.

Askin, Kelly D. 1997. *War Crimes Against Women: Prosecution in International War Crimes Tribunals*, Boston: Martinus Nijhoff.

———. 1999. "Sexual Violence in Decisions and Indictments of the Yugoslav and Rwandan Tribunals: Current Status," 93 *American Journal of International Law*.

Aufricht, Hans. 1944-45. "On Relative Sovereignty," parts I and II, 30 *Cornell Law Quarterly*.

Aydelott, Danise. 1993. "Mass Rape During War: Prosecuting Bosnian Rapists Under International Law," 7 *Emory International Law Review*.

Badie, Bertrand. 2001. "Realism under Praise, or a Requiem? The Paradigmatic Debate in International Relations," 22 *International Political Science Review*.

Baker, Christopher, ed. 1998. *Human Rights Act 1998: A Practitioner's Guide*, London: Sweet and Maxwell.

Bass, Gary Jonathan. 2000. *Stay the Hand of Vengeance: The Politics of War Crimes Tribunals*, Princeton: Princeton University Press.

Bassiouni, M. Cherif. 1999. *Crimes Against Humanity in International Criminal Law*, Boston: Martinus Nijhoff.

———. 1997. "From Versailles to Rwanda in Seventy-five Years: The Need to Establish a Permanent International Criminal Court," 10 *Harvard Human Rights Law Journal*.

Bassiouni, M. Cherif and Peter Manikas. 1996. *The Law of the International Criminal Tribunal for the Former Yugoslavia*, Irvington-on-Hudson: Transnational Publishers.

Beigbeder, Yves. 1999. *Judging War Criminals: The Politics of International Justice*, New York: St. Martin's Press.

Biersteker, Thomas J. and Cynthia Weber, eds. 1996. *State Sovereignty as Social Construct*, Cambridge: Cambridge University Press.

Bloch, D.S. and E. Weinstein. 1998. "Velvet Glove and Iron Fist: A New Paradigm for the Permanent War Crimes Court," 22 *Hastings International and Comparative Law Review*.

Bodin, Jean. 1992. *On Sovereignty: Four Chapters from the Six Books on the Commonwealth* translated and edited by Julian H. Franklin, Cambridge: Cambridge University Press.

Bognanno, Mario F. and Kathryn J. Ready, eds. 1993. *The North American Free Trade Agreement*, Westport, CT: Quorum Books.

Brody, Reed and Michael Ratner, eds. 2000. *The Pinochet Papers: The Case of Augusto Pinochet in Spain and Britain*, The Hague: Kluwer Law International.

Brown, Bartram S. 2000. "The Evolving Concept of Universal Jurisdiction, 35 (2) *New England Law Review*.

Brownmiller, Susan. 1975. *Against Our Will: Men, Women and Rape*, New York: Bantam Books.

Brownmiller, Susan. 1994. "Making Female Bodies the Battlefield." In *Mass Rape: The War Against Women in Bosnia-Herzegovina* edited by Alexandra Stiglmayer, Lincoln: University of Nebraska Press.

Brysk, Alison. 2000. *From Tribal Village to Global Village*, Stanford: Stanford University Press.

Bull, Hedley. 1977. *The Anarchical Society: A Study of World Order in Politics*, New York: Columbia University Press.

Burhenne,Wolfgang E. and Thomas J. Schoenbaum. 1973. "The European Community and Management of the Environment: A Dilemma," 13 *Natural Resources Journal*.

Burley, Anne-Marie and Walter Mattli. 1993. "Europe Before the Court: A Political Theory of Legal Integration," 47 *International Organization*.

Canon, Bradley C. and Charles A. Johnson. 1999. *Judicial Policies: Implementation and Impact*, Washington, D.C.: CQ Press.

Carpentier, Michel. 1972. "L'action de la Communauté en matière d'environnement," 153 *Revue du Marché Commun*.

Carter, Ralph G. and Donald W. Jackson. 2002. "The International Criminal Court: Present at the Creation?" In *Contemporary Cases in U.S. Foreign Policy: From Terrorism to Trade* edited by Ralph G. Carter, Washington, DC: Congressional Quarterly Books.

Cassese, S. 1991. "La Costituzione Europea," *Quaderni Costituzionali*.

Cerna, Christina M. 1992. "Structure and Functioning of the Inter-American Court of Human Rights," *British Yearbook of International Law Annual*.

Chalmers, Damian. 1997. "Judicial Preferences and Community Legal Order," 60 *Modern Law Review*.

Charnovitz, Steve. 1991. "Exploring the Environmental Exceptions in GATT Article XX," 25 *Journal of World Trade.*

Cichowski, Rachel A. 2000. *Litigation and Environmental Protection in the European Union, Max-Planck-Projektgruppe Recht der Gemeinschaftsgüter,* Bonn: Max-Planck.

Clayton, Richard and Hugh Tomlinson. 2000. *The Law of Human Rights,* Oxford: Oxford University Press.

Clements, Luke. 1994. *European Human Rights,* London: Sweet and Maxwell.

Close, George. 1978. "Harmonisation of Laws: Use or Abuse of the Powers under the EEC Treaty?", 3 *European Law Review.*

Coan, Christin B. 2000. "Rethinking the Spoils of War: Prosecuting Rape as a War Crime in the International Criminal Tribunal for the Former Yugoslavia," 26 *North Carolina Journal of International Law and Commercial Regulation.*

Coleman, William D. and Geoffrey R.D. Underhill, eds. 1998. *Regionalism and Global Economic Integration,* London: Routledge.

Condé, H. Victor. 1999. *A Handbook of International Rights Terminology,* Lincoln, NE: University of Nebraska Press.

Connelly, Alpha. 1994. "Ireland and the European Convention on Human Rights: An Overview." In *Human Rights: A European Perspective* edited by Liz Heffernan, Dublin: Round Hall Press.

Copelon, Rhonda. 1994. "Surfacing Gender: Reconceptualizing Crimes Against Women in Time of War." In *Mass Rape: The War Against Women in Bosnia-Herzegovina* edited by Alexandra Stiglmayer, Lincoln: University of Nebraska Press.

"Danish Government Puts EC on Notice that it Values Environment Above Unity," *International Environment Reporter* (August 12, 1987).

Danner, Allison Marston. 2001. "Constructing a Hierarchy of Crimes in International Criminal Law Sentencing," 87 *Virginia Law Review.*

Davidson, Scott. 1993. *Human Rights,* Buckingham: Open University Press.

———. 1992. *The Inter-American Court of Human Rights,* Brookfield: Ashgate.

Davis, Patricia H. 2000. "The Politics of Prosecuting Rape as a War Crime," 34 *International Lawyer.*

De Witt, Bruno. 1999. "Direct Effect, Supremacy and the Nature of the Legal Order." In *The Evolution of EU Law* edited by Paul Craig and Grainne deBurca, Oxford: Oxford University Press.

Dehousse, Renaud. 1998. *The European Court of Justice: The Politics of Judicial Integration*, New York: St. Martin's Press.

"Denmark Wins Assurances From EEC Partners That National Laws Will Not be Compromised," *International Environment Reporter* (February 12, 1986).

DePalma, Anthony. March 11, 2001. "NAFTA's Powerful Little Secret: Obscure Tribunals Settle Disputes, but Grow Too Fat, Critics Say," *New York Times*.

Deutsch, Karl W. et al. 1957. *Political Community in the North Atlantic Area: International Organization in the Light of Historical Experience*, New York: Greenwood Press.

Dicey, A. 1965. *An Introduction to the Study of the Law and the Constitution*, London: Macmillan.

Donahue, John D. and Mark A. Pollack. 2001. "Centralization and its Discontents." In *The Federal Vision: Legitimacy and Levels of Governance in the United States and the European Union* edited by Kalypso Nicolaidis and Robert Howse, Oxford: Oxford University Press.

Dorr, Neal. 1994. "An Introduction to Human Rights Developments since 1945." In *Human Rights: A European Perspective* edited by Liz Heffernan, Dublin: Round Hall Press.

Due, Ole. 1994. "The Law-making Role of the European Court of Justice Considered in Particular from the Perspective of Individuals and Undertakings," 63 *Nordic Journal of International Law*.

Ehlermann, C.D. 1987. "The Internal Market Following the Single European Act," 24 *Common Market Law Review*.

Endsley, Harry B. 1995. "Dispute Settlement Under the CFTA and NAFTA: From Eleventh Hour Innovation to Accepted Institution," 18 *Hastings International and Comparative Law Review*.

Enloe, Cynthia. 1993. *The Morning After: Sexual Politics at the End of the Cold War*, Berkeley: University of California Press.

Epp, Charles R. 1998. *The Rights Revolution: Lawyers, Activists, and Supreme Courts in Comparative Perspective*, Chicago: University of Chicago Press.

Evans, Malcolm D. and Rod Morgan. 1999. *Preventing Torture: A Study of the European Convention for the Prevention of Torture and Inhuman or Degrading Treatment or Punishment*, Oxford: Oxford University Press.

Ference, Benjamin. 1999. "A Prosecutor's Personal Account: From Nuremberg to Rome," 52 *Journal of International Affairs*.

Finer, Samuel E. 1997. *The History of Government*, Oxford: Oxford University Press.

Flynn, James. 1987. "How Will Article 100a(4) Work? A Comparison with Article 93," 24 *Common Market Law Review*.

Folnegovic-Smalc, Vera. 1994. "Psychiatric Aspects of the Rapes in the War Against the Republics of Croatia and Bosnia-Herzegovina." In *Mass Rape: The War Against Women in Bosnia-Herzegovina* edited by Alexandra Stiglmayer, Lincoln: University of Nebraska Press.

Forsythe, David P. 2000. *Human Rights in International Relations*, Cambridge: Cambridge University Press.

————. 1991. *The Internationalization of Human Rights*, Lexington: Lexington Books.

Fram, Alan. (December 7, 2001) "Senate Votes Against International Criminal Court," Associated Press.

Gamarra, Eduardo A. 1994. "Market-Oriented Reforms and Democratization in Latin America." In *Latin American Political Economy in the Age of Neoliberal Reform: Theoretical and Comparative Perspectives for the 1990* edited by William C. Smith, Carlos H. Acuna, and Eduardo A. Gamarra, New Brunswick: Transaction Press.

Gantz, David A. 1998. "Resolution of Trade Disputes under NAFTA's Chapter 19: The Lessons of Extending the Binational Panel Process to Mexico," 29 *Law and Policy in International Business*.

Garrett, Geoffrey. 1995. "The Politics of Legal Integration in the European Union," 49 *International Organization*.

Garrett, Geoffrey, R. Daniel Kelemen, and Heiner Schulz. 1998. "The European Court of Justice, National Governments, and Legal Integration in the European Union," 52 *International Organization*.

George, Stephen and Ian Bache, *Politics in the European Union*, Oxford: Oxford University Press.

Gerard, Alain. 1975. "Les limites et les moyens juridiques de l'intervention des Communautés Européennes en matière de l'environnement," 11 *Cahiers de Droit Européen*.

Gibson, James L., Gregory A. Caldeira, and Vanessa A. Baird. June 1998. "On the Legitimacy of National High Courts," 92 (2) *American Political Science Review*.

Glenny, Misha. 1992. *The Fall of Yugoslavia: The Third Balkan War*, New York: Viking Press.

Goldstein, Leslie Friedman. 2001. *Constituting Federal Sovereignty: The European Union in Comparative Context*, Baltimore: The Johns Hopkins University Press.

Grabitz, Eberhard and Christoph Sasse. 1977. *Competence of the European Communities for Environmental Policy: Proposal for an Amendment to the Treaty of Rome*, Berlin: Erich Schmidt Verlag.

Gradam, Judith and Michelle Jarvic. 2000. "Women and Armed Conflict: The International Response to the Beijing Platform for Action," 32 *Columbia Human Rights Law Review*.

Griffith, Robin. 1992. "International Trade Treaties and Environmental Protection Measures," 1 *Review of European Community and International Environmental Law*.

Grille, Enzo. 1997. "Multilateralism and Regionalism: A Still Difficult Coexistence." In *Multilateralism and Regionalism after the Uruguay Round* edited by Riccardo Faini and Enzo Grille, Basingstoke: Macmillan Press.

Grotius, Hugo. 1925. *De Jure Belli Ac Pacis Libri Tres*, Oxford: Oxford University Press.

Grugel, Jean and Wil Hout. 1999. "Regions, Regionalism and the South." In *Regionalism across the North-South Divide*, edited by Jean Grugel and Will Hout, London: Routledge.

Guarnieri, Carlo and Patrizia Pederzoli. 2002. *The Power of Judges: A Comparative Study of Courts and Democracy*, Oxford: Oxford University Press.

Gulmann, Claus. 1987. "The Single European Act—Some Remarks from a Danish Perspective," 24 *Common Market Law Review*.

Gutman, Roy. 1993. *Witness to Genocide: The 1993 Pulitzer Prize-Winning Dispatches on the Ethnic Cleansing of Bosnia*, New York: MacMillan Publishing.

Haas, Ernst. 1958. *The Uniting of Europe: Political, Social and Economic Forces, 1950-1957*, London: Stevens and Sons.

Hancher, L. and Hanna Sevenster. 1992. "Comment," 30 *Common Market Law Review*.

Herman, Lawrence L. 1998. "Sovereignty Revisited: Settlement of International Trade Disputes—Challenge to Sovereignty—A Canadian Perspective," 24 *Canada-United States Law Review*.

Higgins, Rosalynn. 1984. "The European Convention on Human Rights." In *Human Rights in International Law* edited by Theodore Meron, Oxford: Clarendon Press.

Hix, Simon. 1999. *The Political System of the European Union*, Basingstoke: Macmillan Press.

Hoefgen, Anne M. 1999. "There Will be No Justice Unless Women Are Part of that Justice," 14 *Wisconsin Women's Law Journal*.

Hoekman, Bernard and Michel Kostecki. 2001. *The Political Economy of the World Trading System: From GATT to WTO*, New York: Oxford University Press.

Howse, Robert. 2000. "Adjudicative Legitimacy and Treaty Interpretation in International Trade Law." In *The EU, the WTO and the NAFTA* edited by J.H.H. Weiler, Oxford: Oxford University Press.

Hudec, Robert E. 1993. *Enforcing International Trade Law: The Evolution of the Modern GATT Legal System*, Salem, NH: Butterworths.

Huntington, Samuel P. 1993. *The Third Wave: Democratization in the Late Twentieth Century*, Norman, OK: University of Oklahoma Press.

_____ 1973. "Transnational Organizations in World Politics," 25 (3) *World Politics*.

Ivkovic, Sanja Kutnjak. 2001. "Justice by the International Criminal Tribunal for the Former Yugoslavia," 37 *Stanford Journal of International Law*.

Jackson, Donald W. 1997. *The United Kingdom Confronts the European Convention on Human Rights*, Gainesville, FL: University Press of Florida.

Jackson, John H. 2000. *The Jurisprudence of GATT and the WTO*, Cambridge: Cambridge University Press.

Jacqué, Jean-Paul. 1986. "The 'Single European Act' and Environmental Policy," 16 *Environmental Policy and Law*.

Joerges, Christian. 1997. "The Impact of European Integration on Private Law: Reductionist Perceptions, True Conflicts and a New Constitutionalist Perspective," 3 *European Law Journal*.

Juda, Lawrence. 1992. "A Note on Bureaucratic Politics and Transnational Relations," 4 (2) *International Studies Notes*.

Kahler, Miles. 1995. *Regional Futures and Transatlantic Economic Relations*, New York: Council on Foreign Relations Press.

———. 2002. "Legalization as Strategy: The Asia-Pacific Case," 54 *International Organization*.

Kaiser, Karl. 1971. "Transnational Politics: Toward a Theory of Multinational Politics," 25 (4) *International Organization*.

Kavass, Igor I. 1992. *Supranational and Constitutional Courts in Europe: Functions and Sources*, Buffalo: William S. Hein.

Keeling, David T. 1992. "The Free Movement of Goods in EEC Law: Basic Principles and Recent Developments in the Case Law of the Court of Justice of the European Communities," 26 *International Lawyer*.

Kelemen, R. Daniel. 2001. "The Limits of Judicial Power: Trade-Environment Disputes in the GATT/WTO and the EU," 34 *Comparative Political Studies*.

Kelman, Herbert C. 1977. "The Conditions, Criteria, and Dialectics of Human Dignity: A Transnational Perspective," 21 (3) *International Studies Quarterly*.

Keohane, Robert O. 1996. "International Relations, Old and New." In *A New Handbook of Political Science* edited by Robert E. Goodin and Hans-Dieter Klingemann, Oxford: Oxford University Press.

———— and Joseph S. Nye. 1977. *Power and Interdependence*, Boston: Little Brown.

———— and Joseph S. Nye. 2001. *Power and Interdependence*, Third Edition, New York: Longman.

———— and Joseph S. Nye, eds. 1971. *Transnational Relations and World Politics*, Cambridge: Harvard University Press.

———— and Joseph S. Nye. 1974. "Transgovernmental Relations and International Organizations," 27 (4) *World Politics*.

Khansari, Azar M. 1996. "Searching for the Perfect Solution: International Dispute Resolution and the New Trade Organization," 20 *Hastings International and Comparative Law Review*.

King, Henry T., Jr. 2001. "Universal Jurisdiction: Myths, Realities, Prospects, War Crimes and Crimes Against Humanity: The Nuremberg Precedent," 35 *New England Law Review*.

Krämer, Ludwig. 1998. *E.C. Treaty and Environmental Law*, London: Sweet and Maxwell.

Krasner, Stephen D. 2001. "Abiding Sovereignty," 22 *International Political Science Review*.

Kromarek, Pascale. 1990. "Environmental Protection and Free Movement of Goods: The Danish Bottles Case," 2 *Journal of Environmental Law*.

Langeheine, Bernd. 1989. "Le rapprochement des législations nationales selon l'article 100a du traité CEE: l'harmonisation Communautaire face aux exigences de protection nationales," 328 *Revue du marché commun.*

Lawson, R.A. and H.G. Schermers, eds. 1997. *Leading Cases of the European Court of Human Rights,* Leiden: Ars Aequi Lilbi.

Lenaerts, K. 1990. "Constitutionalism and the Many Faces of Federalism," 38 *American Journal of Comparative Law.*

London, Caroline and Michael Llamas. 1995. *Protection of the Environment and the Free Movement of Goods,* London: Butterworths.

Lutz, Ellen and Kathryn Sikkink. 2001. "International Human Rights Law in Practice: The Judicial Crusade: The Evolution and Impact of Foreign Human Rights in Trials in Latin America," 2 *Chicago Journal of International Law.*

Lutz, Robert E. 1996. "Law, Procedure and Culture in Mexico under the NAFTA: The Perspective of a NAFTA Panelist," 3 *Southwestern Journal of Law and Trade in the Americas.*

MacCormick, Neil. 1993. "Beyond the Sovereign State," 56 *Modern Law Review.*

———. 1999. *Questioning Sovereignty: Law, State and Nation in the European Commonwealth,* Oxford: Oxford University Press.

MacDonald, R. St. J., F. Matscher and H. Petzold, eds. 1993. *The European System for the Protection of Human Rights,* Boston: Martinus Nijhoff.

MacKinnon, Catherine A. 1994. "Rape, Genocide and Women's Human Rights." In *Mass Rape: The War Against Women in Bosnia-Herzegovina* edited by Alexandra Stiglmayer, Lincoln: University of Nebraska Press.

Maduro, Miguel Poiares. "Contrapunctual Law: Europe's Constitutional Pluralism in Action." In *Sovereignty in Transition* edited by Neil Walker, Oxford: Hart Publishing, forthcoming.

———. 1998. *We the Court: The European Court of Justice and the European Economic Constitution,* Oxford: Hart Publishing.

Malkin, Peter Z. and Harry Stein. 1990. *Eichmann in My Hands,* New York: Warner Books.

Malloy, James M. 1987. "Politics of Transition in Latin America." In *Authoritarians and Democrats: Regime Transitions in Latin America* edited by James A. Malloy and Mitchell A. Seligson, Pittsburgh: University of Pittsburgh Press.

Mancini, G. F. 1989. "The Making of a Constitution for Europe," *Common Market Law Review.*

Mansfield, E.D. and H.V. Melner. 1997. *The Political Economy of Regionalism,* New York: Columbia University Press.

Maravilla, Christopher Scott. 2001. "Rape as a War Crime: The Implications of the International Criminal Tribunal for the Former Yugoslavia's Decision in *Prosecutor v. Kunarac, Kovac and Vukovic* on International Humanitarian Law," 13 *Florida Journal of International Law.*

Marquis, Christopher. February 6, 2003. "U.N. Begins Choosing the Judges for New Court," *New York Times.*

Mattli, Walter. 1999. *The Logic of Regional Integration: Europe and Beyond,* Cambridge: Cambridge University Press.

McCrudden, Christopher and Gerald Chambers, eds. 1994. *Individual Rights and the Law in Britain,* Oxford: Clarendon Press.

McDonald, Gabrielle Kirk. 2000. "Friedmann Award Address: Crimes of Sexual Violence: The Experience of the International Criminal Tribunal," 39 *Columbia Journal of Transnational Law.*

Meron, Theodor. 1993. "The Case of War Crimes Trials in Yugoslavia," 72 *Foreign Affairs.*

———. 1995. "The Humanization of Humanitarian Law," 94 *American Journal of International Law.*   •

———. 1993. "Rape as a Crime Under International Humanitarian Law," 87 *American Journal of International Law.*

———. 1994. "War Crimes in Yugoslavia and the Development of International Law," 88 *American Journal of International Law.*

Merrill, Thomas W. 1992. "Judicial Deference to Executive Precedent," 101 *Yale Law Journal.*

Merry, Sally. 2001. "International Research on Women and Violence: Rights, Religion and Community Approaches to Violence Against Women in the Context of Globalization," 35 *Law and Society Review.*

Minow, Martha. 1998. *Between Vengeance and Forgiveness,* Boston: Beacon Press.

Moravcsik, Andrew. 1995. "Explaining International Human Rights Regimes: Liberal Theory and Western Europe," 1 (2) *European Journal of International Relations.*

Mortelmans, Kamiel. 1996. "Community Law: More than a Functional Area of Law, Less than a Legal System," 1996 *Legal Issues of European Integration.*

Morrow, Lance. February 22, 1993. "Unspeakable," *Time.*

Moshan, Brook Sari. 1998. "Women, War and Words: The Gender Component in the Permanent International Criminal Court's Definition of Crimes Against Humanity," 22 *Fordham International Law Journal.*

Murphy, Craig. 1996. "Seeing Women, Recognizing Gender, Recasting International Relations," 50 *International Organization.*

Nebesar, Darren Anne. 1998. "Gender-Based Violence as a Weapon of War," 4 *Journal of International Law and Policy.*

Neier, Aryeh. 1998. *War Crimes: Brutality, Genocide, Terror and the Struggle for Justice,* New York: Times Books.

Niarchos, Catherine. 1995. "Women, War and Rape: Challenges Facing the International Tribunal for the Former Yugoslavia," 17 *Human Rights Quarterly.*

Nicolaidis, Kalypso. 2001. "Conclusion." In *The Federal Vision: Legitimacy and Levels of Governance in the United States and the European Union* edited by Kalypso Nicolaidis and Robert Howse, Oxford: Oxford University Press.

O'Donnell, Guillermo. 1994. "The State, Democratization, and Some Conceptual Problems." In *Latin American Political Economy in the Age of Neoliberal Reform: Theoretical and Comparative Perspectives for the 1990s* edited by William C. Smith, Carlos H. Acuna, and Eduardo A. Gamarra, New Brunswick: Transaction Press.

O'Neill, Onora. 1990. "Justice, Gender and International Boundaries," 20 *British Journal of Political Science.*

Padilla, David J. and Elizabeth A. Houppert. 1997. "The OAS and Human Rights in the Caribbean." In *Democracy and Human Rights in the Caribbean* edited by Ivelaw L. Griffith and Betty N. Sedoc-Dahlberg, Boulder, CO: Westview.

Palmeter, David and Petros C. Mavroidi. 1998. "The WTO Legal System: Sources of Law," 92 *American Journal of International Law.*

Park, Sung-Hoon. 1997. "Regionalism, Open Regionalism and GATT, Article XXIV." Unpublished paper presented at conference on Regional and Global Regulations of International Trade, Macao: Instituto de Estudos Europeus de Macau.

Periera, Lia Valls. 1995. "Toward the Common Market of the South: Mercosur's Origins, Evolution and Challenges." In *Mercosur: Regional Integration and World Markets* edited by Riordan Roett, New York: New York University Press.

Petersmann, Ernst-Ulrich. 1995. *International and European Trade and Environmental Law after the Uruguay Round*, Boston: Kluwer Law International.

Phelan, Rossa. 1997. *Revolt or Revolution: The Constitutional Boundaries of the European Community*, Dublin: Sweet & Maxwell.

Philpott, Daniel. 1999. "Westphalia, Authority and International Society," 57 *Political Studies*.

Politi, Mauro and Guiseppi Nesi, eds. 2001. *The Rome Statute of the International Criminal Court*, Burlington, VT: Ashgate.

Pratt, Kathleen M. and Laurel E. Fletcher. 1994. "Time for Justice: The Case for International Prosecutions of Rape and Gender-Based Violence in the Former Yugoslavia," 9 *Berkeley Women's Law Journal*.

Provine, Doris Marie. 1997. "Women's Concerns in the European Commission and Court of Human Rights." In *Law above Nations* edited by Mary L. Volcansek, Gainesville, FL: University Presses of Florida.

Rawlings, Richard. 1993. "The Eurolaw Game: Deductions from a Saga," 20 *Journal of Law and Society*.

Ray, Amy E. 1997. "The Shame of It: Gender-Based Terrorism in the Former Yugoslavia and the Failure of International Human Rights Law to Comprehend the Injuries," 46 *American University Law Review*.

Rehbinder, Eckard and Richard Stewart. 1985. *Integration Through Law: Europe and the American Federal Experience, vol. 2, Environmental Protection Policy*, New York: Walter de Gruyter.

Reid, T.R. August 16, 1993. "Openly Apologetic, Japan Recalls War's End," *Washington Post*.

Reisman, W. Michael. 1990. "Sovereignty and Human Rights in Contemporary International Law," 84 *The American Journal of International Law*.

Reitman, Janet. July 22, 1994. "Political Repression by Rape Increasing in Haiti," *Washington Post*.

Risse, Thomas and Kathryn Sikkink. 1999. "The Socialization of International Human Rights Norms into Domestic Practices: Introduction." In *The Power of Human Rights: International Norms and Domestic Changes* edited by Thomas Risse, Stephen C. Ropp, and Kathryn Sikkink, Cambridge: Cambridge University Press.

Robertson, A.H. and J.G. Merrills. 1993. *Human Rights in Europe: A Study of the European Convention on Human Rights*, Manchester: Manchester University Press.

Romano, Cesare P.R. 1999. "The Proliferation of International Judicial Bodies: The Pieces of the Puzzle," 31 *New York University Journal of International Law and Politics*.

Rosenau, James. 1990. *Turbulence in World Politics*, Princeton: Princeton University Press.

Rourke, John T. 2002. *Taking Sides: Clashing Views on Controversial Issues in World Politics*, Guilford, CT: Dushkin/McGraw Hill.

Rubin, Alfred P. 2001. *"Actio Popularis, Jus Cogens and Offenses Erga Omnes?"*, 35 (2) *New England Law Review*.

Ruggert, Matthias. 2001. "Pinochet Follow Up: The End of Sovereign Immunity," 48 *Netherlands International Law Review*.

Sandholtz, Wayne and Alec Stone Sweet, eds. 1998. *European Integration and Supranational Governance*, Oxford: Oxford University Press.

Scharf, Michael P. and Thomas P. Fisher. 2001. "Forward." In "Symposium: Universal Jurisdiction: Myths, Realities and Prospects," 35 (2) *New England Law Review*.

Schmitt, Carl. 1988. *Political Theology: Four Chapters on the Concept of Sovereignty*, Cambridge: MIT Press.

Schwartz, Stephen. 1994. "Rape as a Weapon of War in the Former Yugoslavia," 5 *Hastings Women's Law Journal*.

Sciarra, S., ed. 2000. *Labour Law in the Courts - National Judges and the ECJ*, Oxford: Hart Publishing.

Sellers, Patricia Viseur and Kaoru Okuizumi, 1997. "Intentional Prosecution of Sexual Assaults," 7 *Transnational Law and Contemporary Problems*.

Serra, Jaime. 1997. *Reflections on Regionalism*, Washington, D.C.: Carnegie Endowment for International Peace.

Shabtai, Rosenne. 1995. *The World Court*, Boston: Martinus Nijhoff.

Shapiro, Martin. 1981. *Courts: A Comparative and Political Analysis*, Chicago: University of Chicago Press.

Shaw, Jo. 1995. "Introduction." In *New Legal Dynamics of European Union* edited by J. Shaw and G. Moore, Oxford: Clarendon Press.

Shelton, Dinah. 1988. "Improving Human Rights Protections: Recommendations for Enhancing the Effectiveness of the Inter-American

Commission and the Inter-American Court of Human Rights," 3 *American University Journal of International Law and Policy*.

Siefert, Ruth. 1996. "The Second Front: The Logic of Sexual Violence in Wars," 19 *Women's Studies International Forum*.

Slaughter, Anne-Marie, Alec Stone Sweet, and J.H.H. Weiler, eds. 1998. *The European Court and National Courts - Doctrine and Jurisprudence: Legal Change in Its Social Context*, Oxford: Hart Publishing.

Sloan, Robert D. and Pascal Cardonnel. 1995. "Exemptions from Harmonization Measures under Article 100a(4): The Second Authorization of the German Ban on PCP," 4 *European Environmental Law Review*.

Smith, James McCall. 2000. "The Politics of Dispute Settlement Design: Explaining Legalism in Regional Trade Pacts," 54 *International Organization*.

Solis, Gary D. 2000. "Obedience of Orders and the Law of War: Judicial Application in American Forums," 15 *American University International Law Review*.

Steiger, Heinhard. 1977. *Competence of the European Parliament for Environmental Policy*, Berlin: Erich Schmidt Verlag.

Stein, Eric. 1981. "Lawyers, Judges and the Making of a Transnational Constitution," *American Journal of International Law*.

Steiner, Henry J. and Philip Alston. 2000. *International Human Rights in Context: Law, Politics, Morals*, Oxford: Oxford University Press.

Stephens, Beth. 1999. "Humanitarian Law and Gender Violence: An End to Centuries of Neglect?", 3 *Hofstra Law and Policy Symposium*.

Stiglmayer, Alexandra. 1994. "The Rapes in Bosnia-Herzegovina," *Mass Rape: The War Against Women in Bosnia-Herzegovina*, Lincoln: University of Nebraska Press.

Stone Sweet, Alec. 1992. *The Birth of Judicial Politics in France: The Constitutional Council in Comparative Perspective*, Oxford: Oxford University Press.

———. 2000. *Governing with Judges: Constitutional Politics in Europe*, Oxford: Oxford University Press.

———. *The Judicial Construction of Europe*, Oxford: Oxford University Press, forthcoming.

———. 1999. "Judicialization and the Construction of Governance," 31 *Comparative Political Studies*.

————. 1997. "The New GATT." In *Law Above Nations* edited by Mary L. Volcansek, Gainesville, FL: University Press of Florida.

———— and Thomas Brunell. 1998. "Constructing a Supranational Constitution: Dispute Resolution and Governance in the European Community," 92 *American Political Science Review*.

————. 1999. *Data Set on Preliminary References in EC Law*, San Domenico di Fiesole: Robert Schuman Center, European University Institute.

———— and James A. Caporaso. 1998. "From Free Trade to Supranational Polity: The European Court and Integration." In *European Integration and Supranational Governance* edited by Wayne Sandholtz and Alec Stone Sweet, Oxford: Oxford University Press.

———— and Wayne Sandholtz. 1998. "Integration, Supranational Governance, and the Institutionalization of the European Polity." In *European Integration and Supranational Governance* edited by Wayne Sandholtz and Alec Stone Sweet, Oxford: Oxford University Press.

————, Wayne Sandholtz, and Neil Fligstein. 2001. *The Institutionalization of Europe*, Oxford: Oxford University Press.

Sunstein, Cass. 1990. "Law and Administration After *Chevron*," 90 *Colorado Law Review*.

Tate, C. Neal. 1995. "Why the Expansion of Judicial Power?" In *The Globalization of Judicial Power* edited by C. Neal Tate and Torbjorn Vallinder, New York: New York University Press.

———— and Torbjorn Vallinder. 1995. "The Global Expansion of Judicial Power: The Judicialization of Politics." In *The Globalization of Judicial Power* edited by C. Neal Tate and Torbjorn Vallinder, New York: New York University Press.

————, eds. 1995. *The Global Expansion of Judicial Power*, New York: New York University Press.

Taylor, C. O'Neil. 1997. "The Limits of Economic Power: Section 301 and the World Trade Dispute Settlement System," 30 *Vanderbilt Journal of Transnational Law*.

Tessler, Mark and Ina Warriner. 1994. "Gender, Feminism and Attitudes Toward International Conflict: Exploring Relationships with Survey Data from the Middle East," 49 *World Politics*.

Thompson, Ginger. January 17, 2002. "As a Sculpture Takes Shape in Mexico, Opposition Takes Shape in the U.S.," *New York Times*.

Touscoz, Jean. 1973. "L'action des communautés européennes en matière d'environnement," 9 *Revue trimestrielle de droit Européen.*

Tridimas, Takis. 1998. "Member State Liability in Damages for Breach of Community Law: An Assessment of the Case Law." In *New Directions in European Public Law* edited by Jack Beatson and Takis Tridimas, Oxford: Hart Publishing.

Usher, John A. 1988. "The Gradual Widening of European Community Policy on the Basis of Articles 100 and 235 of the EEC Treaty." In *Structure and Dimensions of European Community Policy* edited by Jurgen Swarze and Henry G. Schermers, Baden-Baden: Nomos Verlagsgesellschaft.

Usher John A. 1985. "The Scope of Community Competence - Its Recognition and Enforcement," 24 *Journal of Common Market Studies.*

Vallinder, Torbjorn. 1995. "When the Courts Go Marching In." In *The Global Expansion of Judicial Power* edited by C. Neal Tate and Torbjorn Vallinder, New York: New York University Press.

Van Schaack, Beth. 1999. "The Definition of Crimes Against Humanity: Resolving the Incoherence," 37 *Columbia Journal of Transnational Law.*

Vega-Canovas, Gustavo. 1999. "NAFTA and the EU: Toward Convergence?" In *Regional Integration and Democracy* edited by Jeffrey J. Anderson, Lanham: Rowman and Littlefield.

Vermulst, Edwin and Bart Driessen. 1995. "An Overview of the WTO Dispute Settlement System and its Relationship with the Uruguay Round Agreements," *Journal of World Trade.*

Volcansek, Mary L. 1986. *Judicial Politics in Europe,* New York: Peter Lang.

————, ed. 1997. *Law Above Nations: Supranational Courts and the Legalization of Politics,* Gainesville, FL: University Press of Florida.

Von Glahn, Gerhard. 1992. *Law Among Nations: An Introduction to Public International Law,* New York: Macmillan.

Von Moltke, Konrad. 1977. "The Legal Basis for Environmental Policy," 3 *Environmental Policy & Law.*

Wald, Patricia M. 2001. "Establish Incredible Events by Credible Evidence: The Use of Affidavit Testimony in Yugoslavia War Crimes Tribunal Proceedings," 42 *Harvard International Law Journal.*

————. 2001. "The International Criminal Tribunal for the Former Yugoslavia Comes of Age: Some Observations on Day-to-Day Dilemmas of an International Court," 5 *Washington University Journal of Law and Policy.*

Walker, Neil. 2002. "The Idea of Constitutional Pluralism," 65 *Modern Law Review.*

Weiler, J.H.H. 1999. *The Constitution of Europe: Do the New Clothes Have an Emperor?* Cambridge: Cambridge University Press.

———. 1993 "Journey to an Unknown Destination: A Retrospective and Perspective of the European Court of Justice in the Arena of Political Integration," 31 *Journal of Common Market Studies.*

———. 2000. "The Principle of Constitutional Tolerance." In *The Europeanisation of Law: The Legal Effects of European Integration* edited by Francis Snyder, Oxford: Hart Publishing.

———. 1994. "A Quiet Revolution," 26 *Comparative Political Studies.*

———. 1997. "The Reformation of European Constitutionalism," 97 *Journal of Common Market Studies.*

———. 1990-91. "The Transformation of Europe," 100 *Yale Law Review.*

——— and Ulrich R. Haltern. 1998. "Constitutional or International? The Foundations of the Community Legal Order and the Question of Judicial Kompetenz-Kompetenz." In *The European Court and National Courts - Doctrine and Jurisprudence: Legal Change in its Social Context* edited by Anne-Marie Slaughter, Alec Stone Sweet and J.H.H. Weiler, Oxford: Hart Publishing.

Wellens, Karel. 1996. *Economic Conflicts and Disputes before the World Court* (Boston: Khuwer Law International, 1996).

Wheeler, Marina. 1993. "The Legality of Restrictions on the Movement of Wastes and Community Law," 5 *Journal of Environmental Law.*

Wheeler, Nicolas J. 2001. "Humanitarian Vigilantes or Legal Entrepreneurs?" In *Human Rights and Global Diversity* edited by Simon Casey and Peter Jones, London: Frank Cass.

White, Eric L. 1989. "In Search of the Limits to Article 30 of the EEC Treaty," 26 *Common Market Law Review.*

Wincott, Daniel. 1995. "Political Theory, Law and European Union." In *New Legal Dynamics of European Union* edited by J. Shaw and G. Moore, Oxford: Clarendon Press.

Wood, David M. and Birol A. Yesilada. 1996. *The Emerging European Union,* White Plains: Longman Press.

Wright, Quincy. 1943. *Human Rights and the World Order*, New York: Commission to Study the Organization of Peace.

Yuan, Lee Tsao. 1997. "Growth Triangles in Singapore, Malaysia and ASEAN: Lessons for Subregional Cooperation." In *Asia's Borderless Economy: The Emergence of Subregional Economic Zones* edited by Edward K.Y. Chen and C.H. Kwan, Sydney: Allen and Unwin.

LIST OF CONTRIBUTORS

Donald W. Jackson received his Ph.D. from the University of Wisconsin, Madison in 1972. He was a Judicial Fellow at the Supreme Court of the United States in 1974-75. He currently is the Herman Brown Professor of Political Science at Texas Christian University, where he also directs TCU's London Internship Program. His current research interests include democratic transitions in Central America (focusing especially on the rule of law), leading to a series of articles on El Salvador and Guatemala that he has written with Michael Dodson, also of TCU. A second research interest focuses on transnational and international human rights enforcement. This has led to a book on the European Court of Human rights, *The United Kingdom Confronts the European Convention on Human Rights* (1997), and to a forthcoming chapter in an edited book on the creation of the International Criminal Court.

Joseph Jupille received his Ph.D. from the University of Washington and is currently assistant professor of political science at Florida International University. He is author of *Procedural Politics: Issues, Interests, and Institutional Choice in the European Union*, and coeditor, with James A. Caporaso, of a special issue of *Comparative Political Studies* on "Integrating Institutions: Theory, Method, and the Study of the European Union." Jupille's dissertation won the 2001 Prize for Best Dissertation in European Union Studies from the European Community Studies Association (ECSA). He has been an EU-US Fulbright scholar and a Social Science Research Council (SSRC) International Dissertation Fellow.

Kimi King is associate professor of political science at the University of North Texas. Her interdisciplinary research interests include civil rights and liberties, conflict resolution, judicial decision making, legislative control of the bureaucracy, and administrative agency decision making. She has authored or coauthored articles in *Political Research Quarterly*, *American Politics Quarterly*, *Presidential Studies Quarterly*, and *Social Science Research*.

Miguel Poiares Maduro, professor, Faculdade de Direito da Universidade Nova de Lisboa and Advocate General at the European Court of Justice, earned his doctor of law degree at the European University Institute where he was awarded the Row and Maw Prize and the Prize Obiettivo Europa (Best Doctoral Thesis of the EUI). He has been a US-EU Fulbright Research Scholar at Harvard Law School. He is co-director of the Academy of International Trade Law and coeditor of the Hart Publishing Series Studies on European Law and Integration and the Special Book Review Issue of the *European Law Journal.* He is the author of *We The Court: The European Court of Justice and the European Economic Constitution* (1998).

James Meernik is associate professor of political science at the University of North Texas. He is the author of articles in the *Journal of Politics, International Studies Quarterly, Political Research Quarterly, Journal of Peace Research, International Interactions, Legislative Studies Quarterly,* and *American Journal of Political Science.*

David M. O'Brien is Leone Reaves and George W. Spicer Professor of Government and Foreign Affairs at the University of Virginia. He is author and coauthor of several books, including *Supreme Court Watch* (Annual); *Constitutional Law and Politics* (two volumes); *Storm Center: The Supreme Court in American Politics,* 3rd ed.; *The Politics of American Government; The Public's Right to Know: The Supreme Court and the First Amendment; What Process is Due? Courts and Science Policy Disputes; Abortion and American Politics;* and *Views from the Bench: The Judiciary and Constitutional Politics.*

Doris Marie Provine is director of the School of Justice Studies at Arizona State University. She is a graduate of the University of Chicago (B.A., 1968) and also has degrees in law (J.D., Cornell, 1971) and political science (Ph.D., 1978). She has served as a member of the faculty of Syracuse University. Provine's research and teaching interests center on the role of courts in politics. She has published books on how the U.S. Supreme Court selects cases for review, on the differences between lawyer and non-lawyer judges, and on how trial judges actively work to settle cases. She has also written on the work of the European Court on Human Rights and on law and justice in France. Her current work is concerned with the racial dimension of the contemporary war on drugs. She has received two National Science Foundation grants and was selected as a Mellon Fellow and Judicial Fellow. During 1999–2000, she served in Washington as program officer for the National Science Foundation in the Law and Social Sciences Program.

John F. Stack, Jr. is professor of political science and law and is director of the Jack D. Gordon Institute for Public Policy at Florida International University. His research focuses on constitutional law, transnational relations, world politics, and ethnicity. He is the author, editor, or coeditor of nine books, the most recent of which is *Congress and the Politics of Foreign Policy*, coedited with Colton Campbell and Nicol Rae (2003).

Mary L. Volcansek is dean of the AddRan College of Humanities and Social Sciences and professor of political science at Texas Christian University. Her research interests focus on comparative judicial politics and the institutional connections of courts to the larger political environment. She has written or coauthored five monographs and three edited volumes. Her most recent monograph is *Constitutional Politics in Italy: The Constitutional Court* (2000).

TABLE OF CASES

European Court of Human Rights

United States Courts

Index